STAIN

Job
Lot

Industrial Sociology:
Work in the French Tradition

The Authors

Nicole Abboud
Michel Burnier
Daniel Chave
Sami Dassa
Pierre Desmarez
Pierre Dubois
Claude Durand
Sabine Erbès-Seguin
Riva Kastoryano
Danièle Linhart
Dominique Monjardet
Catherine Paradeise
Pierre Rolle
Michael Rose
Pierre Tripier

Industrial Sociology: Work in the French Tradition

Edited by
Michael Rose

Translated by
Alan Raybould

Original French text
Edited by
Claude Durand
and the Groupe de Sociologie
du Travail

$) SAGE Publications
London · Newbury Park · Beverly Hills · New Delhi

Originally published as *Le Travail et sa Sociologie*
© Editions L'Harmattan 1985

This translation © Sage Publications 1987
Abridgement and Introduction © Michael Rose 1987

This edition first published 1987

Published with the support of the Centre National de la
Recherche Scientifique, Paris and the Université Paris 7.

All rights reserved. No part of this book may be reproduced or utilized in any form or by any means, electronic or mechanical, including photocopying, recording, or by any information storage and retrieval system, without permission in writing from the Publishers.

SAGE Publications Ltd
28 Banner Street
London EC1Y 8QE

SAGE Publications Inc
2111 West Hillcrest Drive
Newbury Park, California 91320

SAGE Publications Inc
275 South Beverly Drive
Beverly Hills, California 90212

SAGE Publications India Pvt Ltd
C–236 Defence Colony
New Delhi 110 024

British Library Cataloguing in Publication Data
Industrial sociology: work in the French tradition.
   1. Industrial sociology—France
   I. Rose, Michael, *1937 Nov. 24–* II. Le travail et sa sociologie. *English*
   306'.36'0944   HD6957.F8

Library of Congress Catalog Card Number 87-050308

ISBN 0-8039-8053-1

Phototypeset by Sunrise Setting, Torquay, Devon
Printed in Great Britain by J. W. Arrowsmith Ltd, Bristol

For S.G.

Contents

Translation: a note	vii
Abbreviations	xv

1. Introduction: retrospection and the role of a sociology of work
   Michael Rose — 1

2. Foreword to the French edition
   Claude Durand — 30

PART ONE   SOCIOLOGY AND SOCIOLOGISTS OF WORK TODAY

3. An inventory of current research on work (1983)
   Pierre Dubois and Riva Kastoryano — 39

4. Ten years of the sociology of work: the headings of the *Bulletin Signalétique* in 1972 and 1982
   Daniel Chave — 58

5. Sociological research and social requirements
   Claude Durand — 65

6. The frontiers of the sociology of work
   Sabine Erbès-Seguin — 77

PART TWO   SITUATIONS AND STATEMENTS: THE EVOLUTION OF THE SOCIOLOGY OF WORK

Introduction to Part Two — 95

7. The sociology of work: science or profession?
   Pierre Desmarez and Pierre Tripier — 95

I   The Origins — 98

8. Proudhonism and Marxism in the origins of the sociology of work
   Pierre Rolle — 98

9   In search of the founders: the *Traités* of the
    sociology of work
    Dominique Monjardet   112

II *The Sociology of Growth*   120

10 Darras on 'the distribution of the pay-off'
    Catherine Paradeise   120

11 Trends and interventions in French society
    Pierre Tripier   135

12 Critics, outsiders and the dishonoured: from the
    seminar, 'Social Transformation in Contemporary
    France' to the book *Tendances et Volontés de la
    Société Française* (1965)
    Nicole Abboud   144

III *The Sociology of the Recession*   151

13 The division of labour — the Dourdan I colloquium
    Michel Burnier and Pierre Tripier   151

14 Employment: the social and economic issues —
    the Dourdan II colloquium
    Sami Dassa   161

15 The underlying sociology of the Dourdan II colloquium
    Danièle Linhart   168

16 Conclusion: the sociological Utopia
    Dominique Monjardet   172

    Bibliography   178

    Index   181

Translation: a note

Alan Raybould and Michael Rose

Introduction
Only a tiny fraction of social science written in languages other than English gets translated into English. This is deplorable enough, but those items that do get translated are often roughly treated in the process, particularly if they are French. True, there have been some remarkable exceptions. The late Raymond Aron, for example, always seemed to get very well served. And it will not do to say that this was because Aron wrote such a clear, simple prose. Even Louis Althusser was capable of writing in such a style and Jean-Paul Sartre certainly was, in his social science commentaries as in his plays and novels. But these latter writers were invariably made to sound awkward, difficult, arrogantly obscure by their translators.

True enough, some of their English-speaking cultists — the ones who have now deserted them in the main — seemed to require that their social science should have such qualities. All the same, after confronting the task of producing what we hope is a faithful and readable version of a moderately difficult French text, we see better than we did beforehand why translators often get into trouble. It is worth outlining some of the main difficulties we have faced.

Stylistic issues
Far from being a subsidiary problem, the question of appropriate rhetoric has been an urgent one. The published French text consisted of a set of 'written up' conference papers. Writers had been able to consider at leisure their choice of terms and their syntax. Despite considerable differences between chapters in the style and clarity of their French, however, overall they presented very distinct features: sometimes extremely lengthy sentences mixed with three or four-word verbless ones; use of semi-colons or dashes in ways to which an English speaker is unaccustomed; adoption of formal stylistic devices such as rhetorical questions to introduce new themes.

Whether these are seen as ingredients of a distinctly Gallic flavour, or were merely characteristic of the intellectual milieu from which the authors were drawn, is no great matter. What is clear is that these syntactical and rhetorical features form part of the meaning that needs to be conveyed. While it would have been irritating and even absurd simply to have reproduced all these features as they appeared in the French text, it would have been inadmissable to try to mask them completely under a uniform 'anglicized' style. To do that would also have destroyed contrasts between the original papers, some of which have a very distinctively personal style; for example, it seems to us that parts of Rolle's read like an affectionate parody of Proudhon in his most flamboyantly didactic vein; and we have retained the self-deprecating humour which lightens Chave's statistical analysis.

Shared stylistic properties reflect specific cultural factors, one national, the other occupational. In many historical, biographical or bibliographical references, some of them formal citations but many of them passing remarks or phrases, similar important cultural specificities recur. To a French reader, they instantly conjure up an image or create a mood, but for an English reader they may seem to lack even a face meaning. A passing reference to 'les dégâts du progrès', for example, may gain the assent of an English speaker who shares a belief that some forms of scientific progress are harmful. But he or she is unaware that this was the title of a book sponsored by the CFDT union confederation that created a stir on its publication in 1977. To weave the phrase into a sentence — at least, it did here — implies not just assent to it, but amounts to a signal of political position: support for the CFDT line as against that of the CGT, for example.

It would have been tiresome to flag all such half-visible signs — and there must have been many others that completely eluded us. But those which seem crucial have been dealt with by modifying the text or adding a note. The same goes for references to those organizations or institutions mentioned in the text which may be unfamiliar even to the specialist English-speaking social scientist but are important for the argument the writer is putting forward.

Conceptual issues

A reference to a state agency or to an academic body, even when there is no counterpart in Britain or any other country, can be dealt with in a fairly straightforward way. Much greater care is needed in handling concepts.

We have no intention of overstating this problem. Many social science concepts — *norm, inflation, social integration, national income*, etc. — are international, and if there is disagreement over precisely what content they should be given it is an international disagreement. More trickily, some basic sociological terms originated in France, especially in the work of Emile Durkheim, and no doubt originally reflected unique features of French life or politics. 'Solidarity', as in the celebrated 'solidarité organique' attributed by

Durkheim to industrial societies, has roots in the 'solidarité' sought by the early French labour movement. In France, then, the term may possess a special resonance. But this is additional to its core meaning and is no obstacle to cross-national understanding.

But because so many — the majority — of terms can be so thoroughly trusted, we must beware of several which are largely undependable or even systematically treacherous.

False socioeconomic friends

Take, for example, the term 'volontarisme'. This seems to suggest a form of action based on readiness to do something from personal choice or inclination. To some British industrial observers it may bring to mind what was often characterized as the 'voluntary system' of traditional British industrial relations — such 'voluntarism' being characterized specifically by the readiness of employers and unions to reach agreements which would be honoured purely and simply because the two parties to them felt bound by personal commitments. Under the system, the law — that is to say, the state — was excluded from the management of this branch of social affairs.

By contrast, 'volontarisme' is a logic of action which originated in the monarchical prerogatives claimed by the Bourbon kings. The right of the sovereign authority to impose its will was consciously appropriated 'on behalf of the People' by the leaders of the Jacobin phase of the Revolution. It has thus come to signify a method of action based on the rights of the state to impose its *will* ('volonté'): for the public good, to be sure.

In other words, the term means the very opposite of what it appears to mean on the face of things to an English speaker. More than this, the whole notion of volontarisme is deeply engrained in French political philosophy, industrial administration, and to some extent broader culture. Certainly, action that is 'volontariste' may be initiated in a benevolent spirit, or at least in that of 'the greatest good of the greatest number' rather than in one of raw despotism; that is part of its ideology. But ultimately it implies a readiness to impose a carefully prepared course of action stemming from a definite policy.

The theme of volontarisme runs through several of the chapters, notably those by Paradeise, Tripier, and by implication Abboud. It is present in all of them in so far as French work culture and industrial relations are permeated by volontariste impulses on the side of traditionally autocratic private employers or technocratically minded state functionaries. One way of handling the translation problem would have been to adopt the French term itself. But it seemed far less risky to utilize several other English words or phrases, depending on the exact context. 'Interventionism' is the least inaccurate single-word equivalent. But sometimes this has been qualified by 'deliberate' to convey the meaning adequately.

A comparable trap is 'corporatisme'. This term does not figure importantly in this text but illustrates equally well how apparently similar world-of-work jargon can depend on the national context in which it is used. In the English-speaking world, drawing on the analogy of Mussolini's Italy, 'corporatism' has come to mean a tripartite system of socioeconomic management, in which government, organized labour, and an employers' association, reach mutually acceptable decisions guided by an overall view of the national interest. In France, on the other hand, le corporatisme draws on the model of the pre-Revolutionary artisans' and merchants' guilds or 'corporations'. These bodies were inward-looking, commercially restrictive or craft-sectionalist, special interest organizations, that bred a mentality on the part of their members hostile to any wider collectivism. Once again, its French connotations are almost exactly the reverse of the British ones.

And so one could go on. A labour 'militant' in France is not necessarily a 'militant unionist' in the British sense, but simply a unionist who takes an active part in union affairs, thus approximating to the pattern for an 'activist' in a British union; while 'un activiste' in France conjures up the image of someone who is certainly a militant in the British sense of being politically committed or motivated in the cause of labour to the point of being prepared to pursue it by violent methods.

Particular decisions
The chapter requiring the most careful thought was that by Kastoryano and Dubois, which analyses research on several dozen major themes relating to work, employment, unions and business organizations. Anyone wishing to gain a rapid working knowledge of the core vocabulary of the French social sciences of work could well begin by setting the original beside our rendering. We wish to draw specific attention to the following decisions:

bassin d'emploi: 'industrial region', but it also has some of the sense of the official British 'travel-to-work area';
conditions du travail: 'quality of working life';
entreprise: left as 'enterprise', though the authors are thinking of any distinct work-unit, not just private firms;
grève: 'strikes', albeit that some *grèves* are stoppages or interruptions that may not amount to strikes in a British or American sense (e.g. because only the active unionists stop work);

hiérarchie: 'management group' — the French term derives from the bureaucratically organised hierarchy of the church;
insertion professionelle: 'training schemes', though not necessarily of the Youth Training Scheme type;
ouvrier: 'manual worker'. In other parts of the text, ouvrier is usually left as 'worker'. *Travailleur* means any waged or salaried person. (That is 'labour' in the Marxist sense — *un laboureur*, incidentally, means 'a ploughman', while *un manoeuvre* is the equivalent of unskilled labourer.) *Travailleur* is mostly given as 'worker' except where precision called for the awkward 'employed person' or 'employed people'. *Un employé* is a white-collar worker, and *un fonctionnaire* is a Civil Servant, whether white-collar or blue-collar. The vague and unsatisfactory 'manager' is used throughout for the equally vague and unsatisfactory *cadre*;
partenaires sociaux: 'management and labour', or perhaps 'both sides of industry';
participation: 'profit-sharing' along the lines favoured in Gaullist — or rather, original Gaullian — industrial ideology;
polyvalence: we have left inverted commas around the anglicized 'polyvalence' and usually qualified it by an accompanying phrase in other chapters (e.g. job enlargement via the ending of demarcation); it need imply little more than such a growth in 'flexibility' (see a note on this in the final section), but English-speaking social scientists seem to believe it denotes a more complex phenomenon;
pouvoirs publiques: generally 'the authorities' — a 'public authority' in the British sense of a quango like the Port of London Authority is *une régie* (e.g. *la Régie Renault* which supervises the nationalized car industry);
reconversion: 'technical modernization';
représentations du travail: 'images of work';
revendications: 'wage claims and other demands' — the French term sometimes confuses specifically monetary with more diffuse 'demands' though it usually signifies the latter;
système de commandement: 'control system' — we rejected 'authority structure' because this English term — begs the question of whether those who give orders actually possess legitimate authority, while a large part of the task of 'command' is to check (*contrôler*) the work;
travail salarié: 'paid employment' — *salaire* can mean 'salary' but includes wages for hourly-paid work.

We must mention at this point a particular difficulty that occurred in another chapter, Sami Dassa's on the 'Dourdan II' round-table on the division of labour. In his French original, Dassa introduced his own English translations for travail and emploi respectively, in order, presumably, to explicate his use of the French terms. After some heartsearching we have decided that English terms other than those chosen by the author himself establish better the distinction he was attempting to draw.

Terminology in evolution

We conclude by mentioning three key terms referring to novel institutions and processes, whose meaning has been shifting and may continue to do so in future. The first of these is 'groupes d'expression'. The 'groupes' formed a central part of the new workplace industrial relations provisions introduced under the Left government's Auroux laws of 1982, and were intended to function within that apparatus as a whole. In practice, many seem to have been operating little differently from quality circles, although the original aim was to give workers more say, as a presumed right, in determining their immediate working environment and task structures: indeed, some sanguine unionists saw them as a real step towards workers' control. Because the final outcome for the groupes is unclear, and because there exist no bodies in Britain or America equivalent to them, we have left the term untranslated.

Secondly, there is 'précarisation'. Occasional attempts have been made to import this term into English-speaking countries. These have not so far been successful. 'Precarization' hardly slips lightly off the tongue. But the notion has lain at the heart of recent French studies of the labour market, and parallel concerns have existed among radical political economists in the USA for many years and are now apparent in Britain too. Since we cannot suggest any concise one-word, or even two-word, translation, the French has been left together with a footnote or a phrase giving the flavour of the term. One of us, at least, would not be too unhappy to see 'precarization', however ungainly, finally adopted in English.

Finally, 'flexibilité' has been adopted in English. As in France, 'flexibility' may denote either a slackening of regulations or agreements covering (i) pay-rates and methods, or (ii) terms and conditions of employment, or (iii) organization and methods of working. In practice, the term to date has been much more closely associated in France with the second of these areas where legislation, which hitherto was strictly enforced, covers working hours, recourse to temporary or contract workers, or official approval for redundancies. By contrast, in Britain, and the USA to some extent, the central flexibility issues have clustered much more closely around the third area, namely that of work organization, where union power, custom and practice, demarcation, and 'restrictive practices' are at issue: when discussing this area, French writers often prefer to talk about the growth in polyvalence (see above). This difference of experience within the 'organizational space' of industrial societies needs to be borne in mind.

One final note on our own division of labour in the translation exercise. The first main pass was undertaken by Alan Raybould. This draft was annotated by Michael Rose and returned. Problematic terms or passages were then discussed and agreement reached on how to handle them. Those which could not be settled in this way were referred to third parties, preferably French colleagues, for an opinion. Overall, this procedure worked smoothly and amicably.

Abbreviations

ANACT: Agence National pour l'Amélioration des Conditions du Travail. State-funded body providing information and consultancy on work environment and organization of a Quality of Working Life (QWL) type.

ATP: Action Thématique Programmée. Similar to a 'Research Initiative' in Britain, involving an integrated set of projects on an overall theme prescribed by the funding agency.

CDSH: Centre de Documentation en Sciences Humaines. Documentation service operated by CNRS (q.v.).

CES: Centre d'Etudes Sociologiques. Parisian documentation centre and library.

CEREQ: Centre de Recherches et d'Etudes sur les Qualifications. State body researching into work, employment and especially the impact of technical change on skills.

CERP: Centre Européen des Relations Publiques.

CFDT: Confédération Française Démocratique du Travail.

CFTC: Confédération Française de Travailleurs Chrétiens.

CGC: Confédération Générale des Cadres.

CGT: Confédération Générale du Travail.

CNAM: Conservatoire National des Arts et Métiers. The location for the Laboratoire de Sociologie du Travail et des Relations Professionelles.

CNRS: Centre National de la Recherche Scientifique. Umbrella body for state-supported research in all fields. It lays down policy lines, maintains laboratories and institutes, and offers established staff a secure full-time research career.

CORDES: Comité d'Organisation des Recherches Appliquées sur le Développement Economique et Social. Body attached to the Prime Minister's office charged with ensuring that results of important new work are known in government circles.

CRESST: Centre de Recherches et d'Etudes en Sciences Sociales du Travail. One of the main successors of the ISST (q.v.), based in Paris suburbs.

CSO: Centre de Sociologie d'Organisations. Based in Paris.

DGRST: Délégation Générale à la Recherche Scientifique et Technique. Funding agency awarding research contracts on behalf of government ministries.

ECSC: European Coal and Steel Community. One of the transnational agencies forerunning the European Commission.
ENA: Ecole Nationale d'Administration. A supra-university Grande Ecole charged with producing top managers and administrators for state-owned undertakings in particular.
EPHE: Ecole Pratique des Hautes Etudes. Grand Ecole concerned with providing training in research: social sciences catered for in its Sixième Section.
ESRC: Economic and Social Research Council.
FIFI: Modèle Physico-Financier. Econometric model utilized by technocrats and planners in the 1950s and 1960s.
FO: Force Ouvrière.
GIS: Groupement de l'Industrie Sidérurgique. Steel industry association and pressure-group.
GLYSI: Groupe Lyonnais de Sociologie du Travail. Research group based in suburbs of Lyons.
GRECO: Groupement pour la Réconstruction des Cités Ouvrières. Association concerned with urban redevelopment and low-cost housing.
GST: Groupe de Sociologie du Travail. Research group based at the Université de Paris VII at Jussieu.
INED: Institut National d'Etudes Démographiques. State research agency concerned with population studies.
INSEE: Institut National de la Statistique et des Etudes Economiques. State agency for economic research, compiling and publishing official statistical series.
ISST: Institut des Sciences Sociales du Travail. Research centre established in the 1950s for research into work, now superseded by other agencies, notably CRESST (q.v.).
LEST: Laboratoire d'Economie et de Sociologie du Travail. Interdisciplinary research centre based in Aix-en-Provence.
PCF: Parti Communiste Français.
PSU: Parti Socialiste Unifié.
RCP: Recherche Coordonnée sur Programme.
RESACT: Recherche Scientifique et Amélioration des Conditions du Travail.
SWO: Sociology of Work and Organizations.
SEITA: Société d'Etat d'Industrie des Tabacs et Allumettes.

1
Introduction: retrospection and the role of a sociology of work

Michael Rose

Introduction

What is so special about the sociology of work in France that makes it worth translating a book in which our French colleagues review the recent history of their subject and worry about their role as social scientists and intellectuals? There are several excellent reasons. First in importance is the special context, so different from those in Britain or America for most of the recent past, in which the French social scientist of work has existed. Sociologists everywhere understand better than many other people that old Russian benediction: may you live through uninteresting times! Our French colleagues should particularly appreciate it.

In *Servants of Post-Industrial Power?* (Rose, 1979), I argued that Sociologie du travail (it always seems more appropriate to leave the term in French) provided an especially instructive insight into relationships between economic change, intellectual power and government in France in the years 1945–75. The subject profited, above all in the first half of this period, from the hopes of economic planners that empirical research would help them to identify the urgent (but not obvious) human problems of economic growth and suggest solutions, as well as supplying better informed management teaching, highly trained human resources consultants to work with organizations, and, it seems probable, explanations of socioeconomic change as a whole that legitimated the methods adopted to promote and guide it by the planners themselves and their political masters.

By and large they were disappointed. The question-mark I inserted after the main title of the 1979 book may be an unduly coy way of indicating the rejection by the 'sociologues du travail' of such 'service' of economic power. For they did reject it and sought, or were constrained to seek, intellectual and academic power. Some leading researchers gained a great stock of it, at least temporarily; and one or two of these 'barons' did favour a social democratic or corporatist remodelling of government and business that would enable them to participate more closely in shaping the economic life of the country.

But their real influence remained an intellectual one. The auguries for a Left political victory at the polls were not good until well into the mid-1970s. But symbolic power was up for grabs. Competition between the 'grands patrons' of half a dozen leading centres reflected not only differences in theory and outlook, or personal rivalry as gurus to the young, but the dynamics of French academia and the Latin Quarter star system. Nevertheless, most of the barons did retain a common interest in understanding work as a human act, and in the meaning of the employment relationship, which depended on viewing these institutions as historic pointers to the nature of a society as a whole. In the English-speaking industrial sociology of the same period only Robert Blauner (1964) took this question as his main problematic.

Belief in the ontological primacy of work was a legacy of their chief mentors, Georges Friedmann and Pierre Naville (Rose, 1979: Chs 3 and 5). One or two had been briefly influenced by Marxism in their younger days, but they followed Friedmann especially in viewing social development mainly as the product of technological change, not class struggle. As a source of explanation, the latter was explicitly excluded, discounted, or simply overlooked by nearly all of them. (Here too, Blauner was reminiscent of them.)

Sociologie du travail had become a relatively distinct and established tradition of enquiry by 1960, with readily identifiable strengths and weaknesses, and it maintained, for the time being, a leading role within French sociology as a whole. From the first, as Monjardet claims in his chapter on the great sociological *Traités*, there seems to have existed an aim of establishing a clear 'brand-image' and intellectual prominence for Sociologie du travail as a 'modern' discipline. This was backed by an esprit de corps capable of bridging personal rivalries between competing research groups and their leaders. Even the preference for technological explanations was helpful, since they were favoured by planners and higher civil servants.

In the quarter century since then there have occurred great changes both within Sociologie du travail and in its public position. These are comparable in scale to those overtaking the social sciences of work in the English-speaking world, though in some respects they have been in an opposite direction to them. Sociologie du travail has lost its favoured position — and not just because the planners have lost theirs. It has lost some of its social and intellectual cohesion. Yet, it seems to me, it shows evident continuities with the earlier period. We shall note some of them shortly.

First, a note on the origins of the book. It is based on papers given at a conference on the achievements and potential of economic sociology held at the Chateau of Gif-sur-Yvette just outside Paris in early November 1983. The Gif conference centre is run by the Centre National de la Recherche Scientifique (CNRS), and officials from the Ministry for Research and Technology were present at the sessions. The original French version of this book was published with a grant under the Ministry's programme on 'Technology, Employment and Work'.

No doubt the Ministry hoped its support would encourage closer participation in the modernization and reform programme of the socialist government. The anthropologist Maurice Godelier, who had been put in charge of overall CNRS social science research policy, seems to have been particularly keen to get sociologists of economic life involved in the programme he had devised. One aim, no doubt, was to encourage closer participation in it.

The event was organized by the Groupe de Sociologie du Travail (GST) of the Université de Paris VII at Jussieu, whose members take a firm line on academic independence. Thus while many participants were no doubt personally sympathetic to the socialist government, they were extremely wary of becoming more closely involved in its policy-oriented research. The circumstances in which they were originally prepared thus gave a sharper edge to many of the contributions, even when they deal with the perennial dilemmas of the funded researcher in the sociology of work. In this respect, they provide a fascinating glimpse into the cultural politics of the socialist years.

Along with several other non-French colleagues, I was invited to take part in the sessions and give a commentary from my national perspective. These contributions appeared in the French version of this book (Durand, 1985) but I decided, with many regrets, not to have them translated. However useful French colleagues may have found them, these commentaries would have distracted attention from the main thrust it seemed to me this book ought to have once translated into English. That is to say, it should add to the information and appreciation of the central tradition in Sociologie du travail.

Precarious identity

I have a long-standing interest in Sociologie du travail, as an intellectual current and broad cultural force, as well as a scientific achievement and source of information on French economic life. But my aim here is not simply to update the commentaries on the sociology of work in France that I have made elsewhere (Rose, 1975; 1977; 1979; 1981; 1985a; 1985b). Rather, I want to draw attention to issues treated in the Gif sessions which seem to me particularly relevant to the interests and needs of English-speaking sociologists of work as they appear on our current agenda.

Our French colleagues, I believe, are *uniquely* qualified to address some of these issues, because of historical factors and features of political economy that operate especially powerfully in France, though some of them may affect other countries. One such factor is the traditional importance of craft labour as a distinct social group. Another is the special relationship between that group and revolutionary political parties. Another still is pressure on social scientists not merely to investigate carefully delimited social processes but to locate them within a more encompassing interpretation of French society — or rather, of human society — as a whole.

I am conscious, when I itemize such factors, that some of them seem much less characteristically French than they would have done twenty years ago. A considerable internationalization has occurred in the perspectives which sociologists of work bring to analysis. Certain French social theorists have exerted a particular influence in recent years on English-speaking investigators. The determination of English-speaking sociologists to achieve distinction as theorists with a following beyond sociology students is altogether greater than it was, though achievement is less evident.

At the same time, 'Anglo-saxon' technical skills in field research, once despised as 'empiricism' or 'mystification', have for their part become more highly regarded in France. Indirectly, the texts which follow tell us much about this process, whereby this branch of social science, along with many others, broke down some long-standing national barriers. Yet for the moment we must look more closely at the special identity of Sociologie du travail through the eyes of its present-day exponents.

Founding fathers
How solid were the intellectual foundations on which the subject had been raised so rapidly after the 1944 Liberation? As most participants at the Gif conference, certainly those connected with the Groupe de Sociologie du Travail, are the closest lineal descendants of the Liberation pioneers, it is intriguing to observe them undertaking their own assessment of these antecedents. It seems to me that they succeed in doing so with as much objectivity as is possible in such circumstances. They show little sign of falling back on hagiography or ancestor worship.

The method they have chosen most often is to scrutinize selected key texts which seem to mark moments when a given structure of ideas and attitudes, of explicit or implicit paradigms, crystallized and was publicly signalled; moments, we might term them, of achieved intellectual sedimentation. This procedure can result in overlooking the influence of the personal and institutional forces affecting the intellectual community. But it can disclose longer-run modes of thinking or guiding concepts which were utilized to express the intellectual dimension of such relationships.

Dominique Monjardet examines the *Traité de Sociologie du Travail* jointly edited by Georges Friedmann and Pierre Naville in 1961–2, and the *Traité de Sociologie* edited by Georges Gurvitch in 1958. Superficially, these 'treatises' are reminiscent of 'readers' in the English-speaking world in that they consist of contributions solicited from recognized specialists. Yet in France such works aim to be taken as the sign that a discipline has been adequately established and can express and project a coherent view of its subject of enquiry. There is less sympathy for the view that an editor should, like the American or British editor of a reader, feel him or herself under an obligation to include diverging views on any topic in order to remind student readers of the pluralism of theory, method and values. Rather, the aim is to produce a coherently authoritative statement demonstrating the maturity of a discipline through a unified perspective. In sum: the more monolithic, the more respectable.

A second point to note is the obvious one that not only was Sociologie du travail seen as meriting a large slice of space in Gurvitch's *Traité* on general sociology, but also as being so independently important that a whole *Traité* of its own should be devoted to it. True enough, commercial judgments about the size of markets likely to buy any reasonably presentable volume, irrespective of its real intellectual coherence or importance as a fund of reliable knowledge, may have crept in. Nonetheless, publication of a *Traité* was regarded as a matter of real intellectual consequence, as a cultural occasion and scientific claim in itself.

Monjardet's findings are unsentimental. Neither of the *Traités*, he maintains, possesses real intellectual coherence, though the editors and many of the contributors speak or proceed as if they did. The unifying element in each case was more one of attitude: namely, that work is central to human life and that, in modern times, this ontological principle is expressed most graphically in the activity of male workers in heavy industry. Monjardet judges that the Friedmann–Naville work, in particular, was 'demand led' — that is, created for a 'market', or rather, a powerful audience. Beyond its weakness as a theoretical work, he deplores an enthusiasm in it for 'positivistic' American social psychological research on workers' attitudes, and its 'expansionist' tendency to equate 'society' with 'industrial society' and thus 'sociology' with 'industrial sociology'.

Utopia of the planners

The Friedmann–Naville *Traité* had been a long time in preparation and its first volume appeared only in 1961. It therefore reflected attitudes towards economic scarcity and public life which had become seriously outdated by a combination of factors, notably the return of de Gaulle in 1958, the easing of the international tensions of Cold War I, the achievement of French decolonization — above all in Algeria — and the apparent institutionalization of a French economic growth miracle that began to seem a serious rival for West Germany's. This was accompanied by a rapid shift in cultural and intellectual frames:

> 1945–60: to measure the distance travelled between the two dates, it is enough to open a newspaper or a review and to read several book reviews. Not only are the same names no longer dropped nor the same references made any more, but the same words are no longer uttered. The language of reflection has altered. Philosophy, which was triumphing fifteen years ago, today gives way before the human sciences, and this effacement is paired with the appearance of a new vocabulary (B. Pingaud, quoted in Dupeux, 1969:386).

Some of the implications of this change for Sociologie du travail are suggested here by examining two collective works which attempted to assess the process as it occurred. As Durand argues in his Foreword, an alternative approach would have been to examine two or three 'masterworks' which created a stir in intellectual circles during the 1960s. On the other hand, the collective works chosen for examination are much more suggestive of the day-to-day institutional and intellectual forces which began to press on sociologues du travail during the 1960s.

He is right. There is a serious risk of focusing on works such as Mallet's *La Nouvelle Classe Ouvrière* (Mallet, 1965), for example, whose significance was altered by happenings later in the decade. The landmark works examined take us briefly back up into that strange, half-forgotten world of endless vistas of abundance that existed on the high plateau of the postwar growth era. How different from our own that world looked, especially to the economic planners who in France were then widely credited with having guided the country to it from the wreckage of the war.

Catherine Paradeise brilliantly suggests the growth era atmosphere in her analysis of *Le Partage des Bénéfices*. Issued under the odd-looking collective signature of 'Darras', this is the report which arose from a conference designed to make economic planners better aware of what sociologists had to offer them, and to apprise sociologists of the information needs of economists — at least, of those economists who took part. Few sociologues du travail of baron rank actually participated. Thus, this event cannot provide direct evidence on the thinking of the relevant group at this time. However, it does offer important indirect evidence of the intellectual and other pressures which were being brought to bear on the sociologues du travail who were mere knights or esquires.

The meeting was a self-consciously stage-managed and media-friendly encounter between economists and sociologists held in a provincial industrial town, Arras — hence the collective name chosen. Paradeise provides a valuable reading of the subtext of the contributions. The uninsistent arrogance of the economists is nicely captured. They had no hesitation in assuming that planners like themselves (nearly all were econometricians working in state agencies) were more or less in control of a booming economy in a France whose national economic independence could be blithely assumed. When they talk of being responsible for putting into practice a 'general will' defined in the democratic political arena, one is left with the uncomfortable feeling that they may want to believe themselves but cannot quite do so. They unhesitatingly apply a machine analogy to society, which Paradeise aptly pokes fun at. They sound benign. They sound insufferable.

The sociologists were seemingly prepared to accept much of the technocratic analysis. Only an 'anonymous' linking sociological commentary (written in fact by Pierre Bourdieu) raises normative and value questions. Otherwise, the view of French society as increasingly consensual and pragmatic was widely echoed.

In his examination of the second collective work, *Tendances et Volontés de la Société Française*, Pierre Tripier takes stock of a conference called by the Société Française de Sociologie to evaluate the post-1945 movement of French society. He finds a thematic unity that is as much one of attitude as anything else. The sociologues du travail who gave papers once again emerge as fascinated by change but unable to interpret it as anything but the product of technological factors, 'inevitably' introducing a 'natural' cultural crisis over the 'Americanization' it seemed to betoken. The France of the peasantry was to be seen as collapsing under ineluctable yet quite 'normal' trends — urbanization, secularization, and the mass marketing of consumer goods.

Running through this vision, Tripier finds an 'amnesiac' inclination to assume that history began in 1945, with the establishment of the economic plan. Widespread acceptance already existed of the claim that fragmentation and opportunism were replacing a mythical nineteenth-century unity and solidarity in the working class. Despite this implicit evolutionism, there was a covert admiration for the attributed power of the French state to act in such a way as to guide change through volontariste methods as well as to instigate it through the planning mechanism. State power was, Tripier finds, regarded as a positive national resource by practically every participant but the principled anti-statist Michel Crozier.

In her tantalizingly brief comment on Tripier's evaluation, Nicole Abboud is led into making some strong claims about academic gate-keeping and godfathering. As a participant who had just prepared a two-volume report on the recruitment of young workers to occupations (Abboud, 1959 and 1962), she recalls that sociologues du travail were even less well represented at the meetings than Tripier states. And, she alleges, several sociologists, she being one of them, who gave papers on the relationship between education, cultural change and employment, were 'excluded' from the published proceedings of *Tendances et Volontés* for taking a line offensive to the technocrats.

The excluded 'minoritaires', she maintains, pointed to looming difficulties over the economic socialization of the younger generation while refusing to view them as 'natural' obstacles to modernization that could be removed by technocratic planning — even if it were based on elaborate sociological information. To have included such papers would have wrecked the impression that the most important sociologists were doing work relevant to the planners' needs, and had acquired fluency in the planners' own vocabulary of analysis as well as in their vocabulary of motive. For mentioning unmentionable truths their authors were 'dishonoured'.

It is probably now too late to validate such claims. Abboud also seems to be saying obliquely that if only the planners and the politicians had heeded what the excluded were trying to say to them they would have been less thunderstruck by the May 1968 events — though they would not have been able to do much to stop them occurring, they would have seen them coming. In so far as this allegation is correct, she must have drawn some *Schadenfreude* from the turn of events. Additionally so, in that from the mid-1960s, as Tripier points out, many supposedly 'established' economic and social trends began to wobble giddily. Around this time, for example, employment in services overtook that in manufacturing, and the postwar 'baby boom' collapsed. When participants from the 1963 meeting reconvened in 1980 to assess the intervening years, Tripier observes, more than a few words were eaten with due solemnity.

The three latter chapters successfully evoke strong intellectual and professional pressures operating on the research community. But they leave open the question of exactly what impact they had on most sociologues du travail. Such effects are always difficult to determine. But it is certainly true that, in the middle years of the decade, anybody who refused to take continued rapid economic development and growing social harmony as established facts was likely to be treated as an eccentric. The first serious talk of an oncoming postindustrial order began to be heard. With continuing technical change and growing automation in factories, what would become of work and workers? If these terms were defined as Friedmann had defined them, the answer seemed to be: they would both disappear. From 1966, the 'flagship' journal *Sociologie du Travail*, which had been founded as recently as 1959, was beginning to run an increasing number of special issues on topics such as urbanism or social movements, whose relation to the central issue of work, though potentially close, was insufficiently clearly spelled out.

Yet between 1968 and 1973 the technocratic mirage flickered out. So too did the illusion that work and employment were problems that would disappear in the supposed 'post-histoire' of the information society.

Farewell to the working class

First came the events of May 1968. Students took over the streets of central Paris. At first, many observers were incredulous. For political activists of the early 1960s, students exemplified the materialism and narcissism of consumer society. Yet here they were, stoutly proclaiming the end of that society and of the Gaullist regime.

A formerly combative labour force that had been becoming the despair of the French communist party (PCF) and of the union confederation (the CGT) that the PCF dominated, suddenly rediscovered its militantisme. Overnight, unprompted by union leaders — indeed, sometimes against their advice — the workforce paralysed the economy with a general strike and occupied several thousand plants and offices. Employees of all grades and both sexes, not just male blue-collar workers, joined in. Before the occupations ended, several weeks later, a rich new 'stoppage culture' had emerged on many of the larger sites.

So much for the withering away of the strike; so much for the end of ideology; so much for all the other fusty early 1960s doctrines that had sounded so plausible ten weeks earlier. But what was the real meaning of the May–June events of 1968? Luckily, we do not need to agree on the meaning of the events — historians will go arguing about that — to see their importance for sociologues du travail. In the most dramatic way, the events reintroduced concern with all the 'bread-and-butter' issues of work under industrialism: parcellized tasks, tell-and-do authority structures, union rights, strikes, and the predicament of whole forgotten armies of workers — women, immigrants, youth. An instant re-politicization of work occurred.

This process pointed to novel varieties of social conflict. The

French strike-rate rose for several years. But it rose even further in other countries throughout the worldwide 'protest peak' period of 1968–73 (Rose, 1985c). A more remarkable shift occurred in the *content* of strikers' demands, which introduced or upgraded 'qualitative' objectives such as more challenging work and self-management ('autogestion'). Though these pressures sometimes originated in advantaged manual worker groups, and thus seemed to support Mallet's new working class hypothesis, they were as likely as not to be voiced *on behalf of* all employees by a new breed of young radical politician and union leader — notably those connected with the Parti Socialiste Unifié (PSU) and the Confédération Française Democratique du Travail (CFDT).

Much of the dynamism in industrial politics originated with young better-educated, better-off employees in white-collar state employment. It is now possible to recognize how far these more fortunate sections of the postwar generation succeeded in colonizing public debate with their viewpoint and values. In France, the nature of the change in the political agenda was at first masked by the archaic vocabulary in which much of the new industrial politics was conducted: in the ten years following the events, everyone in French industry began speaking like a Trotskyite; even the tougher opponents of workers' control had to sound ready to make some concession to it. Right-of-centre public figures were liable to preface any public utterance about economic life with a ringing condemnation of bureaucracy, subdivided work, or autocratic management 'hierarchies'. It is quite hallucinating to recall how recently, historically speaking, that this was so.

The rhetorical cobwebs veiled the rising influence of the 'post-bourgeois' (Rose, 1985c: Ch.4) groups of younger people who had gravitated towards professional or better white-collar jobs in the public sector. From this secure base, these groups were able to go on advocating radical change well into the second post-1968 period, when rapid economic growth disappeared: presaged in the world currency crisis of 1971, the end of the postwar growth era was confirmed by the first oil crisis in 1973.

Henceforward, the politics that really excited many in these advantaged employee groups, which revolved more around cultural issues and value-stances, especially those bearing on the position of women or the quality of (working) life, was increasingly expressed in an appropriately updated language. The old language of class struggle rapidly reverted to the leaders of workers in production industries, particularly those now under threat from foreign competition and technical change and about to contract sharply in numbers and political influence. By 1980, it was difficult to unearth a middle-class 'soixant-huitard' who was still vocalizing in Trot-speak. As in other western countries, proletarianism was to prove no match for the 'le repli sur soi' expressed in the quest for individuated 'lifestyles' and the busy collective narcissism of yuppie-dom. To be sure, booms radicalize, depressions conservatize.

The language of economic growth was abandoned with greater reluctance by those who had risen and prospered with the virile economic trend lines of the growth era. Giscard d'Estaing even attempted to merge old and new vocabularies by talking in late 1975 about the pursuit of a 'new type of growth' based on the pursuit of qualitative rather than quantitative targets. This virtuosity with concepts aroused puzzled, sceptical, or derisive reactions.

Yet by 1975, 'la crise' had largely replaced 'la croissance' as the commonest term in popular political economy. And so it has remained, with the brief respite of 1981–2 when the Mauroy government attempted a Keynesian solution for unemployment that rapidly showed up the narrow limits of France's economic sovereignty. Meanwhile, the reforming zeal of the post-bourgeois elites, where it has not simply collapsed in sell-outs to new realism *à la française*, has been diverted from public to private life — the position of women, the relationship of 'le couple', and up-market dabbling in sex, drugs, and rock'n'roll: the transformation of Sartre's newspaper *Libération* from journalistic Molotov cocktail to yuppie psychobabbler between 1970 and 1985 expresses the shift perfectly.

For the principled soixante-huitards, and there are still some around, the last ten years have been a nightmare, as they have for their counterparts in other countries. Perhaps anyone who shared those ideals at some point finds it acutely difficult to recall the protest peak years between 1968 and 1973. They undoubtedly restored dynamism to Sociologie du travail. The GST itself made some of the most notable contributions to conceptual thinking and to the empirical literature around 1970, which became widely known and debated by English-speaking students of social class and industrial relations (Mann, 1973; Gallie, 1978; Lange et al., 1982; Lash, 1984).

Many of these studies had direct implications for a debate on the new working class that had become increasingly international. It would have been interesting to have some comment, on the Gif conference record, about how these years were experienced in Sociologie du travail. To my surprise, nobody took up the topic. In private conversations in the mid-1970s, however, there was an obvious pattern, with the younger investigators often cheerfully anticipating major social and industrial change wrought by 'new worker' groups, and their senior colleagues looking towards the future with less confidence and enthusiasm. The scepticism of the latter has turned out to be better justified by the turn of events.

Here, it is vital to remember that the new working class issue had surfaced much earlier in France, following the return of de Gaulle in 1958, in a special bumper number[1] of the non-party Leftist journal *Arguments* which baldly posed the question: 'Where has the Working Class got to?' (*Arguments*, 1958). In a France where the PCF could still count on getting up to one-quarter of the votes cast in a general election, it should be remembered, an answer to a question like that was always much more narrowly associated with issues of political commitment and strategy than with objective validity pure and simple.

At first, relevant survey data were lacking, though by 1965 the controversy was being fed by findings from disparate sources such as the studies of European steel workers financed by the European Coal and Steel Commission (Reynaud et al., 1957; Durand et al., 1958) or in Alain Touraine's (1966) characteristically provocative and idiosyncratic yet invaluable studies of workers' social awareness, which offered evidence of a growing variety in socially held perspectives on economic life. The May 1968 events were repeatedly discussed by social scientists in terms of Mallet's hypothesis, of course, but once again many of them were from other specialisms. What is clear, though, is that the issue is currently regarded as to all intents and purposes closed. Quite simply, the record of politics and industrial relations in the last ten years imposes a negative verdict on the main parts of the hypothesis confirming the research findings of non-French investigators, notably Gallie (1978).

—

La crise and précarité

Inevitably, perhaps, it was the years of deepening economic trouble that got more attention at Gif. Here, we can observe some of the younger researchers who lived through the elation of the protest peak period beginning to struggle with the emergence of an altogether gloomier and more austere world. Analyses of two conferences in this period, the Colloques de Dourdan of 1976 (by Burnier) and 1980 (by Dassa and by Linhart, from two different perspectives), show a quite dramatic contrast in tone to those of Darras and *Tendances et Volontés*.

This cannot be ascribed simply to the very different participants — the Dourdan colloquiums were packed with members of the social science branch of the post-bourgeois elite, for whom the 'productivism' of the technocrats who dominated Darras and *Tendances* was repugnant. Classic Sociologie du travail, as Burnier notes, can be viewed as a sociology of progress. Rationalization of work on the

Fordist mass-production assembly model, it was often suggested, could at least be seen as a stage on the road towards a general adoption of automation, which would liberate workers from Fordist drudgery. For Friedmann himself, automation would be a trivial advance unless it reintroduced craft labour on a wide scale, and Friedmann grew less and less hopeful that it would do so. But a more optimistic futurology was detectable in Naville's work. The young Touraine spelled out a cheerful scenario unhesitatingly.

During the protest peak period, there occurred a widely remarked 'revolt against work' in all industrialized countries, which was read as the spontaneous rejection of Taylorist or Fordist methods of organization and control (Rose, 1985c). Burnier finds the participants at Dourdan I strangely silent on this crisis of do-it-by-numbers and repetitive work, although they did question the principle of the division of labour. There appears to him to be an obsessive emphasis on the subordination of workers in the labour process without any recognition of the extent to which they were now demanding higher quality work, albeit implicitly, in strikes and turnover and absenteeism. This was perhaps most apparent in those contributions which embodied elements of segmented labour market theory, where the division of labour was portrayed essentially as the product of a conscious campaign by capitalists to divide the working class as a political actor. In all events, the mood was one of gathering despondency, with a mistrustful eye to technical change. (There was a more interesting theme too, which we shall come back to.)

By Dourdan II in 1980, Sami Dassa maintains, the gloom had turned deep purple. The theme was that of accelerating socio-economic change, nearly all of whose consequences were viewed as deleterious, with the working class finally being smashed apart by employer drives for *flexibilité* in the three key areas of employment law and practice, work organization and payment systems. Employment was viewed as increasingly dualistic, as employers sought to integrate core groups of workers socially and ideologically into the local workplace, allegedly with some success, while the remainder of the labour force was being driven into 'precarious' temporary or part-time work. For Danièle Linhart as well, Dourdan II reveals an astonishing degree of acceptance of the inevitability of the trends delineated — or, as she puts it, in their 'non-malleability'.

Trends in problems and themes
The foregoing contributions certainly give us insight into how the broad changes in the social and economic climate may have affected the mood and morale of sociologues du travail as croissance

14 Industrial Sociology: Work in the French Tradition

deteriorated into crise. They also provide evidence on trends in topics of enquiry, changing modes of explanation, and some passing commentary on methods of investigation — Dassa notes, for example, that projects reported at Dourdan II were mostly 'short, rapid and lightweight', showing a distinct preference for limited case-studies and qualitative techniques of investigation.

A more analytic approach to preferred topics is provided by two other chapters. Chave confirms the trend since the 1970s towards a growing preoccupation with the labour market, employment structures, and the division of labour. The obverse of this is declining interest in skills and training. This finding surprises me, and he acknowledges that the data on which he relies, drawn from an official abstracting service (the *Bulletin Signalétique*) are affected by the vagaries to which such services are prone.

The Dubois and Kastoryano chapter reports a more extensive survey undertaken by the writers themselves. This suggests complex trends which cannot be readily summarized. One striking development noted by them, however, is that economists are beginning to tackle issues formerly regarded as sociological, with sociologists returning the compliment — if that is what it is. There are more attempts to form interdisciplinary teams. This matches experience elsewhere, and we shall come back to it later. So does the finding that international comparisons are increasingly popular. At the same time, these authors find a serious bias towards studies focusing on production industry rather than services, and on male manual workers, especially those in big public corporations. It is probable that Sociologie du travail has always suffered from this bias.

These surveys are both quantitative, and apply to the years between the early 1970s and the mid-1980s. It is worth setting them in a longer-term context, even if this involves some impressionistic judgments.

By comparison with the early 1970s, as previously noted, the most obviously recessive set of themes are those pertaining to worker militancy, class action, and social consciousness. New working class theorists conjectured the emergence of a cluster of values and forms of action for relatively advantaged groups of workers that would partly revive long-standing objectives in the labour movement, notably the ideal of self-management (autogestion). The working class would not disappear. Rather, leadership of the labour movement would shift to the 'newer' industries. In sharp contrast, a novel theme in recent work has been that of an allegedly final decomposition of the working class: indeed working class *culture* as a whole is said to be vanishing. It seems likely to remain a popular hypothesis among researchers, especially when smokestack industry is disappearing or automating, and remaining plants are getting smaller and relocating to the suburbs or to greenfield sites.

In the Dubois and Kastoryano survey, 'Work and Lifestyles' was the topic chosen more often than any other as the one investigators would most *like* to study, if they had a completely free choice. If I have a correct understanding of it, such an approach is concerned not just with the question of growing heterogeneity in market positions between employee groups, but assumes the disappearance of values and ways of living that might serve to bridge particular sets of interests on those occasions formerly likely to generate solidarity. Surely, though, Dassa is right when he asks whether sociologists may not be prematurely abandoning concern with collective action and fundamentally common ways of life. Maybe it is worth remembering that writers such as André Gorz, in person or in his alter ego as Michel Bosquet, who have recently been crying farewell to the working class were some of the first to bellow hello to the new working class.

But the record itself is clear. Whether the right salutation will turn out to be, as it has been more than once before in the history of sociology, au revoir, or should in fact be farewell, there is no denying that nobody thinks studies of the working class win brownie points in the CNRS of the awful eighties. But it is certainly farewell to the technocracy. This change, barely commented on in the contributions, is particularly noticeable to a non-French observer. To be sure, the bald term 'technocracy', or some equivalent, was rarely utilized in titles of projects or publications. But in texts themselves, in interpretations, in face-to-face discussions, it was everywhere.

This is not to say that the existence of a technocracy was generally treated as unproblematic — if anything the reverse was true. What mattered is that the employment relationship was not regarded as a matter exclusively concerning the private employer and labour. All that has changed. This reflects a profound underlying switch in the frames of reference adopted in official and in popular thinking about the French political economy as a whole since the first oil crisis and the revival of market economics. In short, re-enter the Boss.

Flexibility

New employer policies and the new types of working practices and forms of the employment relationship that go with them are the single most important novel theme in research and reports. This reflects what has actually been happening in French workplaces (de Morville, 1984). French employers were already starting to make an effort to introduce greater flexibility before the first oil crisis. Their bid to do so was justified by pointing to the relative weight in postwar France of 'social charges' such as insurance and pension contributions in total costs, and the pervasiveness and rigidity of legislation controlling all aspects of the employment relationship in a country where unions were weak or divided at workplace level but the political Left was strongly represented in parliament.

On the grounds of *formal* restrictiveness — in practice small employers often got away with murder — the bosses could make out a strong case. Though rightwing governments ruled France for twenty-three years after it, the Gaullist political restoration of 1958 was never exploited to abrogate the highly elaborate welfare and employment protection policies introduced after 1945: indeed, such policies harmonized closely with the paternalism and statism of 'Gaullian' Gaullism. It is worth noting that French practice had a strong influence in determining the norms that lay behind European Community legislation in these areas.

While firms were expanding furiously and profits soaring, the 'Patronat's' (employers in general) complaint that state regulation of employment seriously impeded industrial performance was dismissed as special pleading or simply ignored. What is more, it was public knowledge that the tacit justification for the reception of a massive immigrant worker population in the postwar years was precisely that it allowed sufficient worker flexibility to keep the economic miracle growing. Most immigrant workers lacked the same employment protection as French-born citizens all along. After 1973, however, the drive for flexibility became more insistent, was presented in a more sophisticated language, and resulted in more carefully thought-out practices. More people became sympathetic to it. For a social scientist to say that some workers believe it is in their own interests to accede to greater flexibility, to the extent of colluding with an employer in bending or actually breaking the law, is no longer regarded as heretical.

Preoccupation with flexibility and new employer policies is accompanied by loss of concern with the institutional and normative rigidities in French work organizations and in industrial relations arrangements, exemplified at an earlier period in the best-known work of Michel Crozier and Jean-Daniel Reynaud respectively. The simplest way of accounting for this is to point to the state of the labour market, to a switch towards novel personnel management policies and authority structures in workplaces, or to the weakening of radicalized unionism.

This is not the same thing as declaring that French society, especially French economic society, is now 'débloquée', or that French unionism has become generally collaborative, though it is obvious that class-conscious unionism is in retreat. Policies aimed at producing what managers consider 'positive' forms of identification with work-units on the part of employees must still take account of the undertow of broader French culture and social structure, which continue to sustain, albeit in weaker forms, many of the oppositionist workplace attitudes and behaviour delineated in the 1960s and 1970s.

But there does exist a structural shift towards smaller work-units, which favours de-bureaucratization and weakens unionism. The effect of the Auroux Laws of 1982 (Machin and Wright, 1985) on the willingness of unions to accept any binding involvement in workplace operations remains to be seen, and at the time of writing it is possible that the laws will be repealed in any case. Here too, Dassa offers the interesting comment that in the 1980s French unions have been losing such control over hiring and firing as they once had, while gaining some control over work operations, which many of their leaders and members do not want.

He also evokes the 'death of the employer'. I wish he had been able to explore this idea further. What he seems to have in mind is the effect, in the private sector especially, of an increasingly corporate structure, the dispersion of sites, and the growth of new control practices (whether integrative or précarisant), which may be leading to a lower profile for the 'patron' as an individual. Many French employees may well greet the change warmly because it removes from the control system of the workplace an almost feudal, highhanded particularism and paternalism. Others, those located in rural areas for example, may miss the personalized blend of deference and condescension which characterize such archaic boss-systems.

To sum up the most obvious thematic shifts in research and theory, then, we can say that class action, militancy, technocrats, the blockage or anomie of workplace institutions, and — above all — technologically paced evolutionism have receded sharply, while unemployment (usually seen as an aspect of wider précarisation), the decomposition of the working class, new technology and work organization, employer control strategies, and new work cultures have superseded them.

It is noticeable that the pattern as a whole tends to suggest a growing similarity in the themes tackled by the sociologues du travail and those taken up by their colleagues in other countries, especially in west European countries, above all in Italy and Britain.[2] This was to be expected. It has become plain that west European countries share more structural economic problems with each other than they do with the United States. There is increasingly wide recognition in Europe that if there are to be any solutions to some of these problems they can only be joint solutions, despite the daunting obstacles to cooperation in a period of severe stress and heightened nationalism.

But the current prevailing atmosphere of barren and ugly rivalry, like the face of a football hooligan, is the face of an obvious loser.

This is not a theme to be pursued here. In the final section I want to highlight other kinds of preoccupation, present in many of the contributions, but tackled head-on in three or four of them. Some have always been tacitly shared by economic sociologists everywhere. All of them have attained far greater significance in recent years and are becoming more explicitly recognized as challenges faced in common. They yield a large part of our agenda for the coming years.

Sociology and economics
The alteration that has been occurring in the political economy of France has made many more sociologues du travail eager to bring about a closer liaison between their work and that of economists.

I repeatedly find that the extent of any rapprochement of sociology and economics in France tends to be exaggerated by British investigators, especially those committed to a labour process approach. Moreover, these observers see the initiative as coming from economists, or at least from political economists. Why this impression exists is puzzling. One explanation may lie in the reputation enjoyed a few years ago by personalities such as the economist Christian Palloix or the urbanist Manuel Castells. But these were always rare figures, and their versatility has been oversold. As in other countries, in any case, even when they introduce them, economists regard sociological explanations as purely ancillary, and treat them with suspicion because of their low degree of formalization and unquantifiable character.

Marxist economists, when operating in their academic mode, are hardly less snooty than others in this respect. Though they are often stated with flair and vigour, the more partisan Marxist analyses of the economy — which are nowadays much less influential — habitually resort to a stress on somewhat mechanistically conceived ideological and political factors, not on social ones, though they too prefer to stick to narrowly economic determinants.

The only group of economists to have collaborated closely with sociologists over a number of years on a well-defined set of problems are those attached to the Laboratoire d'Economie et de Sociologie du Travail (LEST) at Aix-en-Provence (Maurice et al., 1986). LEST is not represented among the authors here, and it would be valuable to know more about the organizational and personal aspects of this rare example of transdisciplinary team collaboration. The resulting 'societal' problematic of the Aix group has, however, been evaluated (Rose, 1985a). The LEST approach is reminiscent of others that seem to be at the stage of formation elsewhere, notably in Britain, but this approach clearly needs much more development.

On the side of the sociologists, the capacity to communicate at an adequate level with economists is no greater in France than anywhere else. In *Servants of Post-Industrial Power?* (Rose, 1979) I stated that Sociologie du travail until the mid-1960s could be defined in part by its blissful ignorance of economics, whether in its marginalist or its political economy modes, and by a quite astonishing disregard for the fact that work is first and foremost an *economizing* activity. (Naville was the main exception.) Although several other French colleagues had pointed this out to me — I remember Raymond Aron professing to find it hilarious that Friedmann had never known one end of a demand curve from the other — it was Sabine Erbès-Seguin who deplored it most sharply.

She has continued to be troubled by this failure and returns to it in her paper, pointing to the methodological irony that, despite this lack of economic culture, the interpretations put forward by the sociologues du travail of the 1960s pivoted on a view of social modernity in which the economy took the central place. Erbès-Seguin may touch a chronically raw nerve when she refers to French circumstances. But there is growing recognition everywhere that failure to achieve some integration of, or at least some constructive dialogue between, the two subjects seriously limits the ability of either one of them to make as much sense of the contemporary world as it could do, and hence to have an effect on policy — including the drafting of alternative policies from those actually pursued by government and business.

Of course, it is never the concern, even of a sociologist of economic life, to address *technical* economic issues. But a familiarity with the most important of the technicalities is often indispensable simply for determining what key economic actors, such as employers or unions, are actually *doing*, quite apart from any attempt to understand *why* they are doing what they are doing. By themselves, sociological concepts are inadequate for such purposes, irrespective of the limitations of the economic concepts themselves. It should go without saying that those economists who try to account in strictly economic terms for behaviour that is the product of institutional or normative factors are wasting their time in an analogous way.

In Friedmann's own case, lack of rudimentary economic culture distorted explanation of trends in work and employment towards technological 'imperatives': whereas technical change usually expresses market or cost pressures. A similar problem arose in much of Touraine's analysis of correspondences between industrial civilization and technical and organizational change (Touraine, 1965).

But, to spell things out, for the most part workplace technology changes not because some clever engineer contrives a new machine or process seemingly in obedience to an abstract logic of invention, nor because technocrats — even French ones — are driven by a will to overawe their fellow human beings, nor because the main pressure on managers is to justify their power. All such factors may be relevant. On enquiry, they may even turn out to be, in some cases — cases that are interesting because they prove to be exceptions — the main factors shaping decisions about technical change. But to assume them to be more important than material or financial factors is methodologically perverse.

In a capitalist economy, in fact in any conceivable economy possessing a rational accounting system, technology changes primarily because an employer or manager calculates that it will help cut production costs, increase market share, or raise profits (operating surplus). Now obviously what cannot be fitted readily into the conventional models of decision making that economists apply to such processes are such factors as the manager's *readiness* to calculate rationally, or his or her *ability* to do so successfully. These sociocultural factors can determine the outcome of the economic act itself, and this ought to trouble economists. But that is a different matter. The main point is that nobody can estimate how far social factors impinge on an *economic* process unless they accept that the economic factors the economist is *trying* to summarize in a model must have methodological priority. It only needs to be added that to appreciate such factors does not require a three years' formal training in economics. Half-educated entrepreneurs get by happily enough on instinct. All that is required of us is sufficient intuition to grasp that the social takes second place to the economic in such cases.

Intellectual roots of Bravermania

Up to this point, it has not been difficult to bring out prominent traits and major concerns of Sociologie du travail which enable us to see it in an international context of social enquiry. But it is now necessary to raise one issue which seriously complicates any attempt to situate it in relation to the sociology of work in the English-speaking world in the last dozen or so years in particular.

Any British or American industrial sociologist will remember the years 1974–84 for the furore that followed the publication of Harry Braverman's *Labor and Monopoly Capital* (1974). There is no need to raise a yawn here by going over all the arguments again. However, right from the start (when I was engaged in exploring in depth the Sociologie du travail oeuvre) two things have always astonished me about this controversy, which I failed to experience with the same kind of responses as many English-speaking colleagues. The first source of my difficulty has been the tone of the central verdict handed down by Braverman and summarized by the subtitle of his book (*The Degradation of Work in the Twentieth Century*). This suggests that our economic system seeks mainly to humble skilled workers, when what it mainly seeks is profitable operation. The second source of my trouble arose from the assumption accepted by nearly everyone who took part in the controversy that the perspective put forward was a Marxist one: on this, including many people who called themselves Marxists, nearly everybody uncritically took Braverman at his own insistent word.

In fact, *Labor and Monopoly Capital*, without too much exaggeration, can be interpreted as a brilliantly polemical morality tale about an evil being called Capital and a tragic hero called Craftsman. The whole account embodies and promulgates an ethical framework, whose central tenets are that Skill is of inherent moral worth and that Craftsman, because he possesses it, is the finest of human types. To set out to destroy Skill, because it involves the liquidation of Craftsman, amounts to a crime comparable to genocide. In this light, the book is not an essay in political economy but a jeremiad: a brilliantly delivered one, and possibly a brilliantly crafted one.

The tale had been told before, but never so well: that is to say, never so well *in English*. In France, however, beginning with a rough sketch in *La Crise du Progrès*, Georges Friedmann (1936) had been telling it in French at least as well, possibly even better, between the mid-1930s and the early 1950s. (For a contrast with Friedmann's approach see Durand, 1978.) To me, it has always seemed astonishing that among all those of my English-speaking colleagues who know Friedmann's works, or who have told me they know them, either in the original or in English translations such as *The Anatomy of Work* (original French 1956, trs. 1961), that of all these vigilant scholars only one has commented on the startling similarities between Friedmann's and Braverman's work, if only at the level of mood — the pessimism, the pathos; or of procedure — the type of evidence used, the way it is used. In several places in *Labor and Monopoly Capital*, Braverman explicitly disparages Friedmann's achievement. Nobody ever seems to question whether his characterization is accurate, or what motives he might have had for condemning Friedmann so sharply and, in a sense, so gratuitously.

But there is a deeper similarity. The essential value position put forward by both writers, in terms of its political ideology and social imagery, is an idiosyncratic one. Yet there can be no mistaking some of its central properties: skill is the ultimate measure of all value: craft knowledge is the touchstone of human worth; the craft workshop is a model for a self-governing community. However voluble Braverman's protestations to the contrary, this is not the world of Marx, not even the world of the young Marx who penned searing indictments of mechanized labour and was yet to discover political economy. It is, in all essential and critical features, the world of Marx's arch-rival in politics and as a propagandist. It is the world of Pierre-Joseph Proudhon, patron sage of the Workshop Republic.

'Proudhon? Who he?' Believe it or not, I have actually been asked the question by somebody holding a tenured post in industrial sociology at an English university, and I don't think they were joking. Yet it is difficult to understand Sociologie du travail without appreciating the main lines of Proudhon's thought about work. It is emphatically impossible to understand the French labour movement without doing so. And it has become impossible to appraise some influential recent currents in Anglo-American studies of industrial politics (Burawoy, 1985) and the new economy (Piore and Sabel, 1984) without doing so.

Pierre Rolle's chapter sets out to define the influence of Proudhonian ideas on sociologues du travail. There could be no better advocate of the thesis he puts forward. Rolle has always maintained that it is impossible to understand what is at stake in any sociology of work unless we return to Proudhon's *Philosophy of Poverty*, and then read *The Poverty of Philosophy*, Marx's polemical reply to it (Rolle, 1971; Rose, 1979: Ch.5). Though he reiterates here his belief that Marx got the better of the argument, Rolle acknowledges Proudhon's creativity as a setter of problems, and argues that he has had a disguised influence on the labour movement in France that was almost as great as Marx's own.

Rolle starts by defining sharply the intellectual and ideological context in which Proudhon came to utter his well-known and invariably misconstrued maxim: 'All property is theft!' Inevitably, perhaps, an aphorism like this was always destined to become a standby slogan for sixth-form anarchists, stoned hippies, and the meat-hook branch of the hard Left. For Proudhon, rather, it was merely a rhetorical springboard for performing a spectacular initial leap into an enquiry intended to establish precisely what could *justly* be possessed by any person or group. His conclusion was that, ideally, only producers should possess anything by right. And what producers should possess was not 'the full fruits of their labour' but a set of 'credits'; that is, a set of rights to receive goods from other producers who have already received goods on credit from the producer (or from a joint workshop group). To make such a system operable, coupons would be issued, on delivery of goods, by 'the accountant', who also devises an overall plan for production.

Introduction 23

This is a conspicuously Utopian scheme. But it is clearly not anarchist, for both a system of credit-vouchers or coupons and a plan call for a central authority to administer them. Perhaps, too, as Rolle argues, it is less Utopian than formerly to envisage such arrangements in the late twentieth century, when computer systems might provide a means of handling the formidable tasks of calculation and book-keeping entrusted to the accountant. Likewise, this view of production does constitute an attempt to think beyond capitalist institutions by showing how some of them might be exploited, once hijacked by the labour movement, to yield historically innovative methods of organizing the economy. It is notorious that Marx always wriggled away when challenged to provide a sketch of socialism.

Two things are obviously lacking in Proudhon's analysis. The first is theory of capital stock, which the Marxian notions of exploitation and 'dead labour' later aimed to provide. The second is any recognition of what Marxists would call the ideological (and Durkheimians the moral) dimensions of social life. Most perceptively, Rolle points out that for Proudhon the social is almost as much a direct expression of the economic as it was for old knee-jerk historical materialists. Society is almost reduced to a system of economic exchanges.

Almost, but not quite, and the qualification is essential.

Within the workplace, the relations between producers were to be mediated by a stock of personal authority yielded by the degree of mastery any individual had reached over the work operations performed. In Proudhon's eyes, all individuals possess a kind of 'charge' of authority generated by work experience that is roughly proportional to the range of tasks they can perform to the highest standards as set by acknowledged masters of the skills or craft they exercise.

Technically speaking, this method of evaluation is festooned with booby-traps. And quite apart from its doubtful acceptability to those exercising low craft expertise — let alone those exercising no craft at all — what is startling about this procedure is the degree to which it depends on perpetuating the imagery, indeed the mythology, of traditional craft communities. Proudhon's life-project can be seen as that of securing the continuation of such communities into the indefinite future. This was to be the moral anchor of Friedmann's work too. How astonishingly both anticipate the bestselling message to come from Brooklyn!

English-speaking students of skill who, having swallowed Braverman whole, have believed their problems to be derived predominantly from Marx and to sustain a Marxist political practice, will find Rolle's chapter the most challenging and, I hope, the most unsettling section of the book. Marx himself believed traditional craft organization and skills — indeed, any method of *conceiving* work predating industrial capitalism — was already doomed when he began to write *Capital*, and that, under socialism, Work as a category of thought would appear in discourse only as a quaint archaism signifying a domain of human experience transcended by the movement of history.

Within the logic of the *Marxian* perspective the conclusion was inescapable, just as it is within that of any *Marxist* one. Such logic has a brutal manner towards romantic illusions about preserving outmoded forms of social and economic organization. Rolle contends that Marx's own discussion of work seems to show that he unwittingly absorbed some of Proudhon's ideas. Despite the stupendous originality of both Proudhon and Marx, the broader intellectual currents of their day were refracted through their works. Marx's credentials as a Marxist have often been questioned — the first to do so was Marx himself, when he dissociated himself from a group of would-be followers. Perhaps it is time to open the question of Marx's originality as a Marxian also.

Scientific integrity

The question of what it means to undertake social enquiry, and especially that of how far it is possible and desirable to stand outside the object of study while describing and interpreting it with originality, is disquieting. Answers to it often do no more than elaborate on the enigmatic facets of the role which the social scientist must live through every day of his or her life, sometimes unhappily.

Durand presents a forthright and uncompromising discussion of how the academic researcher should handle state sponsorship of research. The constant stresses which exist in this area were given a novel form in France in the first half of the 1980s. For while the largely unforeseen socialist parliamentary landslide majority following Mitterrand's successful bid for the presidency in 1981 presented social scientists with greater security and better funding, it threw at them the problem of how closely they should allow themselves to become involved in the policy formulation and appraisal of a government with which most of them sympathized.

This might seem to be a problem with which their colleagues in countries where social democratic governments come to power more often confront without suffering undue anxiety. However, we need to remember that a change of government, under the French system, allows the incoming administration unusually wide scope to make sweeping changes of control in the civil service and nationalized industries. In addition, it can take, and invariably does take, other measures to produce loyal and informed support for drastic changes of policy.

Sociologists, like economists, soon found themselves being invited to assist in planning and implementing all manner of changes affecting work and employment. Sociologues du travail had to define the roles they would find acceptable in programmes aimed at increasing employees' organizational involvement and commitment, and at promoting greater harmony and predictability in industrial relations.

For some, the changes envisaged in draft legislation were the very ones they had been advocating for many years. Some risks were obvious. To refuse to assist in implementing reforms could lead to the accusation of dilettantism. On the other hand, acceptance of an openly pro-Mitterrand interventionist role would expose them to the charge of blatant partisanship, with unforeseeable consequences once the political pendulum swung back to the Right.

Such considerations of expediency mask others of a more ethically troubling sort, and it is these that Claude Durand discusses with great sensitivity in his chapter on social research and social needs. Durand reminded the Gif participants that during Giscard d'Estaing's presidency (1973–81) complaints had grown about an increasing pressure for research orientated towards intervention, and had been widely resented within the research community: and rightly so, Durand exclaimed. It was not just a question of a political double standard; though on both sides of the partisan divide there are always people who are ready to advocate one. Nor is it just a question of competence in policy-linked intervention; though as Durand correctly argued, and repeats here, acceptance of an interventionist commitment under *any* administration raises the danger of involving researchers in action for which they are not adequately trained even though they may believe they are.

Such expertise, certainly, can be accumulated; but only at the risk of compromising the quality and reputation of social research as an activity whose central mode should be an ideologically sceptical one, even if it can never be an ideologically detached one. And it lies at the top of a slippery slope leading down to the cynical manipulation of research subjects on behalf of clients with fat pocket-books. All manipulation is ethically unacceptable, whoever is in the manipulator's sights, and irrespective of whether manipulation has a faultlessly 'benign' intention. If researchers say it is immoral to manipulate ordinary citizens or employees even 'for their own good', they must say so too when the targets of manipulation are more powerful figures. 'Policing employers' is no more acceptable than 'nannying workers', if it calls for manipulation.

Rigorous adherence to this rule, Durand states, by no means excludes contracted research for government departments or other clients. But to do such work adequately, and in all meaningful senses honestly, requires independence, an autonomous identity. It also calls for openness of mind and a positive attitude towards freedom of information on the part of the client: proper study of a problem may call for redefinition of the questions posed initially. 'Only the sociologist', Durand insists, 'can be the judge of the frontiers and scope of the field of study — this is his craft'.

Monjardet, in his chapter on the sociological Utopia, presses one of Durand's themes to a disturbingly logical conclusion. If the fundamental task of the sociologist is the creation of knowledge, however fragmentary and empiricist, about the public, he or she must face the possibility that the authorities — which the writer graphically terms 'the Prince' —will try to grab these data and utilize them for their own ends. But sociographic data do not speak for themselves. Nor can the Prince grasp their full meaning. The data-dredging activity should lead, then, to a more 'reflexive' sociology — Monjardet's suggestions are reminiscent of the late Alvin Gouldner's (1971) in certain respects — concerned with decoding the inner meanings which underlie all social reality.

In a pungently ironical style, Monjardet notes how the abstruse theoretical debates that arise among social scientists following competition to decode inner societal meanings also amount to claims on worldly objects — fame, a chair, funding, media exposure, royalties. These scholarly debates are not couched in an everyday language. Nor do they deploy facts that are accessible to unaided common sense. They do not constitute a wilful effort to confuse or baffle the public, though they often may do just that. For however self-seeking the parties to them, however abstruse the concepts coined, however rebarbative the language uttered, this process is vital for social wellbeing. As Monjardet puts it: 'This questioning of discourse, of all discourses, ad infinitum, which cuts across all social practices, constitutes in itself the work by which a society, or at least its different parts, thinks about itself, or at least attempts to.'

The sincerity of the debating parties must, however, be assessed. Sincerity is not automatically signalled by a readiness to identify with an unprivileged social group, and not just because such 'commitment' may be no more than verbal. In fact, complete identification, which the sociologist merely adopts while trying to refine or perfect the discourse of any collective subject, is singled out by Monjardet as worthy of particular scorn. Sincerity can only be gained, he states, once the sociologist renounces, not just publicly but to him or herself, all claims to *power*, including the symbolic power over a public which the radical trendy acquires alongside publishing royalties and fees for appearances on chat-shows.

Ultimately, then, as Monjardet sees things, the explication of emergent meaning, the elucidation and disruption of discourse, is the real vocation of sociologists. They are committed to cultural struggle, rendering it, at least potentially, more productive. But they are not involved in this struggle on their own account; rather as an auxiliary whose self-imposed assignment is that of provocateur. The sociological assignment is for this reason profoundly anti-totalitarian. That is why sociological free thought is banned as firmly in the Santiago of Pinochet as in the Warsaw of Jaruzelski, and treated with suspicion by governments and officialdom in places far closer to home.

Monjardet concludes with an arresting set of thoughts. Sociologists, he declares, must always take themselves seriously as the guardians of Durkheim's notion of a 'morality without principles'. More disturbingly, this role, adequately discharged, approaches that of the original Sophists, who, as Monjardet points out, in ridiculing all given schools of thought bore witness to the very power of thought itself . . . and, for this public-spirited service of shaking to pieces in public the secure frames of publicly held meaning, were periodically seized by an ungrateful public and publicly stoned to death.

The conclusion is disconcerting not just for its austerity. It is also startlingly 'post-modern' in so far as it turns its back on what many French sociologists of Monjardet's generation once accepted unquestioningly as their main obligation as intellectuals: namely, to take a lead in working for a radical Left political settlement — and one that would be permanent. French sociologists are a long way from the hurled cobblestones of the May events. If any cobblestones are to be hurled, following Monjardet they may well find themselves on the receiving end of them. How many of them would have the nerve to face up to such a prospect without flinching? How many of us in other countries would?

It is 1986, not 1968, and it feels like it. We need to adjust to existing circumstances, it is true. But there is a danger of extrapolating the awful present into an indefinite future, just as the technocrats of the 1960s and those sociologists who were most impressed with them imagined the long boom would prove interminable, and just as the radicalized post-bourgeois cohorts of the 1970s acted as if an unebbing tide of change would surge forward for ever. Those sociologists of work who have lived through these interesting times can hardly feel that life always justifies buttoning on a cheerful face. Yet some of us must surely have learned from these vicissitudes that the notion of the cunning of history, 'la ruse de l'histoire', is not a mere verbalism. Without being able to prove Monjardet wrong, I do not believe the main role that awaits us in the years to come is that of victim. But I do not know what that role will be either. In part, it is up to us to invent it.

Notes

1. The original soon became a collector's item. Indeed, copies of the relevant double-issue number were soon 'liberated' from nearly all the main Paris libraries.
2. For an overview of recent Italian research on work and employment see back numbers of the excellent review *Sociologia del Lavoro*, published by the Dipartimento de Sociologia, Universita de Bologna. In West Germany, research has been much more closely tied to applied programmes, notably in the areas of quality of work life and in new technology: see Klaus Dull's chapter in Durand, 1985.

References

Abboud, N. (1959 and 1962) *Le cheminement professionel des jeunes ouvriers*. (Vols. I and II) Paris: Insitut des Sciences Sociales du Travail.
Arguments (1958) Nos. 12–13.
Blauner, R. (1964) *Alienation and Freedom: The Factory Worker and his Industry*. Chicago: University of Chicago Press.
Braverman, H. (1974) *Labor and Monopoly Capital: The Degradation of Work in the Twentieth Century*. New York: Monthly Review Press.
Burawoy, M. (1985) *The Politics of Production: Factory Regimes under Capitalism and Socialism*. London: Verso.
Dupeux, G. (1969) *La France de 1945 à 1969*. Paris: Armand Colin.
Durand, C. et al. (1958) *Niveau de méchanisation et môde de rémunération*. Paris: Institut des Sciences Sociales du Travail.
Durand, C. (1978) *Le travail enchaînée*. Paris: Editions du Seuil.
Durand, C. (ed.) (1985) *Le travail et sa sociologie*. Paris: l'Harmattan.
Friedmann, G. (1936) *La crise du progrès*. Paris: Gallimard.
Friedmann, G. (1956) *The Anatomy of Work*. London: Heinemann; trs. of (1956) *Le travail en miettes*. Paris: Gallimard.
Friedmann, G. and Naville, P. (eds) (1961–2) *Traité de sociologie du travail*. (Vols. I and II) Paris: Armand Colin.
Gallie, D. (1978) *In Search of the New Working Class*. Cambridge: Cambridge University Press.
Gouldner, A. (1971) *The Coming Crisis of Western Sociology*. London: Heinemann.
Gurvitch, G. (ed.) (1958 and 1961), *Traité de sociologie* (Vols I and II) Paris: Presses Universitaires de France.
Lange, P., Ross, G. and Vanicelli, M. (1982) *Unions, Change and Crisis: French and Italian Union Strategy and the Political Economy, 1945–1981*. London: Allen and Unwin.
Lash, S. M. (1984) *The Militant Worker: Class Radicalism in France and America*. London: Heinemann Educational Books.
Machin, H. and Wright, V. (1985) *Economic Policy and Policy-making Under the Mitterrand Presidency 1981–84*. London: Frances Pinter.
Mallet, S. (1965) *La nouvelle classe ouvrière*. Paris: Editions du Seuil; trs. Shepherd, A. and Shepherd, B. (1975) *The New Working Class*. Nottingham: Spokesman Books.

Mann, M. (1973) *Consciousness and Action Among the Western Working Class.* London: Macmillan.
Maurice, M., Sellier, F. and Silvestre, J. J. (1986) *The Social Foundations of Industrial Power: A Comparison of France and Germany.* London: MIT Press.
de Morville, G. (1984) *Les politiques nouvelles du patron et français.* Paris: Editions la Découverte.
Piore, M. J. and Sabel, C. F. (1984) *The Second Industrial Divide: Possibilities for Progress.* New York: Basic Books.
Reynaud, J.-D. et al. (1957) *Attitudes des ouvriers de la sidérurgie à l'égard des changements techniques.* Paris: Institut des Sciences Sociales du Travail.
Rolle, P. (1971) *Introduction à la sociologie du travail.* Paris: Larousse.
Rose, M. (1975) *Industrial Behaviour: Theoretical Development since Taylor.* London: Allen Lane.
Rose, M. (1977) *French Industrial Studies: A Bibliography and Guide.* Farnborough, Hampshire: Saxon House.
Rose, M. (1979) *Servants of.Post-Industrial Power? Sociologie du Travail in Modern France.* London: Macmillan.
Rose, M. (1981) 'Un aperçu étranger sur la Sociologie du Travail française', *Sociologie du Travail* 22(1):55–75.
Rose, M. (1985a) 'Universalism, Culturalism and the Aix Group: Problems and Promise of a Societal Approach to Economic Institutions', *European Sociological Review* 1(1):65–84.
Rose, M. (1985b) 'Un regard anglais sur les sociologues du travail français', in C. Durand (ed.) *Le travail et sa sociologie*, Paris: l'Harmattan.
Rose, M. (1985c) *Reworking the Work Ethic: Economic Values and Socio-Cultural Politics.* London: Batsford.
Touraine, A. (1965) *Sociology de l'action.* Paris: Editions du Seuil.
Touraine, A. (1966) *La conscience ouvrière.* Paris: Editions du Seuil.

2
Foreword to the French edition
Claude Durand

We will refrain from giving a synopsis of the book here, but will simply indicate what the main intentions were and provide a few signposts to guide the reader. Sociologie du travail has had an institutionalized form for thirty years, so it was tempting for a group of researchers specializing in the discipline to venture an appraisal. That presupposed several things.

(1) *An assumption*: that the sociology of work exists as a discipline. We will see that this question is far from resolved.

(2) *A method*: since an exhaustive review of the work in this field would have been wearisome, indeed impossible, it was necessary to stick to important landmarks.

(3) *A unity of analysis*: this lies more in the intent and the procedure than the end results which necessarily reflect the diversity of approach of researchers involved in the field.

(1) The *Traités*,[1] published twenty years ago, should confirm or refute the notion that the sociology of work can be said to exist as a discipline. In fact, the test is not conclusive. The sociology of work is not clearly defined at the outset: in the *Traités* its object is ultimately defined as the field of research in progress. Rather than a sociology of work, it is a question of work studied by sociology (Naville), work as the object of sociology, an object defined by the research done — on machines, workers, work posts, skills.

Yet — and this gives us a clue — work is seen as the central experience of life in society and the notion of work is taken in its broadest sense, not limited to productive activity. Following the Marxian notion of 'abstract work', work is given as a category of analysis.

For the sociology of work, work is a social activity. Work signifies the social relationships of production. By extension, work was to be considered the basis of industrial society, the foundation on which societies develop (Naville). Equally, it is the mainspring of society's action upon itself, on the basis of social movements (Touraine).

This idea of work as a central aspect of sociological analysis was not clearly expressed at the start. It is clarified in later works (notably in *Sociologie de l'Action*, 1965). It is stated explicitly in the foreword which announced the new editorial team of the review, *Sociologie du Travail*, in 1966:

> Although the review follows the problems of industry closely, from the beginning the notion of work which gave it its specificity was understood in its strong sense — the activity through which men master and create their society . . . *Sociologie du Travail* defends a socio-historical orientation: the study of society as the achievement of men, a conception of its transformations as the product of collective work. (*Sociologie du Travail*, No. 4, 1966).

Work becomes a factor explaining social evolution. Because of this, it is more or less assimilated to the notion of *development*, at least within industrial society as other principles (science, knowledge) appear to take its place as motors of social evolution or summon up the notion of postindustrial society.

(2) *The method*. In the first part of the work that follows there is a quite exhaustive study of the themes of recent research in the form of a quantitative analysis of research topics, likely future trends and the relationship with people who award grants and contracts. (In France, hardly any academic social science research is funded privately. But public fund givers can obviously take into account the needs of private firms as they see them.)

The look back into the past in part two has been treated differently. Since an exhaustive study was out of the question, we have chosen to analyse a number of landmarks in the shape of collective works:

(i) The *Traités* of Gurvitch (1960) and Friedmann and Naville (1961) which reflect work done in this field in the 1950s;

(ii) *Tendances et Volontés de la Société française* (1965) and *Le Partage des Bénéfices* (1966);

(iii) *La division du travail* (Dourdan I, 1978) and *L'emploi* (Dourdan II, 1982).

The leap from the first to the last is perhaps too long. Furthermore, some people will criticize us for neglecting some important books, particularly the great professorial theses: but surely these are the fruit of collective work done in research centres. The leaders crop up time and again in the discussions of the disciples, even when the latter are expressing a more critical point of view.

Yet the methodological choices do entail some bias: collective works as they undoubtedly are, the books in question do bear signatures. The *Traités* are the work of professors and directors of research centres. The two seminars from the 1960s are notable for the interest shown by civil servants from the Plan[2] and by the participation of specialists from INSEE; the Dourdan conferences are more centred on the work of a specific research group.[3]

This bias has been corrected, notably by the choice of people presenting papers: the second Dourdan seminar is analysed by researchers from rival centres who express their views bluntly and underline the failings as well as the positive contributions. The founding works (the *Traités*) are dissected by far from faithful disciples. What was left unsaid by the seminar of the *Société Française de Sociologie* (*Tendances et Volontés*) is reinterpreted in the light of papers left out of the book.

So, if there is distortion here, then it might be explained not so much by the books selected as the critical readings of them.

However, we should note that this criticism was itself regulated by collective discussion[4] although it needs to be justified by an account of the perspective adopted. The second check was that afforded by several foreign sociologists of work (Klaus Dull, Michael Rose, Michele La Rosa, Francisco Zapata), each with a specialized knowledge of French sociology of work,[5] who were invited to criticize our diagnoses and compare them with their own experience. They were given the final word at the Gif conference as a sign of our desire for relativity. For reasons given in the introduction, these contributions have not been included in this translation.

(3) *Unity of analysis*. This can be found more in the intent than in the results. We did not aim for an evaluation of the sum of acquired knowledge on the different subjects of the sociology of work. The idea of the cumulation of knowledge is epistemologically contested: each new theory refutes the previous one.

The aim of this work was to highlight the sense and the development of the sociological method at different stages. This is what constitutes the unity of the book over and above the diversity natural to any collective work. Examination of approaches to the sociology of work at specific periods can be presented around three principal axes:

(i) relationship to time;
(ii) relationship to the dominant social actors;
(iii) critical distance.

(i) *A sociology specific to certain periods*. The idea of locating stages was implicit in interpretation. But it is also the idea that sociology expresses the state of society at a given period of its history, that the directions it takes are dominated by the social problems of the moment. For Michel Foucault this is characteristic of all the social sciences: 'One thinks of today.'

From its beginnings, the sociology of work was fascinated by industrial society, a society defined by its development. There was a 'Friedmannian' fascination with technology and a belief in the liberation of the workers following on progress of these techniques. Automation was the natural cure for the alienation of the workers.

Ten years later, Darras began to ask questions about French growth. Analysed in terms of consumption and distribution, have the social consequences of growth lived up to expectations? The study of social morphology ought to show if development has been egalitarian or not.

The seminar of the *Société Française* held around the same time is more concerned with the obstacles to development. The perspective of Michel Crozier is dominant: despite the weight of its traditional structures, French society is modernizing.

These two phases highlight the role of change and progress in sociological explication. In the first phase, progress seems to be the inevitable consequence of technological development. Everything falls before a sort of technological determinism.[6]

But social progress measured globally may be unequal in its distribution and the sociologist, while retaining confidence in technology, can still have doubts about this distribution, concerning him or herself with the position of workers (surveys of worker consciousness) or trying to stimulate more efficient workplace relations (Crozier, Delamotte, Reynaud).

After a break of more than ten years, following the fundamental questions raised by May 1968 when the idea that technological progress equalled social progress lost all credibility and technology was considered an instrument of social domination, a new ideology of modernism is currently re-emerging at a new stage of technical development. New, modernist Utopias are conjured up to justify the economic and social restructuring which constitutes the crisis.

(ii) The second aspect of this attempt to situate the sociology of work focuses on *its relationship with dominant social groups*.

Here, an interventionist[7] perspective is prominent: development is constructed by capitalism, or the technocrats against the working class. Institutions are the work of social actors whose aims and strategies are laid bare. This perspective is clearer in the later seminars than in the first works analysed. But it was there from the beginning, parallel with and antagonistic to that sociology which saw itself as a reflection of society: it is the sociology of contestation, that of the social classes.

It is interesting, and easy, to discover behind Darras and *Tendances et Volontés* the role of the civil servants of the Plan, the administrative elite and the technocrats who also contribute to the diagnoses, in the same way as the sociologists albeit less objectively, since they are closer to the field of action. Sociology is here questioned on its collusion or co-operation with the authorities.

Collaborators and critics are sharply divided — the first controversies being over outside contracts and their ambiguities. It is here that Nicole Abboud de Maupeou discovers in the unpublished papers of the *Société Française* seminar the analysis of social contradictions, a historical relativism and a 'denaturation of change'.

Critical sociology attacks the modernist ideologies in the name of class struggle. The committed sociologist gives voice to worker alienation and exploitation. One school of thought is to link modernism and class struggle — the theorists of the new working class who are not paid enough attention in this retrospective.[8]

In this same vein of class sociology, Dourdan I and II reveal what lies behind employer policies: social control of labour, the division and destabilization (précarisation) of employment, the destruction of working-class resistance through dependence on welfare benefits. Working-class action is not given enough space, we are told. It is true that as regards the themes dominating the social debate — the division of labour, employment — the working class is largely absent from the fight or is allocated only a minor part. But, when unemployment splits up and 'individualizes' working-class action, the sociologist bases his or her analyses on the patterns of social behaviour he or she observes.

Community studies, life histories and monographs are gradually replacing analyses of class and social structures. Societal boundaries are drawing in to encompass little more than local and regional identities. This change of approach, a sort of epistemological reflection of social decomposition, is not peculiar to the last seminar discussed. The June 1982 seminar at Le Creusot organized by the *Société Française de Sociologie* displays even more clearly this disintegration of sociological analysis, this regression of sociology towards a history of events in individuals' lives and social psychology.

There is a trend towards a nominalist approach to social reality which has no place for the analysis of structures, institutions and relationships to the state and focuses instead on the diversity and complexity of particular, individualized social actors.

(iii) *Reflexive sociology*. This is the third great perspective of this appraisal. Alongside the involved or committed sociology, a certain sociology of knowledge demands to be heard — standing above the melee, questioning its own role and prioritizing social criticism.

The first two axes — historical situation, relationship to the dominant actors and social problems of the moment — already presupposed this critical distance. But now it is openly affirmed as such from different vantage-points.

The self-criticism over how sociologists function seeks to link sociological production to the role of the sociologist in society — at the same time advising those in power but keeping some distance from the people of action through critical reflection.

This critical distance as regards sociological procedures is expressed in the manifest interest in epistemological research, the questions raised about the proper method for the desired end. This preoccupation leads finally to a questioning of the frontiers with the other social sciences. The search for common ground seems to prioritize the original link with political economy and its critics (Proudhonian or Marxist). But in the 1950s this line was broken by the attraction of American empirical sociology. Methodology was then strongly influenced by social psychology (attitudes and behaviour at work).

With the antimethodological revision of 1968, a new rapprochement with the economists was affirmed: the Dourdan seminars show a love–hate relationship with economics and for any study of the division of labour or the labour market some debate with the economists is needed. There is an evident attraction towards a body of theory which is better grounded but which is criticized for being too quick with easy answers and which does not have the sociologist's feel for the lie of the land and concern with the concrete.

The link with history is more recent: born of the refusal to get bogged down in statistical methodology and a rejection of structural analyses infused with ideology, the attraction of the historical method takes the form of a return to the concrete, the individual, the community and to culture. A provisional stage, of course, but one which has its part to play, like the previous phases.

This is what distinguishes reflective sociology — its awareness of the relativism of different schools and their insertion in the history of society. That is, it watches itself working and acting.

Notes
1. Friedmann, G. and Naville, P. (1961) *Traité de Sociologie du Travail*. Paris: Armand Colin. Gurvitch, G. (1960) *Traité de Sociologie*. Paris: PUF.
2. By the 1980s, the influence of the *Commissariat Général au Plan*, once omnipresent, had been marginalized by the revival of free market economics.
3. The *Groupe de Sociologie du Travail* (GST), though their contribution is limited to a third of the published papers.
4. In the form of discussions at a GST 'Table Ronde' research seminar, 7/8 November 1983 at Gif-sur-Yvette, organized with the help of the CNRS and the University of Paris VII.
5. Dull, K. (1975) *Industriesoziologie in Frankreich*. Frankfurt. Rose, M. (1979) *Servants of Post-Industrial Power? Sociologie du Travail in Modern France*. London: Macmillan. La Rosa, M. (1979) *La Sociologia del lavoro in Italia e in Francia*. Milan.
6. The analysis of *Sociologie du Travail* in its twentieth anniversary number (No. 1, 1980) also points out this dominant feature of the 1950s. See also Marc Maurice's article in the same issue.
7. *Intervention* by social scientists usually designates consultancy at the level of individual work-units, not large-scale social engineering.

8. See the work of Serge Mallet and the debates in the review *Arguments*, recently republished.

PART ONE
SOCIOLOGY AND SOCIOLOGISTS OF WORK TODAY

3
An inventory of current research on work (1983)

*Pierre Dubois and Riva Kastoryano**

Our aim in this survey[1] was to prepare an overview of research into work under way in 1983–4. The method used to gather most of the data was the mailed questionnaire, sent to more than 1000 researchers at the beginning of 1983. We processed 529 replies, 346 of these having been elicited by the questionnaires, the rest being based on an analysis of annual reports drawn up by the research groups to which the researchers belonged. By adding the latter group of respondents we wanted to get closer to the total population active in this area in the two disciplines most concerned, sociology and economics.

The 529 people researching into work are divided up as follows: 273 sociologists, 143 economists, twenty-four historians, twenty psychologists, ergonomists and physiologists, twelve anthropologists, nine jurists, six political scientists, five geographers and thirty-seven 'others', notably engineers, doctors, administrators, management consultants and personnel officers. Although we did not expect to arrive at fully representative samples in all the disciplines, we can say without too much risk of contradiction that the 'labour force' studying work is, in its great majority, made up of sociologists and economists.

The questions asked were very simple. What is the subject of your current research? What questions does it ask, that is, what are key problem issues? Does it deal with a particular branch, a certain type of enterprise in terms of size or legal status, or with a definite occupational group or grade of employee? Finally, does it involve any international comparison?

An analysis of the replies to those four questions takes up the first part of this text and we will take note at certain points of the differences observed between sociologists and economists. In the second section, which is shorter, we look at the respondents' expressed intentions about research topics they might tackle in future in order to measure any clear trend in comparison with current themes.

---

* Groupe de Sociologie du Travail

Classification by subject of current research

Classification under six headings[2]

Any classification of research topics under a series of headings is by definition arbitrary. Thus we need to explain the principles which led us to arrive at our different headings and subheadings. In so far as this survey concerns actual research on work and work is carried out in a structure which is the work organization or firm (which for sake of simplicity we will term the enterprise), we have divided the research topics according to a 'spatial' schema. There are research projects studying:

— the environment in which enterprises exist;
— the relationship of enterprises to their environment;
— the labour market;
— work in the enterprise;
— reactions to work in the enterprise;
— a population which works in a specific environment but which at the same time has a history or lives in it.

The results based on the 529 research projects are as follows.

(1) *Research into the environment of enterprises*
55 (10.5%)

National or local government policy
— industrial policy, planning	10
— training and research policy	7
— regional development policy (including that of local authorities)	8
— health and social policy (welfare payments)	5
— policies bearing on labour and employment legislation	3
Industrial relations system	7

The policies and functioning of
— worker or employee organizations	14
— employers' organizations	1

(2) *Research into enterprises (location, development, strategies, performance, their controllers)*
119 (22.7%)

History of industrialization during a given period or in a given region	11
History of a given branch of activity	16
Spatial division of labour, international division of labour, technology transfers	8
Special types of production unit	
— small or medium-sized firms	3
— newly created or relaunched firms	3

— worker co-operatives 1
Controllers' groups in companies 4
The functioning, features and aims of enterprise decision-
making systems 25
— company policy and decisions in the matter of
technology, innovation, research 31
— personnel policy and management of human resources 12
Performance and track record of enterprises. 5

(3) *Research into the labour market and more specifically the characteristics, conditions and context of the access to employment or those resulting in inactivity*
51 (9.7%)
The informal, underground or black economy 2
Local labour market, industrial regions 8
Labour market of a given category (young people, women,
immigrants) 9
Training schemes 15
Redundancy and early retirement 4
Employment and the unemployed 9
Migration, immigration 2
Labour market (unspecified). 2

(4) *Research into work in general (the labour process)*
181 (34.5%)
Recruitment, selection, relationship between educational
qualification and job, promotion, careers, vocational
training 24
Gradings, job structures, salaries 24
Organization and division of labour, quality of working life 34
and more specifically
— job content, qualifications, occupational know-how,
specific trades and professions 49
— *groupes d'expression* and new forms of work
organization 14
— hours of work, distribution of working time 9
Control systems, communication, participation, relations
between the management group and shopfloor,
discipline 12
A combination of several of the above 15

(5) *Research into behaviour at work*
Values, ideologies, images of work 18
53 (10.0%)

Various forms of behaviour at work (absenteeism, restriction
of output) 8
Unionism, activists 8
Wage claims and other demands, strikes 11
A combination of several of the above 8

(6) *Research into a working population situated historically or in a given environment (work/life outside work)*
66 (12.6%)

Social relations, gender relations, social and sexual division
of labour 5
Paid employment/domestic work 8
Work and lifestyles 24
Effects of work on health 7
Social mobility and social trajectories 11
Social class, class action and class cultures 11

Do sociologists and economists study the same thing?

General finding: depending on whether one is a sociologist of work or an economist, one does not have quite the same research topics (see Table 1). There are proportionally more economists than sociologists working on the environment of enterprises, on companies themselves and on the labour market.

Against this, there is a greater proportion of sociologists of work than economists researching into work in general, behaviour at work (*none* of the 143 economists is found under this heading) and the relationship between work and life outside work ('non-work' as it is sometimes called by English-speaking sociologists).

The 'other' sociologists come in between the sociologists of work and the economists except in the work/non-work category where they are relatively more numerous.

Of course, there is nothing surprising about these findings: when they are not studying macro-economics, economists study the economics of companies; the sociologists of work study work and behaviour at work in the company. This is the traditional division of interest: it is perhaps even surprising that the differences are not more clear-cut. Briefly, Table 1 is of interest because it shows:

There are sociologists of work studying national and local government policy, employer and union policy, the labour market and the history, location and strategies of firms.

There are economists studying work in the firm and relationship between work and lifestyles. The absence among the economists of people carrying out research into behaviour at work is worth noting again.

In other words, each broad field of research except one is covered,

TABLE 1
Proportion of researchers found under the different headings depending on current research programmes

Heading	Total population (n=529) %	Economists (n=143) %	Sociologists of work (n=135) %	Other sociologists (n=135) %
1. Environment of companies	10.5	11.2	4.4	12.5
2. Enterprises	22.7	36.4	14.8	16.9
3. Labour market	9.7	18.2	6.7	9.6
4. Work in general	34.5	28.7	41.5	29.4
5. Behaviour at work	10.1	0	16.3	14
6. Work/life outside work	12.6	5.6	16.3	17.6

in various ways, by the different disciplines. Of course, it does not necessarily follow that interdisciplinary research is being done. On the other hand, that would be a lot more difficult to organize if the various areas were still totally covered by only one discipline or the other.

We can refine the analysis further by comparing economists and sociologists of work at the level of precise research topics (see Table 2). Analysis certainly shows that one or other of the two disciplines is more prominent in some of our groups but it also shows that the 'minority discipline' in any given research group may still be taking equal or greater interest than the other in a specific topic within that group. This is the case in Group Four (work in general): certainly, overall there are more sociologists of work here — but the topic of working time is tackled in equal numbers by the two disciplines. Furthermore, the economists are ahead in the study of gradings and salaries and, more surprisingly, when it comes to the organization and division of labour.

The analysis can be pursued further. Economists and sociologists of work comprise only 53 percent of our total population. It is interesting, then, to find out in what topics the economists and sociologists of work are over-represented. Take Case 2 in Table 3: here they account for two-thirds or more of the researchers studying the topic. It is just as interesting to discover in which areas they are under-represented. If we look at Case 3 in Table 3, we find that here they account for less than 40 percent of the researchers studying each theme. We have indicated on the right of the table the other disciplines interested in these themes. Table 3 seems clear enough not to require further commentary.

TABLE 2
Themes and disciplines (only those subheadings on which five or more researchers are working are included)

	List one	List two	List three
1. The environment of companies	Industrial relations system Worker organizations		Industrial policy Regional development
2. Enterprises	Decision-making systems		History of industrialization. History of an industrial branch Spatial division of labour Technological decisions Personnel policies
3. Labour market	Labour market for a given category		Local labour market Training schemes Unemployment/the unemployed
4. Work in general	Working time	Training. Careers. Relationship between qualification and job. Skill. Occupational know-how. Specific trades. New forms of work organization. Control systems, participation, communication.	Gradings Salaries Work organization/division of labour
5. Behaviour at work		Values and images of work. Behaviour at work. Unionism/activists. Strikes and demands.	
6. Work/life outside work		Work and lifestyles Paid employment/housework. Social mobility. Social classes.	

Note:
List one: Sociologists of work ($n=136$) and economists ($n=143$) study these themes in equal numbers.
List two: Sociologists of work are more interested in these themes.
List three: Economists are more interested in these themes.

TABLE 3
The extent to which certain themes are covered by sociologists of work and economists

	List one	List two	List three	Other disciplines concerned
1. Environment of companies	Industrial policy Industrial relations system		Training policies Regional development Worker organizations	Other sociologists Geographers, jurists, other sociologists Historians
2. Enterprises	History of an industrial branch. Decision-making systems	Spatial division of labour Technological decisions Personnel policies	History of industrialization	Historians Other sociologists
3. Labour market	Labour market for a given category Training schemes	Local labour market Unemployment/the unemployed		
4. Work in general	Organization and division of labour Control systems. Communication participation	Gradings/salaries New forms of work organization. Working time.	Training careers/relationship between qualifications and job Occupational know-how. Specific trades	Other sociologists Other sociologists, historians, anthropologists
5. Behaviour at work	Values and images of work. Behaviour at work. Unionism/activists		Strikes and demands	Other sociologists
6. Work/Out of work life	Salaried/domestic work Workers' health Social mobility. Social classes		Work and lifestyles	Other sociologists, historians, anthropologists

Note: List one: Themes covered by proportion of sociologists of work and economists corresponding to their proportion of total population. *List two:* Themes in which they are over-represented (i.e. they account for more than 2/3 of total). *List three:* Themes in which they are under-represented (i.e. below 40%). Here, other disciplines working on a theme are noted.

Let us move on a little further while still remaining at the level of precise research topics (subheadings in our groups) being tackled by at least five researchers. There are thirty-two of them under our classification system. Only one of these is being studied by a single discipline (the spatial and international division of labour, tackled exclusively by the economists). The other thirty-one topics are being studied by at least two different disciplines.

In conclusion, the subjects listed, all more or less closely linked with work, are certainly tackled first and foremost by sociologists *and* economists. Certainly, the sociologists of work are more prominent in certain thematic areas, the economists in others. Nevertheless, Tables 2 and 3 have shown that none of the thirty-two subheadings in our classification (with one exception) is accounted for totally by a single discipline: the walls have come tumbling down and there are no more private preserves.

If a particular topic is tackled by several disciplines, that does not mean, of course, that researchers drawn from different disciplines are working together, complementing each other's problematic and approach: they may even be continuing the battle to impose their discipline in the field and see off the others. This survey shows there are possibilities of multidisciplinary research programmes in all the topics. The question remains of whether they should be instigated and organized, and how this is to be done: our brief did not cover that.

Questions asked by research: technology at the heart of the problematic. One of the questions the survey asked was: 'What are the main questions tackled by your research?' The replies allowed us on the one hand to specify the theme of the research under way and so to classify it under one of the different subheadings; and, on the other, to get some sort of idea of the problematics in play. We have therefore coded the replies to this question in the following way: 'What is/are the explanatory hypotheses? What is/are the explanatory factor(s)? With what independent variables, if you like, are findings to be linked?'

Naturally, the subject can be tested for the effect of new technology and power relations in the firm: for this reason the sum of percentages adds up to more than 100 percent. The results are to be found in Table 4.

The 'technology' factor or the 'incidence of technology or new technologies on . . .' is a long way ahead of the field. It is therefore worth spending a little more time on it, especially as the next two factors are analysed later, since they are the subject of precise questions (Does your research focus on a particular type of firm? Does your research give rise to an international comparison?).

TABLE 4
Explanatory factors listed in order of decreasing importance

	%
1. Technology	27.8
2. Company structure (size, legal status, branch)	17.6
3. Political system or factors specific to country studied	17.6
4. Economic context or crisis	9.8
5. Training system	8.0
6. Industrial relations system or power relations	6.8
7. Labour market	5.5
8. Legislation	5.3
9. Region	5.3
10. Working conditions	4.8
11. Family/Private life	3.2

Note: Each percentage means: there are x% of researchers in our survey testing the effects of (factor) on their subject matter.

So 28 percent of the researchers look at their subject in relation to technology. Two-thirds of these are interested only in the relationship with technology. The remaining one-third open up the explanatory framework: they also look at the link with company structure (size, legal status, branch), or with the balance of power between employer and workers, with features of the labour market, or features of the country in question, with the training system, the economic context or with working conditions.

If those researchers studying the technological choices of companies (our Group Two) are added to this 28 percent, a proportion of around 33 percent is reached. One in three of the researchers who replied gives technology an important place in his or her research: either technology or technological evolution is studied, or these are given an important explanatory role.

What subjects are tested for the effect of technology?
When studying a subject listed in Group One (environment of companies) or in Group Six (work/life outside work), there is little reference to technology (10 and 11 percent respectively). In Group One, the main point of reference, clearly, is the political system or specific features of the country being studied. In Group Six, the main references are family and private life, as well as work and working conditions in the effect they have on the relationship between work and life outside work. Three other factors also feature strongly: the labour market, the economic context, the region. In other words, in Group Six, various problem areas and approaches can be involved.

When studying a topic in Group Two (companies), Group Three (labour market) or Group Five (behaviour at work), technology is taken as a point of reference in a proportion close to that of the total population of the survey. No less than one researcher in four refers to it. In Group Two (companies), three references are at the same level, clearly ahead of the rest — the political system and specific characteristics of the country studied, technology and technological trends, company structure (size, status, branch: the effect on policies brought into play). In Group Three (labour market), two points of reference tie in first place — technology and the economic context. In Group Five (behaviour at work), four references come in equal first: technology, the balance of power between unions and employer, company structure and work. So, with the exception of Group One, the possible core problem areas are not only rarely a single one but in fact crop up in a variety of the research programmes. This is not the case in the following group.

Indeed, in the study of work (Group Four), reference is made to technology in a significantly higher proportion of cases: 42 percent. This is perhaps not so surprising in that the themes of this group most lend themselves to being tested for a relationship with technology. Even so, it is striking that *one researcher in every two* looking at a given aspect of work refers to technology or technical evolution or new technologies. The 'technology' factor is dominant, and blots out or overshadows other explanatory factors (company structure is mentioned in 19.4 percent of the research programmes in this group; training systems in 13.2 percent; political system 10 percent; legislation 8.5 percent; labour market 6.2 percent; balance of power between unions and employer 4.7 percent; economic context 3.9 percent). We do not wish to deny that technology is an important explanatory factor; but it might be worth reflecting at greater length on the trends established by public debate and funding policies, and about the effective precedence over other explanatory options.

To be sure, 'technology', 'technical evolution' has always been taken, particularly in the sociology of work, as an explanatory factor in the evolution of work. Today, evidently, the explanatory power of technology has not diminished: one might even advance the hypothesis, despite the lack of any comparable survey to refer back to, that its weight has increased. This prominence given to technology in explanatory systems might present, if it were to increase further, the risk of simplistic or reductionist explanations. No-one nowadays defends a strict technological determinism; all the same, the number of researchers studying the relationship between technology and a research subject has perhaps never been greater.

Traditions: the predominance of research into industry, the public sector, large firms and manual workers. First, a few facts to situate the French economy:

(1) There are more people employed today in the so-called 'tertiary' sector than in the secondary or primary sectors.

(2) The private sector remains predominant in spite of the post-1981 nationalizations.

(3) Small and medium-sized firms today create more jobs than large ones.

(4) Blue-collar workers today make up less than a third of the active population and their number is falling.

Given these facts, it was tempting to investigate whether current research was looking at sectors or firms where jobs are most numerous or on the increase; and whether it was studying those occupational categories in which jobs are most numerous or on the increase. Far from it. For the most part, researchers are still focusing on industry, the public sector, large firms and manual workers.

Sixty-eight percent, or 213 of the researchers are investigating a precise economic sector: for more than half of them (60 percent), it is industry, and only for a third (30 percent) the tertiary sector; only 10 percent of researchers are interested in agriculture. What is more, not all industrial sectors receive the same attention: there are privileged sectors such as iron and steel and metal-bashing; the car industry; electrics and electronics; and textiles. On the other hand, some sectors hardly feature at all — glass; ceramics and construction materials; shipbuilding and aeronautics; leather and footwear; paper and print; rubber; wood and furniture. It does not seem that the researcher's interest is determined by the economic state of health of the branch: certain sectors in crisis are studied, others are not. Do researchers study only those sectors that are in the public eye or where funds for a piece of research are available?

Less numerous (30 percent) are those researchers working on something involving a company with a precise sort of ownership profile: two-thirds of them are looking at firms in the public sector, a quarter at firms in the private sector and the rest are comparing the two sorts of firms. One might venture the thought that the recent nationalizations have stimulated the development of research in the public sector, and/or that it is easier to gain access to public companies.

Slightly more numerous (43 percent) are those researchers involved in work on companies of a particular size: nearly two-thirds of them (62 percent) are studying large firms (more than 500 workers); only a quarter are studying small and medium-sized firms (100 to 500); the rest are studying very small firms (less than 100).

Slightly more numerous again (48 percent) are those engaged in work on a particular occupational category: nearly a quarter of them (22 percent) are comparing several categories. Nearly 40 percent are studying manual workers (and as the previous group is just as interested in this category, this means that more than half of the researchers looking at occupational groups are studying manual workers). Of the other categories (agriculturists, heads of industrial and commercial companies, liberal professions and upper management, middle management and technicians, office workers) none has the attention of more than 10 percent of those researchers whose main point of reference is an occupational group.

At the end of the 1970s there was much talk of a 'crisis of trade unionism': unions were losing members and their traditional bases of support — the manual workers in heavy industry — without managing to mobilize those groups of workers significantly on the increase — women, non-manual workers and workers in the tertiary sector. When research into work focuses on a precise sector or socioprofessional category (which is the case in a significant number of projects), it is situated for the most part on the same ground as unionism. No-one talks directly of the crisis of research into work, but we ought to ponder the relatively small number of research programmes that focus on the study of the tertiary sector, of small and medium-sized firms, the private sector and categories other than manual workers.

When one calls to mind the studies of the 1950s and 1960s on the motor industry and steel, one can only confirm the weight of tradition: manual work in large car and steel firms continues to fascinate researchers in the social sciences of work.

What is the significance, in the study of a particular subject, of the reference to a branch of activity, or a type of firm? It can signify two different explanatory strategies: in referring to only one branch of activity (which is the case for two-thirds of those researchers who declare such a context), one is seeking to neutralize 'branch' as an explanatory factor, by supposing that is contains a certain homogeneity of technologies, negotiations and staff, in order to advance other explanatory variables (for example, employer strategy according to size or status of company, differential behaviour at work according to sex, age and category).

On the other hand, the looking at several branches and comparing the subject in each of them (which is the case for one-third of the researchers concerned), the branch intervenes as a factor of explanation.

The same commentary can be made for the other two parameters

— size and status of the firm. We have seen that 30 to 68 percent of the researchers mention the location of the research subject in one of these three contexts. Now, it must be remembered that company structure (in the sense of its location in a branch, its size, its legal status) is taken as an explanatory factor by 17.6 percent of researchers. So those who set out to use one of these contexts as an explanatory factor are in a minority (they compare their subject across several branches or firms); the majority situate themselves in a single context, in order to neutralize its characteristics and bring out other explanatory factors.

Trends: the development of international research
For 394 of the 529 researchers polled, we have information relating to the question: 'Does your research give rise to international comparisons or does it concern a foreign country?' Thirty-six percent replied 'yes'. Sixty-four are comparing France with another country, twenty more are comparing France with two other countries, and no less than 49 are comparing France with three or more countries. Ten researchers are studying a foreign country without directly comparing it with France.

Europe, and the EEC countries in particular, are well ahead of the field as far as comparative research programmes are concerned; then comes America, North America in particular, followed by Asia, then Africa. The foreign countries most often compared with France are the UK (44), West Germany (43), Italy (27), Japan (18) and Canada (17). In Europe, the absence of comparisons with Greece (despite its membership of the EEC), with Austria and with Finland should be noted.

Despite the lack of any previous survey as a point of reference, one can safely say that comparative research has flourished in recent years, stimulated by the different opportunities for funding which have arisen due to the perceived gaps in this field. The proportion of researchers engaged in international comparisons is thus noteworthy — it touches 36 percent.

This average percentage does in fact hide large differences depending on the particular research theme. Thus, a full 56 percent of the researchers undertaking work in Group One (environment of firms) are pursuing international comparisons or studying a foreign country. This falls to 48 percent in Group Two (companies), 36 percent in Group Four (work), 30 percent in Group Six (work/life outside work), 25 percent in Group Five (behaviour at work) and 20 percent in Group Three (labour market). Even in the latter case, though, one researcher in five is engaged in comparative work.

Future research preferences: significant developments

The final question we asked was: 'What research topic would you wish to pursue in the years to come and why?' It is thus a question of preference, not an indication of those programmes that will actually be started, as wishes need to be funded if they are to be fulfilled.

Only those researchers who answered the relevant question (346) are considered here. A significant minority (23.7 percent) gave no reply. Was this because of a lack of preference, or because their current research is long-term, or because they first want to take into account the opportunities that arise when bids are invited for research contracts? We are unable to comment on this issue.

A small percentage (5.2 percent) want to work in areas beyond the scope of topics covered in this survey. All the rest (71 percent) envisage pursuing research in areas covered in the survey, but perhaps with a change of focus. 29.2 percent would move from one group to another (for example, from 'work' to 'companies'); 13.6 percent would change themes within the same heading; 28.3 percent would prefer to continue their present research or start another closely related to it, that is, within the same subheading. In spite of the wording of the question, which might have encouraged respondents to say they would change topics, a significant minority of researchers do not envisage any important change of theme in the years to come.

In our classification, which groups of topics would researchers abandon and which would they gravitate towards? Three groups show similar trends. Few researchers (about a quarter) would abandon these three for another topic-group; but, on the other hand, these same groups are 'attractive' in the sense that researchers currently listed under other headings want to work here eventually. With few intending departures and a significant number of newcomers, the implication is clear: if the wishes of the researchers were obeyed, these three groups would have a greater proportion of researchers than at present. The three are: Group One (environment of companies), Group Two (companies) and Group Six (work/life outside work).

Group Five (behaviour at work) is exceptional: more than half the researchers working in this field today want to leave it eventually; against this, a significant number of researchers currently occupied elsewhere wish to move into this area in time. With many leaving, and many arriving, we have a 'high turnover' group renewing its workforce but retaining the same overall weight.

The last two groups, Group Three (labour market) and Group Four (work) and the first in particular, would see their importance wane. Indeed, they would be abandoned by the majority of researchers currently active in them — no less than two-thirds of the researchers engaged in work on the labour market would like eventually to 'change group'. These departures would not be compensated for by new arrivals from other fields of research (the labour market group in particular does not find many new takers).

These different movements — departures and arrivals — and their impact on the respective weight of each group in the field taken as a whole give the results tabulated below. Two percentages are given for each group, the first being the proportion of researchers currently working in the group, the second the proportion of researchers expressing a wish to initiate projects there. The key to popularity of each subheading is as follows:
  − − sharp decline
  − decline
  = no change
  + trendy
  + + hyper-trendy.

(1) *Research into the environment of companies*
         10.5% 14.2%
National or local government policy
  — industrial policy, planning   + +
  — training and research policy   + +
  — regional development policy (including that of local authorities) =
  — health and social policy (welfare payments)   + +
  — policies bearing on labour and employment legislation   + +
Industrial relations system   =
  The policies and functioning of
  — worker or employee organizations   =
  — employers' organizations.   − −

(2) *Research into enterprises (location, development, strategies, performance, their controllers)*
         22.7% 25.2%
  History of industrialization during a given period or in a
     given region   − −
  History of a given branch of activity   +
  Spatial division of labour, international division of labour,
     technology transfers   =
  Specific types of production unit
     — small or medium-sized firms   − −
     — newly created or relaunched firms   +
     — worker co-operatives   +

54 Industrial Sociology: Work in the French Tradition

Controller groups in enterprises   – –
The functions, features and aims of enterprise decision-making systems   =
— company policy and decisions in the fields of technology, innovation, research   +
— personnel policy and management of human resources   + +
Performance and track-record of enterprises.   =

(3) *Research into the labour market and more specifically the characteristics, conditions and context of the access to employment or their resulting in inactivity*
9.7% 5.7%

The informal, underground or black economy   – –
Local labour market, industrial regions   – –
Labour market of a given category (young people, women, immigrants)   – –
Training schemes   – –
Redundancy and early retirement   – –
Employment and the unemployed   – –
Migration and immigration   + +
Labour market (unspecified).   + +

(4) *Research into work in general (the labour process)*
34.5% 22.8%

Recruitment, selection, relationship between educational qualifications and job, promotion, careers, vocational training   – –
Gradings, job structures, salaries   – –
Organization and division of labour, quality of working life   –
More specifically:
— job content, qualifications, occupational know-how, specific trades and professions   –
— *groupes d'expression* and new forms of work organization   – –
— hours of work, length and distribution of working time   – –
Control systems, communication, participation, relations between the management group and shopfloor, discipline   =
A combination of several of the above.   =

(5) *Research into behaviour at work*
10.1% 10.6%

Values, ideologies, images of work   =
Various forms of behaviour at work (absenteeism, restriction of output)   – –

Unionism, activists =
Wage claims, other demands, strikes − −
A combination of several of the above + +

(6) *Research into a working population situated historically or in a given environment (work/life outside work)*
12.6% 21.5%

Social relations, gender relations, social and sexual division
   of labour + +
Paid employment versus housework =
Work and lifestyles + +
Effects of work on health =
Social mobility and social trajectories =
Social class, class action and class cultures + +

Out of all these groups, 'work/life outside work' would move ahead fastest if the wishes of the researchers were realized. It would contain 21.5 percent of researchers against 12.6 percent at present, thus moving close to the group 'work' which would have 22.8 percent versus 34.5 percent at the moment. The subheading 'work and lifestyles' would leap ahead (11 percent of researchers against 4.5 percent today). It would thus be ranked first out of all the subheadings, although currently it is only fifth, equal with two others.

What about the evolution of preferences according to discipline? The economists are the most stable: among them, two topic groups are expanding slightly ('environment of companies' and 'companies'), two are falling back slightly ('labour market' and 'work in general'); the other two show little change. The sociologists would be far happier to change topics: among the sociologists of work, three topics are moving ahead slightly ('environment of companies', 'companies' and 'work/life outside work'), two are unchanged ('labour market' and 'behaviour at work') while 'work in general' is falling back sharply — it would contain no more than 16.7 percent of the sociologists of work against 41.5 percent at the moment.

Conclusions

Finally, then, what conclusions can one draw from this survey and how should it be used?

It has allowed us to locate a population researching into the environment of companies, companies themselves, the labour market, work, behaviour at work and the interaction between work and life outside work. It is a large population made up mainly of economists and sociologists, researchers and technicians of the CNRS, researchers attached to a research organization in Paris, researchers engaged in work done by teams rather than individuals. Men predominate in all of the categories. No doubt the most novel feature is that a majority of researchers, besides belonging to their principal organization, also have other connections (such as with GRECO, GIS, RCP, etc.). This was expected, but the extent of these tie-ups suggests there could be a restructuring of the research community in progress or on the way.

The survey has also allowed us to measure the number of research programmes under way on a particular theme through a pre-established classification which has a certain logic but which could have been different. Not all the topics figuring as subheadings are tackled by an identical number of researchers; some topics concern only one or two people, others several dozen.

What are the most significant results of this thematic analysis? We pick out four — two encouraging, two more worrying.

It is encouraging that, at a time when efforts are in hand to develop multidisciplinary research, none of the six areas in our classification is the exclusive preserve of one discipline: the economists or the sociologists of work are more involved in certain fields than others, but they are never alone in any of them — almost all of the subheadings are covered by at least two disciplines.

It is equally encouraging to note the high proportion of researchers (around a third) engaged in international research comparing France with other countries, or in research into other countries.

Two other results are more troubling. First, the importance attributed to technology, either as the subject to be studied or as an explanatory factor in the research. This preponderance may carry the risk of neglecting or minimizing other possible explanations.

Equally worrying is the fact that researchers situate their research in production industry more often than in the tertiary sector, in big firms rather than small and medium-sized ones, in the public rather than in the private sector, and among manual workers rather than other occupational groups: the blue-collar worker of big industrial firms in the public sector remains a source of fascination for the researchers questioned here, and this interest carries the risk of neglecting sectors, types of firms and occupational groups that are growing in importance.

The survey, finally, has allowed us to register the preferences for research topics expressed by the researchers. At present, the group 'work' includes more than a third of researchers which puts it well ahead of the others. But in expressed preferences for future research it falls back significantly. With some groups contracting while others are expanding, we can envisage a more balanced spread between the different groups. The group which is making most headway in terms of future preferences is that of 'work/life outside work' and in particular the subheading 'work and lifestyles'.

Against this, there are some gaps in the survey. First, we have no proper reference point in time and so we cannot establish any clear trend in the themes dealt with here. Given the average length of research programmes, it would be desirable to do a survey of this type every two or three years.

The survey has another limitation. It does not allow us to measure the relevance, the interest, or the novelty of results. It is impossible anyway to measure the results of research still in progress, but, more fundamentally, a census of this type is a poor instrument for evaluating research findings. All the same, it may be a necessary step in that direction. And now that researchers working on similar topics have been located, the way is open for a possible comparison of their findings, subheading by subheading.

Notes

1. The complete report (Pierre Dubois and Riva Kastoryano: *Recensement des recherches en cours sur le travail*, GST, Paris, April 1984) is available from the Groupe de Sociologie du Travail, 2, Place Jussieu, 75251 Paris Cedex 05. In the full report there is a section on the personal details of the 529 researchers (discipline, status, sex, university or research organization, etc.) and an explanation of the method of classification used for the themes.

2. Some of the categories used in this chapter raised special translation difficulties because they reflect particular French traditions of industrial organization, methods of administration, or use of 'purely technical' language. The most important are discussed in the Note on Translation.

4
Ten years of the sociology of work: the headings of the *Bulletin Signalétique* in 1972 and 1982

Daniel Chave*

To contribute to the study of the evolution of the sociology of work in France over the last decade, we thought we could gain an insight into the changes in the spread of themes and research subjects from an analysis of the distribution of keywords by which the CNRS *Bulletin* describes titles of publications.

We looked at two years, 1972 and 1982. The results are based on simplifications and working hypotheses for which we should perhaps be locked up! For example, we have acted as if the list of keywords used by the documentation service in question (the CDSH) had remained the same, which is not the case.

We decided to locate all the publications of French writers and institutions, published in French, in the field of the sociology of work. We were faced with an immediate problem: a certain number of references in the *Bulletin* seemed to us to be misclassified. On the other hand, a considerable number of publications which we felt ought to be in there did not figure in the sociology of work section. We therefore searched for them among the references under the general sociology heading.

Thus, the figures presented here do not represent a faithful picture of what is listed in the *Bulletin* under the heading sociology of work but rather what seemed to us to lie in that field. The selection was not made on any criterion other than that of our familiarity with the themes, topics, people and institutions which, in our opinion, make up our professional field. We hope, without being able to offer any guarantee, that our 'bias' will at least be systematic and this grid will be homogeneous for the two years under consideration. Bias of an equally or more important kind may also arise because the person selecting the list of key terms may change, with the added risk of what might be called 'interpretative drift'.

Once we had collected the titles of publications in our field, we sought out the keywords attributed to each document by the CDSH. Generally, two such words are given. We calculated how often the

* Groupe de Sociologie du Travail

most common subject-words appeared for the publications of 1972 and 1982.

In so far as there is more than one subject-word per title, it is not possible to draw up aggregated indices: in order to do this, we have had to fall back on a tricky process of reduction, giving each title one subject-word only.[1] Then we drew up aggregates of keywords to allow a final comparison. The methodological drawbacks in these operations are well known.

I have set out the results of the attempted comparison with all due hesitation. It should be seen as a basis for reflection on the shifting interests within our discipline rather than an empirical product capable of withstanding close inspection in the world of learning.

General statistics
The *Bulletin* lists some 4969 sociological references for the year 1972. For 1982 it records 4210.

In 1972, the sociology of work section accounts for 420 references. The sociology of organizations has another 74, making 494 in all. By 1982 the two sections had been combined and the section sociology of work and organizations accounts for 567 references.

Thus, between 1972 and 1982 we see: (i) a decrease in the number of references to sociology (from 4969 to 4210); (ii) an increase in the number of references to the sociology of work and organizations (SWO) both in absolute terms (from 494 to 567 references) and, even more so, in percentage terms (from 10 to nearly 15 percent of all the titles listed).

In the *Bulletin* for 1972 we found 80 references in France belonging to our field, 64 coming from the sociology of work section, 16 from other sections.

For 1982, we found 131 references, 120 in the SWO section, 11 elsewhere. That denotes a clear increase in the proportion of French publications listed by the *Bulletin*. The fact that we found fewer references belonging to our field but recorded in other sections in 1982 than in 1972 might indicate that the boundaries of our field of study have been better drawn and have 'firmed up' during the course of the decade.

The total number of references for which we found keywords totalled 77 for 1972 and 125 for 1982. These make up our definitive index.

This movement reflects what we have already seen concerning the increase in the number of references in the *Bulletin* for the sociology of work; but, in our opinion, it also represents an increase in the number of publications in French in the field.

Distribution of the main subject words:

	1972	1982
Workers' self-management	3	1
Automation	2	1
Time-budgets	0	2
Managers (*cadres*)	4	3
Careers	1	1
Unemployment	1	9
Working class	3	2
Working conditions and quality of working life	0	3
Division of labour	0	1
Labour law	0	1
Employment	2	9
Companies	12	11
Ergonomics	2	2
Vocational training	6	3
Strikes	0	3
Immigration	0	1
Industry	9	10
Labour market	0	4
Labour movement	1	1
Organization of work	0	6
Manual workers	1	4
Planning	1	1
Power	0	1
Professions	1	7
Industrial relations	1	3
Salaries	4	3
Unions	9	6
Work	12	14
Female work	2	10
Factory	0	2

Make-up of the aggregates and a comparison
(1) *Work, working time and rotas*:

In 1972, 6 references or 9 percent of the total. 4 relate to time — hours of work, length of working week, holidays. 1 relates to temporary work. 1 relates to life at work.

In 1982, 16 references or 13.8 percent of the total. 9 relate to time — length of working work, rhythms, etc. 6 relate to manual work. 1 relates to the black economy.

This aggregate is therefore proportionately on the increase. The reduction in the working week and flexible rotas make an appearance.

(2) *The division of labour, working conditions*:
In 1972, 5 references or 7.5 percent of the total. 2 concern industrial psychology. 3 concern ergonomics and safety at work.

In 1982, 14 references or 12 percent of the total. 4 relate to safety at work. 2 to ergonomics. 3 to working conditions. 5 to the organization and division of labour.

This aggregate is also on the increase, attributable to the appearance during the decade of the themes work organization, division of labour, quality of working life.

(3) *Women's work*:
We move from three references (4.4 percent) in 1972 to 10 (8.4 percent) in 1982, spread amongst these themes: Women's work/home work — 3 references. Discrimination — 1 reference. Wage workers — 1 reference. Vocational training — 2 references. Private life — 1 reference.

(4) *Pay, skills and vocational training*:
In 1972, 10 references (15 percent of the total): of which 4 were to payment systems: (the move to salaried status, *mensualisation*, 1; wage hierarchy, 3); skills, 2 and vocational training, 4.

In 1982, 8 references (6.8 percent of the total): of which 5 were to salaries: (inequalities between male and female workers, 1; with age, 1; others, 3); skills, 1 (cost of manpower) and vocational training, 2.

The number of references to salaries, skills and training decreases from 10 to 8 and by more than half as a percentage of the overall total of reference.

(5) *Employment, unemployment and the labour market*:
In 1972, 3 references (4.5 percent of the total): of which 2 were to youth employment and 1 to long term unemployment.

In 1982, 22 references (16.8 percent of the total): of which 3 were to the labour market; 9 to employment; 7 to unemployment; 2 to migration and 1 to immigration.

The percentage of publications devoted to employment has tripled and the total number of publications has grown seven-fold during the period 1972–82. The theme 'labour market', absent in 1972, exists in 1982.

(6) *Unions, workers, working class, disputes*:
1972: 15 references (22 percent of the total); unionism: 9; disputes: 1; other (working-class power, theories, etc.): 5.

1982: 16 references (13.8 percent of the total); unionism: 9; disputes: 2; individual relations: 2; working class: 3.

The number of references is stable but the proportion of publications on this theme decreases between 1972 and 1982.

(7) *Professions, skilled trades, cadres*:

1972: 8 references (12 percent of the total); cadres: 4; professions: 1; rest: 3.

1982: 11 references (8.4 percent of the total); cadres: 3; professions: 8.

The importance of this aggregate is roughly constant. There has been a moderate growth in the number of references and a decline in the proportion of publications.

Though the number of works relating to managers, or cadres, has been roughly stable, a rise has occurred in the number of references to the professions.

(8) *Companies, industries, factories*:

1972: 19 references (29 percent of the total); management, etc.: 5; company policies: 2; information technology, etc.: 4; communication of information: 3; various: 5.

1982: 21 references (18 percent of the total); management, etc.: 4; policy and strategy: 2; information, relations at work: 3; industrialization, restructuring: 4; various: 8.

The number of publications is stable but the proportion occupied by this aggregate falls between 1972 and 1982. This aggregate is highly heterogeneous: note, however, the new importance of themes linked to industrial restructuring.

The indexing of works by the CDSH is certainly intended to indicate to a reader consulting the *Bulletin* what the title looked up is about. The index therefore refers to a research topic, but also to areas of main concern, fields of study and concepts. This list of words does not let us know the theoretical stance of each author whose publications are indexed but the evidence concerning the shifting frequency of subject-words during the course of the decade lets us interpret these terms as indicators of a field of interest. So if the status of the terminology remains necessarily ambiguous, the shift in interests becomes fairly clear.

It is true that the shifts we perceive result from a study of several different types of publication. A book first has to pass through the filter of an editor in charge of a series and an assessment of its commercial potential is made by the publisher. A student's choice of thesis topic is linked to the field of interest of his or her supervisor; it also reflects the candidate's feel for what is in the air, the centre of debate at the moment the choice is made. A review article has to convince an editorial committee of its quality and appositeness. A research report is the end result of a call for tenders which reflects the desire for information of a particular part of the administration. It is true also that the reports and sometimes the theses often give rise to the publication of articles and books.

An implicit compromise is therefore reached between what is likely to be financed at the research stage (notably through the procedure of calls for tenders), what is academically acceptable (the approval of thesis and research supervisors as well as editorial boards of reviews) and what is likely to be published (the publisher's decision on the commercial feasibility of publication).

One element is relatively constant from one body of judgment to another — the title of the publication and its recognizable terms which constitute the subject-words and give an indication of the theme to the different judges of appositeness or interest. For example, one might explain the growing proportion of references to the quality of working life and work organization by calling attention to:

(1) Public interest in work dealing with the conditions and organization of work during this period. This has been an academic interest, but one also shared by unions, employers and personnel managers.

(2) The existence, or rather the appearance, of specialist institutions which provide some of the funds: ANACT, RESACT committee of the DGRST, FEQUT, CORDES.

(3) The existence and development of research groups which have a speciality and great experience in work and publications in this field: GST, *laboratoire de sociologie du travail et des relations professionnelles*, GLYSI, LEST.

As for the growing number of publications related to women's work, this should not, in our view, be put down to any specific funding but rather to the growing autonomy of research units working on these themes.

The spectacular growth of the employment/unemployment/labour market themes is hardly surprising given the current economic crisis. It is interesting to note that of the 22 references to this aggregate in 1982, seven, or nearly a third, are INSEE publications. One title comes from CEREQ, another from the Ministry of Labour; seven articles are published in non-specialist reviews.

Two different aspects of the role of state funding of research must be considered:

(1) The institutional funding of specialist bodies such as INSEE and CEREQ.

(2) Funding in the shape of bids for research contracts such as the Action Thématique Programmée of the CNRS: two of the titles listed were given as publications produced as a result of these appeals.[2]

We will not risk an interpretation of the decline in certain aggregates between 1972 and 1982. The decline in number of studies on pay and skills, for example, is apparent mainly in relation to the total proportion of publications rather than in absolute terms. Certain groups, certain researchers continue to work on these themes while others have moved on to new fields of interest.

Conclusion

To sum up, the figures that we have presented suggested four trends:

(1) The number of titles belonging to the field of the sociology of work relative to other areas of sociology appears to be on the increase, in absolute as well as relative terms; it also appears that the field is more sharply defined within the indexing system of the CNRS. The proportion of French publications relative to the total number of references in the archive seems to have grown between 1972 and 1982.

(2) The internal distribution of themes and topics, represented here by the subject-words used to index the documents, has clearly changed — that is without doubt most obvious in the development of work on employment, unemployment and the labour market on the one hand; and the development of themes associated with the division of labour, the organization of work and working conditions on the other. Finally, we should note the decrease in the number of studies on skills, gradings and salaries, as well as vocational training.

(3) The GST's share of publications in 1972 and 1982 seems relatively stable; eight titles in 1972, twelve in 1982 — a clear increase in absolute terms and a slight percentage decrease.

(4) Preferences as to the type of publication seem to have altered over the decade: the number of studies published in the form of review articles is growing but the proportion of articles in the overall number of titles surveyed fell from 80 to 55 percent.

The review *Sociologie du Travail* is one of seven to figure in both years; with seven articles in 1982 against nine in 1972 it retains a leading position among the publication outlets in our field but falls from first to third place. That may be a chance effect of the method of archiving: all the same, other reviews abound in 1982 to support the sociology of work and organizations section of the *Bulletin Signalétique*.

Notes

1. Strictly speaking, it was not necessary to resort to this reduction. While frequency counts produced from multiple codeable responses or values inevitably produce percentages that sum to more than 100, this is usually regarded as acceptable in descriptive statistics provided attention is duly drawn to the procedure.

2. Actions Thématiques Programmées began to make their appearance on the French research scene in the mid-1970s. In several respects, the Research Initiatives introduced by the Social Science Research Council in Britain around 1980 resembled ATPs — and may indeed have been modelled on them. Activity was focused on closely-related issues, often policy-related problems, and at the time this was widely disliked by researchers.

5
Sociological research and social requirements
Claude Durand*

The world of researchers and academics is becoming increasingly aware of a phenomenon which is not new but which is becoming ever more urgent today because of certain pressures: the dependence of sociological research on social requirements ('la demande sociale'), or more precisely the demands of the authorities who are charged with giving voice to this 'social demand' when they engineer a shift in research towards the social problems of contemporary society.

Before appraising the guiding hand and weighing up its advantages and drawbacks, it might be useful first to retrace the history of the relationship between research and this social demand, that is, the economic dependence of researchers in the social sciences.

The history of social demand

The 1950s
The political institutions began the process of defining research orientations after the Second World War. In the 1950s, empirical research developed at the expense of armchair academic research thanks to this process. The new research groups on the Left Bank (Institut de Science Sociale du Travail, or ISST, Centre de Sociologie des Organisations, Laboratoire de Sociologie Industrielle) owed their rapid expansion to the large proportion of research contracts which came their way from the ministries and international organizations. The long series of research projects on technical change[1] was financed by the Agence Européenne de Productivité, the European Coal and Steel Community, the Planning Commissariat ('the Plan') and the Ministry of Labour.[2] Crozier's research into the state tobacco company (SEITA) and automation, as well as that of Benoit and Maurice into workplace relations, benefited from a direct input of funds from the companies concerned. For a discussion of these studies see Rose (1979: Ch. 3).

Even so, there was no real feeling on the part of researchers of dependency on the client. Generally, the researchers defined a

* Groupe de Sociologie du Travail

research theme, sought out someone to provide the funds, and worked out a project which suited the latter without worrying unduly, as the direction of the research became clearer, about the client's opinion — so much so that, depending on the particular researcher's attitude, the research could result in critical findings which did not lend themselves to application (Touraine, Reynaud, Durand, Benoit/Maurice) or in reports with more practical intent (Crozier, Moscovici).[3] Care was always taken to try to avoid any appearance of attachment to the firms chosen for fieldwork and to compensate for the services rendered to the companies by giving unions access to the findings. The ISST guidelines on research in firms were specific on that point.

Research under contract in the 1960s and 1970s
Robert Fraisse[4] has shown how, in this second period, a whole array of analytical techniques dealing with social transformation was marshalled around the methods of industrial planning and urban development. This research gave impetus to medium-term forecasting as well as feedback for assessing the results of growth. For example, the evaluation of the benefits of economic progress was the subject of the Arras conference[5] on 'The Distribution of the Pay-off' with the participation of INSEE economists brought together by Pierre Bourdieu. Twenty years of expansion called for an appraisal of the progress made, an evaluation distribution, whether more or less egalitarian, of its benefits.

The methods used put the accent on surveys, on gaining access to concrete data that could be used in tandem with statistical information. With quantitative systems models in the ascendancy, the services of economists were preferred to those of sociologists. Fraisse notes that, in the distribution of contracts, research bureaux — whether public, private or quangos — were favoured, rather than academic research institutions.

May 1968 was the turning-point: as the economists had failed to see the 'events' coming, people began to turn back towards the sociologists for an explanation of the new social movements. Qualitative methods and monographs were preferred to quantitative research at this moment, as was sociology to economics (with contextual analyses of work, health and urban life). A number of bodies were created to see to the management of research contracts: CORDES at the Plan, the urban research mission at the Ministère de l'Equipement, finance agencies linked to DGRST and the various ministries (Labour, Justice, Industry). The accent was now more on the actors and on social action than on economic mechanisms and the advances in living standards. At the same time, researchers were given more scope to define their own projects, the state fishing amongst the myriad initiatives for anything it might find useful.

Sociological Giscardianism
From 1974, the economic crisis ushered in both a renewed selectivity as to priorities combined with financial cutbacks to compensate for the cost of putting former contract researchers on the permanent staff. These were lean years for sociological research. Intellectuals became more and more alienated from the authorities. The reining in of the state's intervention in the economy and its disengagement from the social consequences of the crisis led to a retreat into more individualistic research strategies: life histories, enquiries into social and cultural subgroups or particular trends.

The absence of any overall political project, plus the epistemological criticism of statistical research was translated into a return to individualism by the sociologists. The trend, at the turn of the decade, was for a return to the concrete, to the particular, to personal biographies, to life histories which reconstitute the collective working-class memory or daily life.[6] Up until then, historians had envied the sociologists' systematic methods, their ambition to explain things. Now we saw the sociologists turning towards history, to the slice of life. This new direction entailed the use of ethnographical methods and monographs, be they monographs on strikes, localities or firms. The faithful reproduction of working-class memory took over from class analysis. No-one was interested any more in the role of the state or of the working class, in the interplay of institutions, of social forces. Conflict was located outside the workplace, outside institutions, its reference points now becoming sexual, ethnic, regional or community-based. In the face of the impotence of bureaucratic centralism, the sociologist began to highlight local individualism and identities: concrete social groups were described, with their multiple referents and their tangle of meanings. Theoretical ambitions wasted away.

The socialist era
The Left came to power with the aim of relaunching the economy and mobilizing the vitality of the nation. The politicians were to try to put research at the service of this grand project. Research was held up as the privileged instrument of technological development. The 'Assises de la recherche' were to mobilize researchers in the service of development. The Assises aimed to stimulate exchange of ideas and genuine debate on priorities through well-funded round-tables and conferences. A huge Ministry of Research and Industry was created. The Utopia of technical progress was back with a vengeance.

In this respect, the Eighth Plan had remained critical and cautious. The report of the technology working group at the end of 1979 asked the question: 'Can technological innovation serve social progress?'.[7]

The text goes on to note that the very fact that such a question had been asked proved that a reply in the affirmative was no longer a certainty.[8] The working group appeared to refuse the thesis of technological determinism and any automatic link between technical progress and social progress.

The group's brief was just as questioning: 'What opportunities and what risks does future technical progress hold for the quality of individual and collective life in France?'

Three years later, in the socialist period, there was to be no room for such nuances. The minutes of the 'journées de travail' (work sessions) of 15 and 16 November 1982 of the Ministry of Research and Industry[9] define technological development as the key to France's international competitiveness, the instrument of its economic recovery and the framework for its social aspirations. Innovation in all directions is envisaged, in the new technologies (information technology, electronics, data processing, telecommunications, space, biotechnology, new forms of energy, agro-industry) are defined as the vital sectors of the economy.

This large-scale technological evolution, of course, is to shape the society of tomorrow. The programme for the electronics branch portends the transformation of individual and social life by the new technologies in many sectors: information, education, health, transport, patterns of living.

Research, then, is to be placed at the disposal of development. In the words of the Chevènement seminar: 'Scientific research and technological development govern our success' (the Chevènement seminar).

This upgrading of research is one of status (research determines the development of new technologies) but at the same time it is also an instrumental upgrading: industrialists and researchers are invited to work more closely together. Researchers must make their results show a pay-off since 'they have a moral contract with the nation'.

This sort of policy has institutional consequences: the legislation on research orientations and programmes is linked closely to industrial policy. The CNRS has announced that it is to create subsidiaries in order to ensure that research pays a dividend and stimulates applications. We must examine the consequences of this policy for the social sciences which there is an effort to put at the disposal of this technological mobilization.

Detraz: putting his foot in it
Several methods could be used to evaluate the progress of the political mobilization of the social sciences, in particular an analysis of how the themes of invitations to bid for research contracts ('appels d'offres') have evolved — we have seen a clear increase in the number of themes related to new technology. We have chosen to concentrate on a particular document — the report of the Detraz enquiry[10] which is probably no more than a symptom of the new policy on research, a little eccentric perhaps, but with the merit of clearly stating its leanings and representing well one of the new currents. Even if this trend is not unchallenged and only partially operative, it represents an important pole of current thinking and has had repercussions both on actual research operations and at the institutional level. This shift therefore merits some consideration.

The dangers of social demand

Scientific rigour and political commitment
It was only to be expected that a socialist government would urge the research community to intervene more in society. After all, these researchers, with a reputation for being on the Left, could now have the opportunity of putting their ideas to the test.

The reasoning behind the Detraz enquiry began with the hypothesis that social science research cannot but have a 'finality', an ultimate aim:

> It is important for the future success of genuine social progress that the scientific and technological effort of the nation should henceforth be directed towards the new objectives and made to bear fruit (from the Minister of Research and Technology's letter which served as the enquiry's brief).

We see again, in this enquiry, that the 1950s' aim of harnessing technical progress to social progress, with the new idea, an interventionist one, that the interdependence of technical and social aims should be grasped 'upstream', before decisions are taken. Detraz therefore refuses all technological determinism: the state of social relations is to influence the conception of techniques. Technology (both the equipment and the organization of work) is determined by the conditions and aims of the society in which it is developed. And so the social sciences are entrusted with the role of creating the conditions for mobilization behind new technologies to make them an instrument of the objectives expected of technical progress.

Starting from the observation that social reality, the object of research, is the product of social relations and is recognized as constituting one of the social issues at stake, the enquiry concludes that sociologists should allot themselves the right to guide these issues and intervene in their development. Thus, researchers are given the task of transforming worker–employer relations in the workplace.

All that remains is for the researcher to define the correct objective and choose whom he or she is going to work for.[11]

What privileged insight does the social scientist possess, and what special authority gives him or her the right to arbitrate between opposing social objectives? Does this not, purely and simply, subjugate sociology to the political options and ethical choices of individuals, conferring on them a legitimacy which would imply that the sociologist is a privileged citizen?

Consequent on this policy, the enquiry proposes to set up mechanisms and devise procedures with a view to going beyond 'social demand' and making the process of elaborating research themes more democratic, restoring to research its social effectiveness. Thus, a piece of research will be defined in *interaction* with the social actors, foreseeing methods which would enable workers to participate in the research process. Research becomes social action: 'If you're not *with* the workers, you must be against them'. ('Si l'on n'agit pas avec les travailleurs, on les trahit'.) Social debates no longer feature objective scientific observers. The sociologists are invited to take sides in social conflicts — sociology is up for grabs, it becomes a free-for-all.

We do not contest the opening remarks on the biasing of data from necessarily partial witnesses, nor how difficult it is for sociologists to make objective observations since they are themselves contaminated by personal ideologies, by their own social perspective, and since they are immersed in social action with all its political and ideological presuppositions.

But is not interventionist research a rather curious way of resolving the tension between scientific rigour and the bias of political commitment ('engagement')? It entails breaking the objective distance which theoretical analysis and methodological precautions have created in order to immerse oneself in the empiricism of action. Sticking close to the ground does not confer any special heuristic meaning. 'Helping the worker situate himself as an actor' — does the worker need our help there? Does not the mobilization of researchers behind social objectives entail a confusion of roles, a step on the road to becoming the gurus of the labour movement? And why not management consultants?

Research as a factor in industrial relations

So research looks like becoming *one of the issues at stake* in industrial relations: it will become an interested party in social conflicts. Under the pretext of not being 'disconnected from the socioeconomic system', sociologists are going to have to get their hands dirty.

The notion, borrowed from the natural sciences, that an object is modified and structured by the observation is probably true. But does the observation become any more objective if researchers identify with their object, undertake to reveal it to itself, perhaps even manipulate it? Is this active interventionism going to make fieldwork any easier? Industry's well-known mistrust of sociologists can only grow. Experts can switch clients but their status remains that of the expert, and as soon as they seek to help one side they become a threat to the other. How can you lay claim to independent judgment if you throw yourself into the fray? This conception of research carries the risk of involving the researcher in endless diplomatic wrangles.

Everyone knows from experience that researchers and practitioners do not work to the same rhythms. This interventionist research risks transforming research into rapid, botched operations and reducing sociological research to some sort of group dynamic. If we go any further along that path, we're going to be swimming in considerations of applicability and utilitarianism.

Should not our role as social critic be defined in a context providing for more distance from the object, one which would allow us space to stand back from the immediate issues and which is not locked in to any summary interventionism? These criticisms do not imply that we should abandon the idea of improving the ways we put over our findings, of looking for feedback from research reports — a good test for the analyst — but we must do this without making any exaggerated claims about our effectiveness.

Keeping a distance from the authorities

This distance from the political authorities and from social action may be taken as a sign of escapism and fence-sitting. But it is also a guarantee of our freedom of judgment.

If we reckon that our function as social critics is more important than our being available for immediate practical purposes, our research will first of all seek to produce photographs of social reality, or at a pinch diagnoses of it, and therapy will be left to others.

This wary attitude, involving little or no participation, is criticized in government circles[12] as well as by employers and union officials. Policies on the sciences and the universities currently call for 'mobilizing programmes', 'research with practical objectives'. Now, these sometimes express very short-term political preoccupations.

If you compare the list of themes under the heading 'research with practical objectives' in the government documents of 1982 and 1983 you will notice that, from one year to the next, 'living conditions' has disappeared from the list of social and cultural objectives. New objectives in economic policy may explain this change. But should new research be dependent in this way on changes in the political climate?

Under Giscard d'Estaing, the development of research funding towards more and more applied programmes was deplored.[13]

Given the current trend for 'research with practical objectives', the same movement is likely for different reasons, with concern to see social transformation moved on apace — itself laudable — through putting research at the service of society. The call for research projects on 'social life in the workplace' is openly geared to 'the whole batch of reforms currently under way in the country'.

The ambitious policy of the Ministry of Research and Industry under Chevènement[14] lumped together, with this aim, scientific progress and technological development, rediscovering the technicist Utopias of the 1950s when technical progress became synonymous with social progress. The anti-determinist current of the last few years has left sociologists of work little inclined to lend themselves to these new Utopias.

Our freedoms

The best way of justifying our independence vis-à-vis the government (of whatever shade) is to spell out the conditions of our autonomy. The latter finds expression in the conditions under which research is carried out. It manifests itself, of course, on the theoretical and methodological level. It must finally find a guarantee in the consolidation of institutions.

(1) As regards *means*, researchers have contradictory demands. While they refuse to put themselves at the disposition of a narrow, overly prescriptive demand, they nonetheless claim access to documents and to premises for fieldwork. This is a basic necessity for their work. A government anxious to develop research must facilitate access to firms and administrations which are little inclined to a freedom of information mentality and all too ready to hide behind the 'confidential' nature of certain information.

Research under contract had the merit of launching empirical research and shaking the cobwebs off academic research. It also allowed a bolstering of the potential of the various centres through the large-scale recruitment of young researchers. The confrontation with hard facts contributed to a reorientation of methodology and theory, forcing academic research to leave behind its ideological distortions and to face up to the realities of social practice. Without wishing to question these merits, we must, however, avoid a situation in which the whole research effort is dependent on contracts and see to it that each centre has a supply of guaranteed funds for those initiatives it chooses, alone, to make.

(2) Limiting the economic dependency of researchers does not imply that those researchers who are under contract should not preserve their *freedom of analysis and interpretation*. The only judge here is the university institution and it must be free of interference from funding agencies and research subjects alike. The autonomy of the researcher applies from the moment the research problematics are formulated. Every administration tends to see problems as having external causes. We feel that the problematic must by the same token question the role of the body or institution which has sponsored the research. Is a company looking into the efficiency of its payment by results system also prepared to see its own policy objectives on wages analysed? Will the agency of the Ministère du Travail questioning researchers on the effectiveness of work reorganization experiments be ready to accept a study that includes an analysis of its own role in promoting new forms of organization? Research requirements always focus on someone or something else, and not the sponsor, who is excluded from the field of study. Is the body commissioning the research also willing to be an object of research?

Only sociologists can be the judge of the frontiers and scope of the field of study — this is their craft. The definition of a sociological problematic may lead to a perspective completely different from that formulated in the original 'social requirement'. Thus, research into technological innovation is regularly formulated by social actors in terms of the 'social consequences' of technological change, which implies that technological innovation as such is an unchanging given. The success of the sociological approach in this field has been to problematize the terms of the question and show that we cannot conceive of an autonomous 'technical progress' supposedly inducing 'social consequences' — it was necessary to apprehend *at one and the same time*, in the very process of technical innovation and its application, the objectives and social strategies which set the process in motion and send it on a given course. Thus, the study of 'social consequences' cannot be separated from that of economic, financial and technical decision making and strategy.

The sociologist must likewise have a free rein as regards the method and conduct of the research. The researcher is responsible for the work and its conclusions. Scrutinizing and checking results is the province of the profession. Neither the institutions and organizations studied, nor the political authorities, can have any power of sanction or censorship over this work.

Now, if the threat of direct control is practically non-existent, control of production does become a reality with the thorny problem of publications and books. One way of stifling scientific production is to deny the publication of results. While retaining the normal guarantees of anonymity for the people and organizations that are willing to take part, it is extremely important that research findings are widely diffused. This is vital for the development of intellectual life. It is no less fundamental for social utilization of the research effort. Beyond its practical utility, research is first of all knowledge, and science cannot progress without a wide diffusion of this knowledge.

(3) In this freedom of diffusion, the research *institution* should play an important role — it is at once a guarantee of it and the means. The autonomous status of the researcher is a privilege. This type of CNRS status is not common in western countries, where researchers are generally also teachers or lecturers. After a probationary period, CNRS researchers gain copper-bottomed job tenure and have the right to concentrate entirely on problems of their own choosing — or even, in theory, simply to do nothing but sit and think creatively. Nor are they required to teach, though in practice many choose to do so. A minority 'moonlight' in several other part-time posts. But personal competition and academic ambition drive the majority towards a high level of output. Such a system does not exist in the eastern bloc where sociologists are first and foremost practitioners, for whom research is a method for finding solutions to practical problems: sociologists are at the disposal of enterprises and public bodies. The privileged status we enjoy must be preserved as the principal guarantee of autonomy in a social field where expert opinion is sought after by rival interests. The institution of the CNRS will continue to play a role here.

However, its function in the orientation of research is more delicate and controversial. Historically, in the social sciences, the CNRS gradually allowed itself to lose control of its role of shaping scientific policy because the funding of research projects slipped out of its grasp. The diffusion of funds used for the launching of programmes has been increasingly entrusted to external bodies (the Plan, economic and social Ministries) and the periodical reports of the CNRS commissions have become documents simply registering trends decided elsewhere.

Instigating these chosen funding policies is done on the cheap since what is involved is a financial intervention at the margin, as it were, with CNRS continuing to pay the researchers and foot the bill for buildings, laboratories, libraries, etc., making up the infrastructure. Meanwhile, the Plan and the Ministries can limit their action to placing contracts on the basis of 'top-up' funding for extra operating costs, which are nonetheless vital for the research: expenses for fieldwork, secretarial work, the printing of reports.

Faced with this effective influence of the authorities on research policy, the CNRS has finally had to copy its competitors and launch, with its own researchers, operations of a contractual nature (in the form of ATPs — similar to ESRC research initiatives) which will allow it to claw back certain chances for setting a lead in research programming.

This recovery of some rights over programme-setting is at once salutary and dangerous. The CNRS is rediscovering a role it should never have given up. But at the same time it finds itself, due to a similar way of administering funds, under the same type of political pressure as the ministerial sources of finance: a concern with utilitarianism and rapid results. This new trend is even apparent structurally when new interdisciplinary commissions are created.

Three new commissions have been created as a result of the preoccupation with 'making research pay off' which, in administrative terms, means 'getting it utilized'.

The commission for the 'valorization' of research and its application aims to maintain and safeguard the status of those researchers put at the disposal of industry. The commission for scientific information is geared towards the diffusion of research findings and getting cultural spin-offs going. The administrative commission provides a framework for the participation in the activities of state administrations.

A similar utilitarian trend also seems to characterize officially stated plans for higher education, as set out in the recent 'projet de loi' (similar to the British White Paper) where universities are urged to concern themselves with 'responding to social requirements' and to organize their relations with the professions better.

Notes

1. The ISST research into the attitudes of steelworkers, research into the evolution of payment systems, the CERP research on the restructuring of the coal industry and millinery trade, Pierre Naville's work on automation.

2. Nicole Abboud de Maupeou's work on young apprentices.

3. Thus, Crozier went over his findings with managers in the administrations studied and Serge Moscovici took pains to make recommendations on how workers might be kept informed of and participate in technical change. (Barbichon, G. and Moscovici, S. (1962) *Modernisation des mines, Conversion des mineurs*. Paris: Ministère du Travail.)

4. Fraisse, Robert (1981) 'Les sciences sociales: utilisation-dépendance-autonomie' in *Sociologie du Travail*, Volume 23, Number 4.

5. See Darras (1966) *Le Partage des bénéfices*. Paris: Minuit.
6. The papers of the Cresuot seminar organized by the Société Française de Sociologies show this new trend.
7. The title of Paragraph 3 of the first part of the document prepared by the Planning Commissariat in preparation for the 8th Plan: *La Société française et la technologie*. (1980) Paris: La Documentation Française.
8. Surveys in several different fields come up with equally sceptical findings. See 'Les ouvriers et le progrès technique' in *Sociologie du Travail*, 1, 1980.
9. *Une Politique industrielle pour la France*. Published by La Documentation Française.
10. We are aware that this report does not have any official status as regards government research policy. However, the commission was set up and even if this school of thought is not uncontested, its theses can be easily spotted in current research policy. The document is thus useful as an indication of the concrete proposals of the tendency.
11. This choice is not a formality and during recent debates in the discipline researchers who have definite aims (*chercheurs 'finalisés'*) have accused one another of treason and manipulation of the working class.
12. One civil servant from the Ministry of Research and Industry refused us access to his files on the grounds that sociological research 'did not bring any added value'.
13. See Dubois, Pierre: *La Sociologie du Travail ouvrier en France dans les années 70*.
14. Jean-Pierre Chevènement entered the new government immediately in 1981. Before his arrival in power he had run the Centre de Recherche et d'Etudes Socialistes (CERES), a noted focus for radical Left opinion (and often agitation, too) in the Parti Socialiste. After becoming Minister of Education in the later years of the socialist government, he dissolved CERES and promoted a republican traditionalist approach to education, stressing the authority of teachers and self-discipline and civic virtue ('civisme') among pupils.

6
The frontiers of the sociology of work
Sabine Erbès-Seguin*

Work is a complex activity, its definitions varied and ambiguous. The construction of the sociology of work as a specific discipline implied, on the part of its pioneers, the delineation of its own approach and methodology. The difficulties arising from these problems are clearly stated in the *Traité de Sociologie du Travail*. We will only analyse here those relations which, from the point of view of the theoretical differentiation between disciplines, appear to pose the most important problems.

Industrial psychology: conflictual relations
On the surface, the closest discipline to the sociology of work, at least in its 'American' origins, is what might be called the psychophysiology of work. So much so that, in everyday language, we might confuse the two. But, while social psychology certainly shares a common boundary, the two disciplines are in real terms poles apart.

One possible key to the historic links between experimental psycho-sociology with American origins in the 1930s and social psychology is provided by Pagès (in Friedmann and Naville, 1961: 96 et seq.) in what he calls the concept of 'homothemics': 'a science is homothemic when its object of study esteems itself to be homogeneous with it' and especially when, by the very process of reflection that it puts into operation, it plays a role in the evolution of the object studied. Thus, social psychology plays a part in the very processes which condition and constitute work.

This analysis should be read in conjunction with that of Maisonneuve (1950) who considers the concepts of attitude and role to be intermediary notions between psychology and sociology since both, unusually, lend themselves to definition on the individual *and* the collective level.

This analysis highlights the permanent conflict which cuts across the two disciplines: between a subjectivist tendency, represented in France since 1900 by Gabriel Tarde; and a 'societal' ('sociétaire') tendency represented by Durkheim. The controversy here centres on the shape of the order in which collective and individual attitudes are

* Groupe de Sociologie du Travail

ranked. For some — the latest and without doubt the best-known in France at the present time is Olson[1] — society is the sum of individuals. A Weberian strand is also represented in this tendency. For Durkheim, on the other hand, the individual is formed and dominated by society. Now, according to Maisonneuve, the inadequacies of both theses can be overcome thanks to the use of his two concepts: 'the concept of attitude is both individual' (since the attitude translates the position of such and such an individual, the member of such and such a group faced with a collective problem) and 'collective . . . one can envisage [the attitude] of one group vis-à-vis another'. Expanding on the advantages of such a concept from the point of view of scientific knowledge, Maisonneuve points out that he is advocating a dynamic, not a static, apprehension of individual and collective phenomena which are then treated in tandem.

The concept of role is to be treated in the same way: thus, for this author, the main feature of social psychology is that it grasps people 'simultaneously as a *sociable* being and a socialized being'; it grasps them 'at that sort of crossroads where external influences and spontaneity meet . . . [it is] a specialized study, not to be confused with classic psychology or sociology'.

These two approaches, those of Pagès and Maisonneuve, give us a better understanding of the epistemological bases and the academic birth of industrial sociology in the USA, where the psychosocial experiments of the Mayo team came into contact with the systems approach developed by Henderson at Harvard following the biological model.[2] That explains in particular how a psycho-sociology of social control catering for the needs of industry could make the transition into an academic discipline. It also highlights the great importance of the concepts of role and attitude, and one of the origins of all functionalist sociology. We will see other aspects when it comes to the relationship with economics.

The relationship of the physiology of work with the problems of the adaptation of men to work are too obvious to need much space here. It is a matter, as Pagès again puts it, of 'adjusting the material auxiliaries of human activity to the mode of operation which is both the most efficient and the least expensive'. Here we will simply point out the extent to which this collaboration between the two disciplines reinforces the overwhelming priority of the technical factor in the organization of work.

The functions of economic assumptions in sociology
For nearly 100 years two schools of thought have been fighting sporadic battles in a war which is much more than a mere skirmish over frontiers in the analysis of social phenomena. For while the

majority of economists and sociologists admit that economic and social matters constitute a single unbroken process and recognize the specific place that behaviour has in it, there is much more argument over the conception of rationality and particularly the position occupied by behaviour therein.

> From Aristotle to Marx, man in society comes under a single discipline . . . After Marx specialisation wins out over a common training and a single viewpoint with, however, the remarkable phenomenon of a latecomer, sociology, proclaiming its vocation to be *the* science of the sciences of man (Nicolai, 1967: 391).

This is a debate which goes well beyond the boundaries of the sociology of work but one in which we find the preoccupations of certain French sociologists of work at the beginning of the 1960s. Indeed, following T. Hopkins (in Polanyi et al., 1957) sociology is the study of the inter-relations between the various social processes which constitute society. One of the most important of these is the economy, thanks to which members of society are assured of the continuous supply of the material means to satisfy their needs. Yet, says Hopkins, sociologists have shown little originality in elaborating the basic concepts of this process. More often than not, they have been content to take economic theory as their starting-point and have thus worked with the hypothesis, totally without nuance, that *rational action and the market* are respectively the origin and the characteristic form of economic processes. This definition, the basis of Hopkins' critique of Parsonian theory, is interesting in several respects. Above all, it shows how classic sociology was content to take its bearings from economic concepts without redefining or questioning them. One might go so far as to say that only the refusal to redefine the concepts of economics allowed Parsons and Smelser to show that the economy is a sub-system of the social system.

Relations between economists and sociologists in France over the last thirty years can be schematized as follows.

(1) *The rediscovery of sociology* in France after its almost total eclipse in the pre-war years[3] came about first and foremost through the sociology of work. For Friedmann and his successors (who here, if not in other respects, reflect the perspective of Parsons) industrial sociology is *the* sociology of industrial societies. The way in which Friedmann poses 'the human problems' of work shows well that, for him, the great paradigm is technical change and its consequences.

During this period there seemed to be the greatest possible distance between sociologists and economists as well as mutual ignorance — even though each was claiming hegemony over the study of society. Towards the end of this period, one book[4] did begin to ask questions, particularly about the boundaries between the two disciplines, but very few sociologists figured among the authors (four out of thirty-nine) and none of these was a sociologist of work. The latter, for the most part, situated their research in the firm, on people at work, with a few incursions into the field of 'industrial democracy'.

Only Alain Touraine (1963) attempted to build a general theory of action and social movements. Reflecting on the relative absence of sociological studies on economic facts, Lautman (1970) felt that:

> the answer probably lies in the infatuation of that whole first generation of empirical sociologists with the concepts and methods of the social psychologists, who were well ahead in the rank order of technical achievement. From there developed that well-known preference for attitude studies and, for example, for electoral behaviour and the problems of human relations. In France, it is said that professional sociologists have, in the analysis of industrial society, preferred to study disputes and the dynamics of social forces rather than systems of regularity and affinities of structure.

Cuisenier (in Palmade, 1967) for his part, has said that economic sociology has two main tasks: it must restore the meaning given by the actors to their own aspirations and seek to understand economic behaviour as systems of actors in the light of a more general theory of social action. This perspective might be compared to the ambitions of Parsons, though we have already seen how he might be criticized for using economic concepts without defining them.

(2) *After 1968*, there was a period of intense ideological confrontation — among economists as well as sociologists — which made it much clearer that differences are located within each discipline rather than between them. So sociology as a whole, and a fortiori the sociology of work, appeared to represent a particular aspect of an analysis without precise boundaries between disciplines. This position, which tended to be increasingly shared by specialists in the social sciences, flew in the face of the traditional partitioning of disciplines:

> which only takes over — generalising and perpetuating them in the process — the obvious divisions that the practices of industrial society establish between the behaviour, the situation and the institutions of the different categories of social subjects: the company . . . is always, for Political Economy, the only real economic actor; the individual is isolated at his workpost; and the same individual, when socialised, is seen in the organisation of the workshop or company. Distinctions in reality are in this way set up as theoretical distinctions . . . [But] the study of the mass of wage earners (*le salariat*) obliges us to look at work and the firm as groups of relationships, not as fixed realities with an autonomous existence (Rolle, 1971).

It was during this period that the publication in French of the work directed by Polanyi and Arensberg (1975) revived the controversy between economists and sociologists, in particular following Hopkins' critique of Parsons:

> It is the economists who have defined sociological problems existing within the sphere of the economy. With the result that we know next to nothing about types of economies other than our own — and even that we only understand in part due to the lack of any sociology of the market economy.

This lacuna could be explained, say, by the need, recognized by all post-Keynesian economists, to take into account behaviour — no theory can function if it is based on economic rationality alone: part at least of the explanation would thus be *transferred* to sociology and/or psychology. The next step in this type of approach was taken by Parsons when he *embraced* the economy in a general explanation of the social system — but at the price we have already seen.

However, it is interesting to note that Polanyi and his associates questioned the sociological (and economic) view of societies in a study of non-commercial ('non marchandes') societies whose functioning cannot be explained by an economic theory based on the predominance of the market. That demonstrated the ethnocentricity of economists.

The issue here is the role of the 'global social phenomena' (to use Marcel Mauss's term) in the explanation of particular phenomena, the *way* that the economic and social system is taken into account in the analysis.

Parsons, following Max Weber, whose ideas he had introduced into the USA, thought that all societies, taken as wholes, tended to be differentiated at the subsystem level, each of these, including the economy, having a specialized function. Against this, Polanyi and Arensberg's central hypothesis, supported by their analysis of non-market societies, was that the economy does not always have the essential function that it has in industrial societies. Concepts from economic theory are therefore of no use when trying to account for how these other types of society function. The universal rationality postulated by classical economists is just a myth. In this respect, and this alone, Polanyi says he agrees with the analyses of Marx who is perhaps alone in avoiding ethnocentricity.

For both Polanyi and Marx, an economic process only has reality in an 'institutionalized' form, that is, in the words of Polanyi, 'in the context of social structures which constitute its structures of meaning' ('sémantique'): 'The study of the changing place of the economy in society is nothing more than the study of the way in which the economic process is institutionalised at various times and places.'

But Polanyi soon parts company with Marx. Indeed, he does so in his very intentions. Polanyi declares that the main interest of the theory he is proposing lies in its compatibility with functional theory, and so he takes pains to ensure this is the case. Moreover, in his foreword to the French edition, Maurice Godelier stresses the areas of agreement of the authors with functionalist theory:

> The economy within a [system of] sociology always functions within a structural context. The universal function of the economy is to provide society with the means to achieve its objectives while adapting itself to the context of an external environment. The analysis must not begin with individuals but with societies envisaged as totalities.

The essential difference between Parsons and his critics in this book lies in the role of the market — whether it is central or not: for the critics, the fact that the economy might exist as a separate institution is a historical exception and not linked to the tendency for each societal whole to differentiate itself. As a result, 'Parsons' general theory is precluded from any generalisation since it is a party to ethnocentric bias'.

The same sort of divisions between perspectives persists into the present period which one can date from the end of the 1970s, though the terms of the debate have become clearer with the arrival in force of the 'new economists' inspired by the Chicago school. Their approach is based on the paradigm of rational choices made by isolated agents.[5] Olson's book, which appeared in 1966 but was not translated into French until 1978, may serve as a landmark and a base for this tendency, taken up and developed by certain sociologists. Thus, Raymond Boudon considers social phenomena as the product of the behaviour of individuals, endowed with intentionality and coherence. This debate directly challenges sociologists, as Caillé (1981) has correctly pointed out: 'Is there still in existence a sociology with scientific ambitions which is anything more than a partial reading of Political Economy?'

Caillé's central theme is that if there is a convergence between economics and sociology, it is because discussions on society are situated within the framework of a given type of economic system: they deal with the way it works rather than ways in which it might change. Thus, the structure of interests is a given. It is then enough merely to analyse the calculations made by actors on the basis of these interests: 'It is because a society is not identical with itself that economic axioms result in the hiatus which produces history. But the axioms of self-interest cannot explain it.' It seems here that we are touching on one of the main aspects of the ambiguity inherent in the relationship between economics and sociology. To bring this out we have had to move some way beyond the boundaries of the sociology of work.

History and the role of change in sociological explanation

If we contend that the analysis of social relationships, in particular relationships to do with work, cannot be confined within a rigid framework, we are allotting history a decisive place: this is the only way of not artificially separating the study of change from the totality of processes involving such relationships. Only a historical perspective allows us to spot the scale of socioeconomic transformations, often imperceptible in a 'slice' of reality, but equally it helps us move away from the simple study of disconnected events.

Certainly, the historical perspective is particularly important for analysing periods of so-called crisis. Yet the immoderate recourse to that word 'crisis' is often compounded by the lack of any precise analysis, so great is the temptation to consider the period in question as exceptional. Now, any crisis is both the cause and the end result of a series of processes. To go beyond a mere location of events, only the historian can allow us to avoid a whole series of traps, in particular those pointed out by Starn (1976): considering normal processes as pathological; underestimating long-term trends by concentrating on short crises. This author notes that one of the great contributions of the French historical school (the *Annales* school) is to have studied 'the growth and development of an underdeveloped European economy.[6] For them, it is the long period from the fifteenth to the eighteenth century which counts, not the short crises.' He cites in particular the contributions of Braudel (1979) and Richet (1968).

Elsewhere, Le Roy Ladurie (1976) analyses the different historical dimensions of the notion. While defining a crisis as a 'negative and temporary break in a trend or tendency', he shows how necessary it is to distinguish 'several time-scales' by analysing, from the thirteenth century until the present day, forms of crisis of varying periodicity. Starting from this level of analysis therefore has the beneficial effect of first of all showing the *relativity* of the situations in which we locate the relationships under consideration: this gets rid of the apocalyptic aspect that can paralyse analysis.

The most important work in France on the historical construction of capitalist labour relations has been done by Michelle Perrot (1974). The study of 'strikes in their infancy' is also the study of a difficult industrialization and the depiction of a moment in the long history of social conflict. Perrot thus takes her place amongst those contemporary historians who are really sociologists of the past. But reading her description of the transition of strikes from the status of a criminal offence to that of institutionalized conflict, from wildcat stoppages, often disavowed by the embryonic unions, to organized bargaining, one is sometimes surprised to discover contemporary echoes in the working-class world of a century ago. Relatively surprised, one ought to say, perhaps, since despite the transformations in French industrial society, basic social relationships have not changed.

What is surprising is that, in comparing Perrot's analysis to those of authors with ostensibly similar objectives (e.g. Tilly and Shorter, 1974; Goetz-Girey, 1965), radically different perspectives are evident, and it is only in the aftermath of 1968 that comparable approaches can be found (Dubois et al., 1973; Durand and Dubois, 1975). Two elements of explanation combine to throw light on the change in methods of analysis. Each study is decisively shaped both by the period under observation and by the cultural context of the author. The very subject of the study becomes different depending on this. Reflecting on a period when strikes are barely lawful (the 1864 law) or when unions are not yet really legal (the 1884 law) and are often only formed on the occasion of strikes, Perrot is led to define the strike first of all as a social phenomenon, 'a rich and dense working class object', 'a dynamic relationship between social groups'. She concentrates on the internal structure of strikes, and it is through the constituent parts of this analysis that she introduces external determinants. We will see further on the interest of relationships established in this way. Her thought is also influenced — the reflections scattered throughout her book bear witness to this — by the experience of May 1968 and the use that, as a historian, she could make of the similarities between the two periods.

The way in which historically situated phenomena are interpreted has been at the centre of sociological debate, particularly on the place of change in society. In the field of work, debate has centred on the relationship between technical change and the evolution of work. Different conceptions of society appear through the various analyses.[7] Society may be depicted as a more or less permanent given. Analysis can be effected at any level of social organization (company, workshop, etc.): what is important is that it is here located in a framework where pre-existence (if not permanence) is assumed in relation to the phenomenon studied:

> ... an industrial society might be one in which production occurs in plants like those of Renault or Citroën. From that elementary definition

one might effectively deduce a number of traits inherent in an industrial economy . . . An industrial firm introduces a new type of division of labour (Aron, 1962).

Work relationships thus assume a subordinate character and are analysed by reference to the higher logic of the industrial system. It was this type of reasoning which inspired Taylor's model of 'scientific management'.

Of course, no society is stable, mutations occur and society therefore has to adapt: technical progress, for example, is a source of change, but that is injected into a model whose broad outlines remain unchanged. What has to be modified are the methods of production, the machines — and the workers then adapted to this. Much of American sociological reflection in the 1930s was inspired by such considerations.

Between this perspective and that which regards society as possessing a constant future, there is a difference of emphasis rather than a real break. The accent is put on the transformation of the social framework rather than on the simple existence of this framework. When, in effect, one studies a phenomenon at a given point in time, when one 'slices' through reality, the conditions of analysis are the same as in the first perspective: the logic of the system exists before any relations concerning work, and conditions these.

The origins of this line of thought may be found in the ideas of Auguste Comte on the constant improvement of human societies. In fact, for him, the industrial society rising before his very eyes had three dominant features: production was geared towards maximum output and industry was based on the scientific organization of work; the use of science to organize work would allow a powerful development of resources; and industrial production brings with it a concentration of workers which in turn creates new social phenomena.

So we meet again the two principal notions already referred to: (1) social relations at work are subordinate to a pre-existing industrial system, and (2) the belief in a scientific organization of work.

Auguste Comte thought that the opposition between workers and entrepreneurs was secondary, the result of poor industrial organization which could be corrected by reforms. Almost the same terms would be used by Taylor nearly 100 years later.

Thus, one can say that the two positions just summarized are identical and that the first represents one moment of an analysis expressed in the second in the form of a continuous evolution.

Conflict precedes institutions and is the only motor of change
This perspective is above all — but not exclusively — that of the Marxists who consider that:

> In the process of production, human beings do not only enter into a relationship with Nature . . . In order to produce, they enter into definite connections and relations with one another . . . The social relations within which individuals produce, the social relations of production are altered, transformed, with the change and development of the material means of production, the forces of production. The relations of production in their totality constitute what is called the social relations, society, and, moreover, a society at a definite stage of historical development (Marx, 1848).
>
> The history of all hitherto existing society is the history of class struggle (Marx and Engels, 1848).

Time and again in the work of these authors we come across basic principles: history is the work (the unconscious achievement) of people; the motor of history is class struggle; classes emerge from economic conditions, that is, from the structure and conditions of production.

Thus, the perspective has been turned upside down: first one situates the relations of production as a function of the economic conditions under which production is carried out, and then the forms of social organization linked to them are deduced. In the previous perspectives, a form of social organization, a society, was assumed to exist before any relations to do with work — the exact opposite. Marxists first take the relationships of work and describe them as conflictual due to the forms of property ownership which create class antagonisms.

Referring to Marx's analysis in *Das Kapital*, Friedmann and Naville (1961) offer the following interpretation: 'Ultimately, the motive element which explains the evolution or revolution of social structures seems to reside in this interaction between man and his surroundings by the intermediary of technical means (*la technique*).'[8]

This perspective is taken further by Naville and Rolle (in Friedmann and Naville, 1961). Automation represents for them the tangible expression of the logic of capital accumulation: to realize a profit, it is necessary to reduce the contribution of human labour, which not only subordinates it to capital, but transforms the content and the form of this labour.

Other non-Marxist commentators on social relations also place conflict at the heart of their analyses. Industrial, and especially postindustrial, societies are characterized, says Touraine, by the conflict which arises between social actors for the control of development, the dominant socioeconomic issue. But this conflict is rather described as a struggle between different social groups, each trying to ensure for itself the dominant role in a game where the stakes are the same for everyone. Here, it is not a question of any transformation of the productive bases of society, but a modification of the issue at stake which is accepted by all: development. In postindustrial society, it would be less a matter of producing than of creating and then exerting control over what was created.

To conclude on this point, we can say that change is an empirical reality. Industrial and even more so postindustrial society (if indeed it is any different) is characterized by constant modifications in the forms and techniques of production. But change does not mean transmutation, that is, the substitution of one system for another.

From the point of view of sociology, the nuance is of the utmost importance. Change in certain aspects of the system can easily be incorporated in the analysis of that system. From this point of view, all sociology is also the study of change. But mutations — economic, social and political — can only be analysed by first of all establishing what are the social relations and then deducing from them the forms of social, political and economic structuration.

The choice of one viewpoint or the other entails different types of explanation, whatever the field or level of analysis chosen.

Consequently, only historical examination allows an undistorted analysis of one or several precise moments in collective relations by situating them with respect to previous periods. The malaise which comes from a static approach, in which change intervenes as a factor from outside, arrives to disturb seemingly stable relationships, disappears now, since the movement being studied is perceived from the beginning as defined and situated by reference to a process. It is then possible to find a periodization which draws out the broad features of a period as well as the turning points.

The sociology of work and the myth of civil law
In spite of a long standing sociological tradition of reflection on the types of legal intervention in particular societies, contemporary sociology of work, in France at least, seems strangely silent on the function of the law in the social relations of work. Or rather, sociologists of work have hinted at two contrasting types of response to a question never explicitly put: either, studying the direct manifestations of the balance of power between employers and workers (the strike, more often than not), they indicated in this way that the law was for them a superstructure; or, analysing the relations concerning work as a game in which the actors themselves determined the rules, they conferred on this law the status of an institution which was

autonomous within the functioning of society.[9]

In contrast to this almost total lack of sociological analysis on labour legislation, the ground is well covered by jurists, especially when it comes to critical reflection on case law. This state of affairs is well summed up by Pierre Legendre (1977).

> The law is an over-protected area, efficiently defended against scientific enquiry, especially in France, this most centralised and (to use a word) pontificalist of countries. Legal questions have the curse on them, the speech of non-specialists skirts around them, sticking close to carefully checked and approved formulas, borrowed preferably from dead and prestigious masters such as Hegel and Marx.

Now, it is only through an epistemological reflection on legal concepts themselves that one can grasp the way in which the law — particularly labour law — operates on social relations.

Labour legislation was formed and developed in spurts, followed by periods of calm during which the reforms were gradually assimilated, or sometimes rejected, by society. To analyse it, with its ambiguities and contradictions, lays bare the rather chaotic way in which it was constructed and brought into use, reflecting the state of social relations at given periods.

The first contradiction relates to the very origins of this law, derived as it is from an individualistic civil law. Yet it is mostly a collective law. For example, it is hard to maintain that there is no fundamental difference between a contract of 'pure' civil law, such as a contract of sale, and a work contract. Yet a large part of jurisprudence makes use, in divergent ways, of the ambiguity in the definition of the labour contract (cf. Erbès-Seguin, 1983). Jurists recognize the difficulties inherent in the labour law in general and in the legal nature of the company (see, e.g., Camerlynck and Lyon-Caen, 1972). Yet in law socioprofessional relations still closely copy the model traced by interpersonal relations: striking, the collective weapon of the workers, drawing its effectiveness from the very fact that it is a concerted stoppage, is recognized as an individual right. It aims to limit or counter the individual right of ownership of the instruments of work. Employers respond to it in the individual mode using the notion of a 'right to work'.

The right to strike is without doubt one of the clearest examples of the ambiguities in labour legislation. Retracing its history, Jean-Claude Javillier (1976) highlights three historic stages: from the 'strike-as-criminal offence' ('grève-délit') to the 'strike-as-misdemeanour' ('grève-faute') to the 'strike-as-right' (grève-droit'). This aspect of collective relations, the strike, is one of the most closely regulated and among the most symbolic in the evolution of a still-evolving labour law. The preamble of the Constitution of 1946, then that of 1958, recognized the right to strike 'within the limits of the laws which regulate it', according to the time-honoured formula. Now, it is an individual right, reflecting the general spirit of French law; but, almost by definition, it can only be exercised collectively. The history of the right to strike can be seen as the model frequently reproduced in our society by many working-class conquests: as the importance of the victory becomes clearer, so does its institutionalization increase, along with the complexities of the ways this functions and of the bodies set up to interpret its terms. What is more, the contradiction between an individual right and the collective exercise of this right rapidly becomes apparent. A move from an offence to a right in labour relations is a movement within narrow limits, but a movement all the same from an individual liberal logic to a collective social logic.

We find ourselves here at one of those complex, imprecise boundaries between law and sociology: in what areas and to what extent can an offence become, first, tolerated and then a right? At what point does the 'legalization of the working class' (see Edelman, 1978) become an element of social integration? Consequently, over and above the individual right/collective right ambiguity looms the more general problem of the relationship between the norm and social forces. Legislation only becomes effective in so far as the norm, once it has been decreed, either as government policy or as the result of pressure applied successfully, manages to be translated into a modification of previous practices. The problem is then posed in these terms: what is required for the rules which tend to limit ownership rights to be applied in reality? The application of social legislation is in part a function of the balance of power at a given moment in time and in a particular place. Where the workers are strong, they impose the application of laws. There again, that is not true in all cases: there is a world of difference between the rules on working conditions and those on 'comités d'entreprise'. Pressure from the dominant groups is felt more keenly when new norms imposed by the workers in a moment of strength (for example in 1945 with the law on comités d'entreprise) look likely to challenge one of the foundations of the established order.

The judiciary can intervene in several ways — potentially at least — in that there are often lingering problems in deciding whether something is a criminal offence, a misdemeanour or a right. No doubt this is something of a caricature, but one might demonstrate that ambiguity by noting that the term used depends on whether the action or relationship is considered as a function of the individualist logic of civil law or the more social, or collective, logic of labour law.

One might even venture that the fewer economic risks or implications attached to a particular relationship, the more chance it has of being institutionalized. For example, an injunction on workers occupying their workplace is not always served, indeed no court action is sought, if the financial consequences for the firm are small — if it is insolvent or if stocks are high, for instance. On the other hand, an injunction on the removal of stock is always served (Casassus and Erbès-Seguin, 1979).

A second consideration is that legal intervention can come from different branches of the law and from different types of judicial authority which have different roles, and this opens up a diversified field of intervention for social groups. Besides the omnipresent civil legal code, properly speaking, two branches derived from it may intervene in workplace matters: labour law and commercial law. Furthermore, the state may intervene directly, in the shape of the Workplace Inspectors in particular, which brings the principles of administrative law into the picture. 'Inspecteurs du travail' have considerable powers to oblige employers to follow the laws applying to employment and the workplace. While they may sometimes overlook the infringements of 'social' provisions relating to the workplace — notably those covering worker representation — they are often tough in applying rules about safety or hours of work. Much more than the British factory inspectorate, they are likely to perceive themselves as an active agent of the state.

The scope for intervention and the forms it takes in each branch are diverse. 'Gaps' appear of varying size as regards problems to do with work and successive layers of the law are more or less divergent, depending on the historic circumstances at the time of their appearance. For example, a law on bankruptcy or redundancies would probably not be formulated in the same terms during growth years as during a recession. Its wording, and particularly its content under the pressure of various social groups, would in part be a function of the degree of urgency of the problem to be tackled. Besides, the margin of freedom for any intervention also varies according to other forms of collective pressure, depending, one might say, on how central the particular problem is to the great social issues of the period.

So, if the law is linked to social forms, and far from being a simple construct of rules, it is also constantly being renewed (Raguin, 1970). Struggles over the enforcement of legal regulations but also (especially, perhaps) the divergent appreciations and actions allowed by legal concepts that are only precise on the surface, provide much scope for sociological research, still at an embryonic stage in this field.

Conclusion

The formative years of the sociology of work, up until the end of the 1960s, were characterized by the subdiscipline being turned in upon itself and by the growing number of field studies. Research programmes diversified at the beginning of the 1970s. In particular, from studying only behaviour at work, sociologists started to look at relations to do with work, the organization and system of decision making in firms, work and out-of-work life, the labour market, and so on.

This period saw the opening up of debate on the external boundaries of the subdiscipline: the relationship with psychology, but also with anthropology which was at that time one of reciprocal near-ignorance, despite the recent rediscovery of social anthropology. Economic paradigms often remained sited upstream from sociological analysis — which has given rise for decades to theoretical controversy.

However, the main theoretical debates in the subdiscipline have been set off by reflection on the history of work and the object 'work'. For ten years, if that, research has been carried out in collaboration with historians but this still remains intermittent. Come what may, the movement towards the pulling down of barriers both within and around the sociology of work is becoming more and more visible, and is linked to genuine self-analysis on the part of sociologists of work.

The golden age of empirical research was also that of economic growth and of the first phase of funding by contract (1960–74 or thereabouts). Now we are seeing researchers beginning to question the way in which their objectives are determined. This, together with the opening up of interdisciplinary work, is a necessary condition for any really cumulative growth in knowledge.

Notes

1. See Olson, Mancur (1978) *The Logic of Collective Action*. Cambridge, Mass: Harvard University Press. Note that Olson is neither a sociologist nor a psychologist but an economist.
2. See in particular the development of this approach, still in the USA, as related by Pagès in the Friedmann–Naville *Traité* (1961).
3. With some exceptions, notably Halbwachs and Simiand.
4. G. Palmade (ed.) (1967) *L'Economique et les sciences humains*. Dunod: Paris.
5. cf. the Brochier colloquium, University of Paris I, January 1981.
6. Postwar Sociologie du travail was linked directly to the Annales school through Georges Friedmann who had a position on the editorial board of the increasingly famous periodical more or less from the start. It would be worth exploring further the links between what were, in effect, two Parisian 'movements'.
7. One approach to this problem is given by Balle in *Sociologie du Travail*, No. 1,

1980, 'Sociologie du Travail et Changement Social'. She analyses how the authors who have published articles during the review's first twenty years contributed to the construction of a sociology of change.

8. Though often translated as 'technology' (which it certainly covers), 'la technique' ultimately designates not just the knowledge enabling the construction of a new technology, but the implicit 'software' of a device, product or process made by traditional methods. See the Note on Translation.

9. Two types of study of a sociological nature should be noted however — some close to the sociology of organizations on industrial tribunals, one from a historical perspective on the notion of industrial accidents. Other aspects of the law have long been studied — see *Sociologie du Travail*, No. 1, 1981.

PART TWO
SITUATIONS AND STATEMENTS: THE EVOLUTION OF THE SOCIOLOGY OF WORK

INTRODUCTION TO PART TWO

7
The sociology of work: science or profession?

Pierre Desmarez*
Pierre Tripier†

Is the sociology of work a science or a profession, or both? And if it is both, how do you explain that? These questions were touched on frequently during our discussions, at the seminar of 7–8 November 1983, but they are not dealt with systematically in any of the other contributions published in the French language version of the book that followed.

That is why, in this introduction, we have chosen to take a different tack to the other essays here that look at the record of past achievements in sociological explanation, preferring instead to look at the questions asked by American industrial sociologists about their profession.

The relationship between a science and a profession certainly exercised our North American colleagues during the 1950s. Two factors made such a debate urgent: McCarthyism, which had disturbed academic freedoms; and the decision of psychologists to form themselves into a legally recognized profession.

In the ensuing debate, which produced a clash between, in particular, Talcott Parsons and E. C. Hughes (see Parsons, 1952; 1959; Hughes, 1952; 1954; Goode, 1957), Hughes suggested, in an attempt to focus the arguments, the following categorization: science, profession and politics. He contended that these three activities were distinct and validated his claim by his answers to three questions: who determines the division of labour? What is the nature of the norms followed? Where do the main resources come from — who is it you address yourself to in the first instance?

In *a science*, the division of labour is dictated by tradition or university bureaucracy, while the nature of the norms is fixed by the scientific community, in particular by the natural scientists who enjoy

* Université Libre de Bruxelles
† Université de Paris X, Groupe de Sociologie du Travail

a certain pre-eminence in the matter of proof; the clients are other academics, especially those in more established disciplines, and sometimes society or its secular arm, the state.

A *profession* differs from a science on one crucial point — the nature of the clientele that provides the resources and its relationship with the professionals: this clientele has a real, physical existence (which was not always the case as regards the scientific community) in the form of individuals or groups who sanction, by their requests, the output of the professionals. The latter must constantly make compromises between the norms of their community and the needs of clients.

Finally, *the politician* fixes his or her own place in the division of labour, as far as possible; politicians do not act in accordance with any external norms but in line with their own personal beliefs. They expect nothing from the outside world, except perhaps to see it transformed in the direction they desire, following their opinion of what constitutes a 'good' society.

We feel that Hughes's classification is useful as an analytical tool to help explain how the sociology of work was first established and then evolved.

Thus, if you take American sociology of work from the end of the last century, you can see that, in the first few decades, sociologists were guided by 'political passion'. Their work had a sort of moral basis. For them, events were taking place in society which were quite unacceptable: society therefore had to change. Sociology could be the instrument of this transformation. To this end, sociologists had to speak to all citizens, not just their peers; they had to share their knowledge with everyone. Far from claiming any exclusive hold on competence, they had to share their findings and put their analytical capabilities at the service of others. Understanding the real world meant changing it (cf. Cohen, 1983; Desmarez, 1984).

At the end of the 1920s, faced with both a conservative backlash in American society and precise demands from the government and some employers, sociologists redefined their status in terms of 'science' and 'profession'. They now felt they did not have to make personal political choices in their work: science was to be separated from its application. In the same movement, they 'put some distance'[1] between themselves and the layperson and arrogated to themselves a monopoly on the cleansed body of knowledge: they advocated the elevation of their discipline to a science, its autonomy vis-à-vis all the contingencies of the outside world, and simultaneously set themselves up as experts competent to advise their institutional clients on the implications of any decisions they were about to take.

Sociology thus presented itself as a 'pure', 'objective' science, capable of finding within itself its own bases, problematics and legitimacy. This act of enclosure provided both a protective shield and a symbol of justification: results might be distorted by the uses to which they were put in the outside world, but the discipline itself remained intrinsically pure.

It was precisely at the moment it met an eminently solvent clientele in the form of the state, various foundations and large firms, and was becoming an instrument of management and administration that the discipline constructed for itself a field of autonomy and considered its problematics as essentially scientific, covering up its professional roots but still feeding itself through them in terms of available funds, surveys and even its public utterances.

Under these circumstances, two phenomena came about. On the one hand, politically committed behaviour tended to disappear or, to say the least, became very much the domain of a minority, concealing as a result one of the societal roots of what were to become guiding principles in the sociology of work.

On the other hand, as this academic community put on weight — in more than one sense — with more researchers, more teachers, more surveys and more theories, it was to seek to find within itself all the elements of its principles. It was to create a cultural tradition which would direct newcomers to purely academic references — books, articles, theses, the founding fathers — which would have the virtue of hiding from the newly initiated the roots of their science and the fact that they were continuing to feed off the results and interests which originated in consultancy in firms.

The necessary academic arguments, playing down the professional roots of the science, created the false impression that they represented only one of the themes distinguished by Hughes and in so doing allowed the other two to work away in the shadows and impose their viewpoints under the mantle of science.

Note
1. The theory of religious people distancing themselves from the profane elaborated by Durkheim in his *Elementary Forms of Religious Life* seem to us a marvellous depiction of this scientific purging (in the various meanings of the term). See also Bloor (1976).

I. THE ORIGINS

8
Proudhonism and Marxism in the origins of the sociology of work

*Pierre Rolle**

Introduction

Marx and Proudhon: do we really need to revive this debate which caused a great stir in some working-class circles — though very few intellectual ones — during the nineteenth century? Supposing it has some relevance for the present day, could not the essence of this message be phrased in more contemporary terms? If we are not engaged in the history of ideas, but rather, trying to throw some light on the contemporary world, what do we gain by referring to it?

It is not so easy to belong to one's time and become adept in making observations about it. Have we really got rid of the old problematics? It is not a bad exercise to make certain of this by taking our bearings and measuring the distance travelled. It is not a bad thing, either, in this case, to observe how, through a blending of the commonsense views of the period and the application of commonly-held theories, a field and an interpretation were marked out — and they are exactly those later occupied by the sociology of work. Perhaps we will then be able to edge aside some old certainties: those old dogmas which, hidden away in the very principles of our analyses, continue to work away dimly in the background even though, refuted when strictly formulated, they no longer stand up in the light of day.

When we read Marx, we are reading a host of authors who only exist now thanks to him. 'All history is the history of class struggle' — that is Saint-Simon and Augustin Thierry. 'To each according to his needs' — the guiding principle of communism — that is Cabet. 'The first relationship of man to man is the relationship of man to woman' — Fourier. In other words, Marx tried to give shape to a whole number of theories, facts, scraps of information and analyses from which he drew inspiration, or against which he argued. If we wanted to try and discover the real logic of his way of construing them we

---
* Groupe de Recherches Sociologiques, Nanterre

would have to restore his 'borrowings' to their proper context. If we want to understand Proudhon, and we will begin with him, then it is necessary to go over the ground again, as with Marx, resituating him among the economists and what are called the 'publicists' of the time.

The economists of the time? Do we mean Ricardo? Do we mean Smith? Not at all! The great economist of that era was Jean-Baptiste Say.

Proudhon: the contradictions of property
Proudhon came to public notice in a France dominated by Jean-Baptiste Say. Say was considered an authority on English political economy. For some people, he had even formulated its principles better or improved on it. As you probably know, Proudhon's first book deals with property. And, as he put it: 'property is theft'.

Allow me one small digression here, since we are talking about Marx and Proudhon. Naturally, there were some logicians who mocked the assertion that 'property is theft'. It was meaningless, they complained, since, if property were theft, there was no longer any property, and if there were no property, then there could be no theft. An utter contradiction. There must be property for there to be theft. So Proudhon got himself criticized. But Marx defended him against these logic-choppers: saying that property is theft is a declaration that there is a relationship between the two that perpetually transforms one of the affirmations into the other; and that this relationship is much more important and interesting than simply dissecting the concepts, opposing them and showing their coherence, as formal logicians would do. In other words, Marx was conferring on Proudhon the title of dialectician. So what is this polarity of property and theft? I will give you the ideas I have on how, for Proudhon, property could be both a system, a necessary social institution, and theft, an injustice. How did he move beyond this contradiction?

Proudhon distinguishes right away between *property* and *appropriation*. Why is property theft? Because one should accept Say's assertion that property is the precondition for work. This proprietorship must therefore be, in its first form, the ownership of the product of labour. From that point of view, it is entirely legitimate. But, at the same time, it is ownership of the means needed to perform work, the objects on which the worker works, and the workplace where work is done. Ownership in this sense outweighs ownership in the first sense and encompasses it, with the result that the title of what is stated to be the property of labour becomes the property of the non-worker. The ownership of (performed) work is not in itself scandalous, it is even thoroughly necessary, as we saw; and socially, it is not the sort of rigid exclusive right or unchanging institution that property is pictured to be under bourgeois law.

In fact, even if you own the product of your own labour, you cannot get very far with it. Right away you need to exchange it for other products. You need to 'alienate' it, in the legal sense of transferring ownership — which is, after all, the first and most essential meaning of the term.

So there is an error here about property, a mistaken opinion, a difficulty, a confusion. People have got a false impression of property since some have made it a religion — and Proudhon ridicules that in some marvellous pages. According to Proudhon, this absolute affirmation of possession is perhaps the true essence of religion. People build up what today we would call ideologies from it, and parties too, parties of property-owners. This right of property, ambiguous and confused, is the product of a good number of more or less prestigious opinions, on the part of a certain number of goodly people. The painful conclusion must be that people are fighting under a banner, that of property, which is unjust and false.

So what can we say about such a society which, in the view of Jean-Baptiste Say, will be relatively harmonious? There are people in this society propagating a false, a completely false idea. That is inconceivable, because then we are driven to say that individuals are living in a society whose real principles completely escape them. We would be obliged to refute their opinion purely and simply, substituting the idea of a society constructed in a way quite different from what they imagine. Thus, some people at least are not living their history. There would appear to be a class which is useless, indeed absurd, and imbued with ideas that are valueless except in the religious sphere. In order to avoid this conclusion — worrying for any theory of society as well as social science methodology — Proudhon invented the theory of the series of antinomic dialectics.

Series
The point of departure is the notion of series, that is, groups of opinions, which develop according to their own logic, hold themselves to be independent of others and which are in perpetual interaction. Take, for example, *credit*. What is credit? It is the possibility of obtaining money, of lending it to someone and getting back more money than we gave — a quite scandalous system: a deduction in advance on work which, as we will see, is the first form of all *society* according to Proudhon. If we went no further, we would have to say that people who lend on credit are a useless, even harmful, stratum of society and should be cut away. Thus, there seem to be opinions that we would not give scientific credence to and classes or groups of individuals that we would have to declare politically harmful. In

other words, we undertake a revolution both in scientific method and in the political system: no less than that.

But wait. If we look at credit in a different way, we might rediscover that primary harmony that Say spoke about and Proudhon also appeals to, that relationship between supply and demand through the medium of time. If the system of supply and demand is considered at one precise moment in time, you won't find a perfect balance because what is produced today will be bought tomorrow. And if some article or good can be produced today and bought tomorrow, or bought today and produced tomorrow, it is because of the existence of credit. So from this second point of view credit can be justified. Credit exists merely because there is no solidarity among workers. We therefore have to reconceptualize credit. There are people who will sing its praises, while others will denounce it, and each opinion develops, in its own sphere, and establishes an overall interpretation of the social system.

Now, if there is somebody around with a scientific grasp of things — and Proudhon greatly hoped he was that person — this person would understand that these two groups of perceptions must be fitted back into the overall unity that none of the social agents can picture but whose existence the sociologist is obliged to presuppose. This development of opinions which allows me to utilize them as information, yet without simply becoming a captive of any one set of them, is the dialectic of *series*. It is a dialectic because it brings into contact intellectual developments, systems of opinion, which lead on from one to another and which we have to bring into contact, or rather, to set against each other. But in setting them against each other, what do we hope to achieve? We aim to achieve a synthesis which, as in the case of credit, will justify both those who are its critics and those who glorify it, in order to arrive at a more general view of things which is never the vision of a social agent but that of the sociologist. The latter can faithfully represent opinions without simply echoing them. This is the dialectic of 'antinomies' (Proudhon's technical term for 'contradictions') which we will return to since it is here that Marx is most ferocious in his criticism of poor old Proudhon.

So property is scandalous yet necessary in many different ways. In Say's system, there is this flaw, this difficulty, that he did not notice because he was still a captive to old theological prejudices — more precisely, the idea of property in the traditional sense of the word.

The primary unity that Say thought existed between supply and demand was not there for Proudhon: on the contrary, there are crises.

Should we declare that Say was completely wrong, then, that it is false, this law Say put forward about market opportunities ('débouchés'), holding as it does that a level of demand must exist corresponding to a given level of supply which *necessarily* brings a buyer out into the market? Not at all. It is not false, but simply *falsified*, under current social circumstances, by the existence of ownership in the means of production which allows monopolists (we can call such a person a 'capitalist' between ourselves, even if Proudhon does not use the term) to take their cut, as a result of which the relationship of different sets of production costs to each another cannot find their true level. Say's law is essentially correct but will only be fully realized when the opportunity enjoyed by monopoly capital of holding labour to ransom is suppressed. Only then will there be a balance between production costs, one set matching another, representing the exchange of *labour* against *labour*: when this happens, the fundamental harmony that Say presupposed will at long last be realized.

Planning to resolve contradictions
What is Proudhon's solution? And first of all, how did he analyse the industrial system of his day?

Well, this necessary conformity assumed by the theory — an underlying relationship between utility or use-value on the one hand and price or exchange-value on the other — which was to be the means, according to Say, through which work was in theory to be shared out between the different branches of activity according to immediate social need, did not exist. Exchange value is freed by what we shall call the capitalist. It is 'liberated' and moves in line with supply and demand. At any moment it allocates to utilities (that is, goods and services) a set of prices which do not correspond to the basic scale of worth fixed by society. It is thus totally disruptive. But as it is disruptive because of the existence of the monopoly capitalist, harmony could be restored if we once more linked social need directly to *work*.

This is what Proudhon called *constituted value* ('valeur constituée'). Constituted value is both an economic category and a system of work organization. It is one and the same thing. Constituted value is the possibility for a given piece of work to be exchanged against another piece of work of the same quantity. That is to be brought about by absorbing the capitalist's functions in work. The bourgeoisie will dissolve into the proletariat, Proudhon says, with the advent of an extremely interesting and very modern system that he calls 'accounting' — though one might call it something quite different today. The placement of goods must be guaranteed; that is, the social need to which the goods respond will need to be verified, measured and decided in advance. A society's total needs are therefore measured and listed. Quite simply, we are talking about a *plan*. Clearly, the relationship between the prices of things and their usefulness will be in harmony from the moment that decisions are made in advance on the number of people necessary to obtain all the products we need. As a result, the cost of production alone will be what counts: utilities will cancel each other out in the system of exchange. The number of people working in the various branches will be in total harmony with social needs, identified by the 'accountant', this demi-god of the modern world; relative production costs will be absolutely identical from one product to another.

Each article produced will be credited with a labour time which will allow it to be exchanged for another costing exactly the same labour time. That will be made possible by contracts, because Proudhon's planning, to use the modern term, is such that it does not need to be dictatorial: it will be enough for workers to make agreements with each other.

And all this will recreate the harmony which, for Say, was theoretically necessary but which did not exist in the sad reality of society in Proudhon's day. From such harmony would come the possibility glimpsed by Proudhon of eliminating money. Since the utility of a piece of work would be recognized by all, and would be exchanged without problem and without the least loss against any other piece of work taking the same amount of time, the function of money could be taken over by a work 'chit' or coupon. In a shop, you would say: 'I've worked this amount of time as stipulated in my contract to make so many cars, so give me what that's worth, the work coupon corresponding to this time which I will exchange for anything I please which contains exactly the same labour time.'

Proudhon said this work coupon and network of shops had to be *national*: for the most part, he is only against the state on the surface. Thus, as you would suspect, nationwide accounting is called for. And a nationwide organization for such a system is conceivable. Proudhon is only against the state in that he declares the state to be the source and guarantee of credit in its present form and it is to be destroyed for that reason. For the rest, on the contrary, he envisages a terribly statist system. The possibility of exchanging through work coupons all that we currently haggle over through the laws of supply and demand would eliminate all the difficulties that this makes us endure in the concrete world. Freedom and the inevitable will be reconciled through the opportunity each worker has of entering into contracts in this national system — the contract is the exact and necessary form of reconciliation between individual liberty and social determinism. It is through contracts that the distribution of forms of work will be realized in all the sectors.

In other words, it is a question of how many workers will work in any one sector, not *how* they will work. Work has its normal, necessary form and the form that Proudhon finds normal and necessary is, of course, *craft* work. Here, the division of labour pays attention to the unity of the workshop. There are those who claim that the existence of various classes never signifies a division, a tension, or a contradiction within society. In the same way, for Proudhon the division of labour within the workshop is — to use a term that is not his — *organic*. Each individual does a particular operation whose complexity is very easy to determine — all that is necessary is to relate the sequence effected by an individual to the whole of the labour process to discover a perfect measure of the skill[1] required. So each individual takes charge of a segment of the system. But you can only do a particular operation perfectly if you are in a position to see and grasp the whole of the labour process. Anyone who only sees a segment necessarily comes under the authority of someone who understands the entire process. There is only one legitimate line of command, says Proudhon, that of worker to worker. Doing this segment leads, simply by doing it, to an enhancement of skills which allows one to take on a wider set of operations. Moreover, this occurs not because the worker is taught it, or asked to do it, or demands it, but through the very execution of the task. Thus, as you work you improve your skills by virtue of a real learning process ('apprentissage') in the whole of the labour process until, finally, having done the rounds of all the posts, you have all the necessary skills — you are an expert and it is now your turn to introduce the new workers to the job and guide them through the stages.

When an individual enters a workshop, he or she sees the posts and knows he or she will occupy all of them during the course of his or her life — they represent his or her career in a tangible form. There is never any definitive block in this career path, never any complete break since its development, its enhancement ('promotion'), does not come from any operating system (which could change) but is inherent in the working practices. Under these circumstances, one could imagine a more or less extensive division of labour depending on the number of people working in a particular sector. This is the principle of the division of labour as the Greeks sought to practise it in their time. If you needed only a few carpenters, they would be grouped in units of production where there was little division of labour. If, on the other hand, a great number of them were needed, they would share out the tasks. At the least, the carpenters would become distinguished from the joiners, and even among carpenters there would be some differentiation according to particular tasks.

The extent of the division of labour is explained by the number of people in a workshop. As the number of people grows, as property — we shall see this later — has the two-sided character of perpetually increasing human wants and the number of people required in each sector, so is the labour process broken down into smaller and smaller operations. At this point, as if by a miracle, work becomes so simple it can be mechanized. First there is the division of labour, then comes the machines. And the machine is the antithesis of the division of labour because it recomposes work. So people ought to be in favour of machines. The machine eliminates this minute division of labour which in practice often entails a definitive subordination of individuals in the simplest of posts. Gradually the machine reconstitutes the process as a whole: automation liberates people.

Here, I am beginning to talk in the modern idiom, of course, but that is what happens. However, the machine has the disadvantage of transforming the division of labour into a system which is no longer altogether organic. Posts become separate from each other, an apprenticeship on one operation does not lead on to an apprenticeship on a more complex operation. As a result, on the negative side, the machine transforms an organic division of labour into a rigid one, let us say. (I was about to say 'mechanical division' but this other term is needed.) But at the same time that this rigid division of labour is a factor aggravating the dispossession of the worker, it is also working towards liberating him or her. And for Proudhon that is quite logical: if the problem stems from the machine, only the machine can resolve it.

Let me sum up. First, Proudhon sees a possible harmony between exchange value and use value. They may have become differentiated in a given period and consequently disrupted the whole of the economic system, resulting in crises, but that is not a fundamental law of the system. Harmony can be restored through 'constituted value'.

A second point is this: on one side there is the economic system where the products of work are exchanged, and on the other there is work — and work has a form that is normal or even 'natural'. You might take note of the fact that the effect of the disorderly speeding up of the number of exchange transactions is to transform the functioning of the workshop — but you cannot escape the fact that this transformation is like that of the change in value which lies behind it: it is a product of historical contingency and a basic harmony can always be restored to the workshop.

A third point: we do not need to study these processes at one and the same time. There is a place for the sociology of work, and this is why I claim that Proudhon is our founding father. Since work has a 'normal' form, we have to study how it is transformed and influenced from the outside. When this essential form does not exist in reality, there are riots, strikes and labour coalitions (which Proudhon considers as monopolies in just the same way as property ownership), all of them undesirable manifestations that can disappear from the moment that work becomes normal again.

It is possible to study exchange processes on the one hand and production on the other: that splits social science into two parts and each can quite easily be practised independently of the other.

Thus, the system of exchanges is such that social need does not appear directly to the worker. You will notice that we have most of the themes of classic sociology of work — to put it another way, the worker does not understand why he or she is working. The unity of work is no longer clear. The needs that his or her labour satisfies are no longer apparent. This is the very source of the psychological and sociological strains of work. But from the moment that exchange-value is once again linked to use-value, society will assume its real form (hardly visible up till now), namely, as nothing more than a system for exchanging labour. What is called political economy is only a system of exchange which had the appearance of possessing its own special logic for a while during Proudhon's time but which would become once again exclusively the science of the exchanges of work (themselves conditioned by labour) in a harmonized society. That is why we can rightfully study the normal forms of work without bothering to get involved in exchange systems. Better still: we, as sociologists, have the key to the problem the economists are forever trying (without success) to throw light upon. In effect, the 'normal form' of work and exchanges in terms of units of work, will define the harmonious economy of the future.

Proudhon and Marx

Let us recall how Proudhon looked at things using his notion of 'series'. You have to be in favour of the division of labour. It brings with it the full development of aptitudes, a more rational organization of production, and increased productivity, as they say today, all resulting in higher wages for workers. But you have to be against the division of labour, too, because the individual who could once undertake all the operations that make up a labour process can no longer do so. If he or she learns one task thoroughly, he or she is no longer in a position to perform others. Another component of the whole process — the machine — has a direct relationship to this series of tasks, or to parts of this series. You have to be in favour of machines — and against. They have their good and bad sides. These two series yield a body of opinions, attitudes, ideologies, theory, practice, too: practice above all, perhaps, since some workers were to throw machines through windows while others were to be busy producing these machines. You can only make sense of this if you see that the good and bad sides of each of these series can be reconciled in a synthesis: one has to be against machines but hope at the same time that they will continue to develop until the workplace is fully automated.

Marx spoke of the 'great automaton', following Ure, Babbage and many others. At that time, the 'automatic system' meant linking all the machines in one workshop to the same source of energy. A central steam engine worked all the machines by means of belts. The inevitable multiplication of these links would make the workshop a more and more automatic system. Marx's great automaton which he predicted as from 1848 (in his reply to Proudhon) had been conceived of by many others. But it did not come about in the way Marx expected because it took a form much larger than the workshop. Energy is no longer simply something which links machines in a workshop but, in the form of electricity, it organizes and unifies a whole number of operations effected in numerous systems of production. The great automaton of Marx is today a great automaton on the scale of human society.

All classic political economy, among which we can include Proudhon, ignores what Marx was to call 'dead labour'. Proudhon's theory, which is that of Smith and Say, has on one side the products, such as are identified by the accountants, balanced by revenues on the other. All this prevents him from seeing, like Smith himself and many classical economists, that there is a particular thing, dead labour, which does not correspond to any revenue, bizarre as that may seem.

So Proudhon does not have a valid theory of exploitation. Anyone setting up a new production unit from their own resources receives the remuneration corresponding first to this particular grouping together of work and second to the novelty of the scheme they are offering to society. It is at their risk, but if they succeed, the remuneration they receive is in no way due to any act of exploitation. However, you could see exploitation here if you reckoned that individuals receiving the reward for their own work are part of a collectivity whose productivity is greater than the sum of its parts. And the surplus of productivity finds its way into the pockets of the monopolist. That is the only thing in Proudhon that might resemble exploitation. It is also one of the forms of exploitation suggested by Marx in *Das Kapital*.

Furthermore, Marx never parted company completely with Proudhon. He states in several places that there is a collective productivity which does not correspond to the sum of particular productivities and that this collective productivity is pocketed by the capitalist. That would draw us into the theory of exploitation which, to say the least, is neither very simple nor much to the point. No doubt that is not where Marx's work ought to be attacked.

Abstract work, concrete work
Fortunately, I do not have to present this body of work, but simply to indicate hypothetically what is the basic difference between Marx and Proudhon, which is also what concerns us directly as sociologists of work. The main thing to bear in mind is an idea, apparently his alone, that Marx puts forward and that we ought to reflect on and try to improve: the idea of abstract work. Proudhon only talks about concrete work, what individuals effectively do at a particular time in a particular job, resulting in a complete confusion between worker and work. For me, it seems that what is essential yet always difficult for us sociologists of work to grasp is the great importance Marx saw in what he calls abstract work.

For Marx, any analysis of concrete work cannot fail to hit upon serious problems. Abstract work is naturally not the abstraction of work, the concept of work you have when you ignore each particular manifestation.[2] Marx ridicules that idea, saying it can be left to the philosophers. If it were that, it would be something just as real — the living abstract, the effective abstract, the efficient abstract. Abstract not because it has less reality than concrete work but because it has more. Abstract in the sense that one can understand it in itself, distinguish within all the surrounding factors which determine it a reality that one is not obliged to relate to any previous reality whatsoever. Abstract work is not an abstraction from the worker or the workplace. That is the point — abstract work is deemed abstract because it must not be attributed to the act of any particular person or group of workers. That is why, it seems to me, this term is so confusing for people like us who do not really read Hegel. Abstract in the sense of 'separate'. And, indeed, one can separate work in its basic determinant from concrete work, which does not mean that this distinction is such that one cannot naturally re-establish a certain relationship.

But it is precisely in this separation that we must begin our analysis of the relationship. If we want to find an example which might demonstrate what Marx understands by abstract work, we have to look to science — energy, for example, compared with the different forms of energy. Energy obeys laws which govern all sources of energy. It is therefore a reality in itself, not to be confused with any specific form of energy: it even explains how one is transformed into another. I chose this example on purpose because, as you know, this period was obsessed with the problem of energy, the laws concerning the dissipation of energy, what today we call entropy. This phenomenon meant there was an irreversible evolution in the cosmos as a whole, hence the theories about the disappearance of humanity in the form of a maximum entropy — death by going lukewarm, let us say!

The period was also preoccupied with a certain manner of conceptualizing what Marx calls, not very clearly, to be frank, categories. This is neither a concept in the philosophical meaning of the term nor an abstraction in the everyday sense, but a reality which does not cut itself off from its concrete realizations and acts through all its concrete determinants in an autonomous way.

Another example is Clausewitz's theory of war. War can only exist as a concrete fact, waged by human beings, and yet you can discover laws of war which are not purely and simply abstractions formulated on the basis of such and such a war. I do not know if we have resolved this problem — I think not: it seems to me that it would certainly be a useful epistemological exercise for our sciences to reflect on the idea of category as one tried to imagine it at this time without quite getting there.

But that is perhaps how one should consider abstract work in Marx, as a work operation obeying its own laws. First, it appears through all we know, that is, the possibility of adding up quantities of work: subdivisions of labour; the sharing out of work; work careers. We do not have to presume that the movement of workers has to be observed as a sort of journey between moments and places where they can be localized because they are there, at their work post. The worker is a worker before arriving at the work post. We do not have to ask ourselves what links the fact of being pupil, apprentice and worker in different posts, supposing that between them there are only forms of conditioning, correlations and influences.

There is an area, a space as they say today, where all that goes to make up a unit of the operation of work never coincides exactly with the particular operation that an individual worker does. Abstract work is a category that we are obliged to imagine behind all the movements of society and which is signified even in what Proudhon says (in a confused way, according to Marx). For instance, equality supposes that one is comparing quite different sorts of work. There is thus the possibility of measuring concrete pieces of work which at first sight are quite dissimilar — which takes us back to something that necessarily we will have to call abstract work. It will be called something different depending on the way in which it is understood. 'Simple work' is probably also abstract work but measured in a different form, like 'general work', 'social work', the average of all these forms that Marx refers to equally. Each analysis of concrete work requires us to restore a fundamental form of mobility, of transformation, of transfer from one individual to another, and all this obliges us to suppose the existence of abstract work. And this abstract work, which is a necessary category of knowledge, is at the same time a clearer and clearer reality. Greater and greater mobility: transfers, comparability, what is called 'skill' and as such is likely to be compared across the most different of labour processes, all that signifies that work, ever more clearly, acquires characteristics which do not coincide exactly with concrete work.

In other words, and briefly, the separation that Proudhon observes between work and the worker is not a specific distinction which is produced at a given moment in time and which one may hope will go away, but a fundamental distinction, so that henceforth we have to speak of work on the one hand, the worker on the other, and try to understand their concrete relations but starting from the principle of their separation. It is due to this basic separation that we have to speak not of any disruption of the market economy, 'a bad moment that will pass', when work and the worker would no longer coincide but where their future coincidence might be presumed and foreseen, but of an irreversible separation between work and worker. This irreversible separation signifies a new social form that is to be called 'capitalism'. The term has since become so common that one does not always see what it meant for Marx. But if the fundamental distinction that Marx makes can still be discussed today, it is still an element of analysis, part of the problematic.

André Gorz published some time ago a book in which he explained how the 'salariat', the wage-earning mass, came into being, and as a result he was in a position to indicate how the end of the salariat could be envisaged: an end that everybody has been looking for since the eighteenth century! What's more, it's an extraordinary form of production which spends its time trying to find a way of eliminating itself!

Gorz declared that work, probably uniquely in human history, due to fragmentation in work tasks, had taken on a less and less qualitative form, which allowed the service of the worker to be quantified and compared. This quantification yielded the salariat or the waged masses. That meant, just as Proudhon said, that the salariat is an end point of a movement of the economic and industrial system, which reaches the stage of contradicting its own principles. We must hope not for the advent of something new which would be the elimination, pure and simple, of this economic system which brings forth the salariat, but for the restoration of the first principles of a market economy which would make the salariat disappear simply by restoring quality to the input of the worker. The theory of the new working class was pure Proudhon.

Declaring like Marx that the salariat is not a falsification but a form of remuneration which overloads the ever-increasing antagonisms between abstract and concrete work, meant there was no turning back. The problem was not to discover a 'real' market economy but to go beyond the market economy.

Naturally, if I am right in my interpretation, the theory of skills is perfectly Proudhonian and, in so far as it claims to relate prices to uses, it only finds justification in Proudhon. One could also develop this perspective to show that quite a few of the realities of our world and the other one (the socialist world) are much more Proudhonian than Marxist. That is why I have suggested the idea that Proudhon is of more interest today than Marx, even if, in turn, I state that this truth is conditional and transitory and that, in the final analysis, Marx may turn out to have been right after all.

Notes

1. *Qualification* in the French text.
2. In the original, 'determination'. The latter term is used in English, it is true, but it has an unfortunate tone in both languages which suggests that necessitarian factors lie behind the appearance of any 'particular manifestation' of an object, while in fact the writer may wish to suggest, as Rolle does here, that contingency plays an important part in creating the object as encountered by human observers.

9
In search of the founders: the *Traités* of the sociology of work

*Dominique Monjardet**

My rereading of the great founding texts[1] of the sociology of work, the Friedmann–Naville *Traité* (henceforth FN) and the 'Industrial Sociology' chapters of the Gurvitch *Traité* (henceforth G), drafted by and under the direction of Friedmann, was guided by a hypothesis which can be stated as follows.

(1) There is no satisfactory definition of the sociology of work in these texts;

(2) Nor is there any explicit agreement on themes or even any obvious consensus on fields, subjects or methods;

(3) Yet foreign observers (see Dull, 1975; Rose, 1979) share with the young generation of researchers that followed the feeling that there was a 'school' grouped around Friedmann whose attachment to the master was not enough to account for the identity, and even less the robust staying power, of sociology of work which has endured in France until the present day;

(4) Might not the common point, the founding principle (still alive today) be something much more implicit, a type of conviction or belief that the activity called 'work' was, and would remain, the central, essential experience of life in society? More than any other social or anthropological experience, this activity shapes action, produces values, determines orientations and behaviour, underlies the production of symbols, etc.;

(5) A corollary of this was that the central character in industrial society was the *worker* in a restricted sense of that term: the skilled male worker in heavy industry (preferably politically aware and organized).

Behind this presumed conviction one detected, of course, traces of working-class messianism — a legacy of rubbing shoulders with Marxism and/or the French Communist Party. Summed up like that, this hypothesis implies two other questions.

One is historic: might not the progressive decomposition of this implicit belief explain how, after appearing to be a relatively united

* Groupe de Sociologie du Travail

school, French *sociologie du travail*, broke up, exploded even, its 'great names' scattering in all directions?

The second is contemporary: are not the 'main-streamers', among whom I number the Groupe de Sociologie du Travail in Paris, at least as far as the project of its founders is concerned, working on the basis of the same convictions, though they are still just as implicit? Would that not explain the lack of interest in extraindustrial matters, in female workers, etc., on the one hand and, on the other, the gaps or recurrent difficulties in elaborating theory?

I set out with the idea of rediscovering the traces of this hypothesis in the canonical works. Of course, it all depends on what you mean by 'traces' — if you look hard enough you find some, but I had to admit defeat: the hypothesis is not proven, this was not the idea behind the sociology of work at the time.

Besides, the question was badly put. After rereading the texts, it seemed to me that it should have gone roughly like this: how did it come about that what looks like the rebirth of sociology in France after the Second World War arrived by giving priority to the sociology of *work*? We are left with a double question. Upstream, what motivated Friedmann's team — intellectually, politically, ideologically, culturally — to concentrate on that particular field? And downstream, to what demands (political, administrative, or from unions) was this orientation attempting to respond?

Briefly, I concluded that I had been quite mistaken in thinking that upstream factors determined the outcome. It seems a lot more plausible to me that downstream factors — such as the market — provide the better answers.

A groundless hypothesis

If you look hard enough, particularly in the more ideological sections of the *Traités* (and especially Friedmann's introduction and conclusion in FN), you could come up with a few quotes (they look rather quaint nowadays) about work, such as: 'the specific feature of humankind', 'a common denominator and a condition of all human life in society', 'what occupies man essentially', and so on.

You can find things like that scattered throughout the *Traités*. Look at Naville, too:

> Behind the methods, you find quite frequently, besides simple prejudices, unconscious theories, psychology, or quite simply political and moral imperatives, institutional commands, even. One should always beware of possible presuppositions or assumptions of this type, *especially when it comes to work, that irreplaceable motor of all forms of social life* (FN: 45, emphasis added by DM).

However, one should be wary of drawing conclusions from this about some metaphysic of work being omnipresent,[2] especially as quite the opposite sentiments can also be found: 'It is clear that for a growing number of individuals, the centre of gravity of their existence will be found from now on in activities outside work' (FN: 23).

Similarly, the second part of the hypothesis is only verifiable at the margin and in a negative sense. Certainly, neither of these texts deals seriously with anything other than heavy industry: independent craftspeople, small and medium-sized firms, the occupations of the countryside — everything outside manufacturing is ignored, and this is admitted: the authors note that they ought to go and investigate these other areas. Nor is there anything on female workers, with the exception of fifteen pages by Guilbert and Isambert-Jamati in FN on female employment. The central figure is definitely the male manual worker in heavy industry.

But it is difficult to argue that all this is intentional. It is a fact that there were hardly any books or research which might allow these other things to be tackled seriously and this lack is deplored as such.

Thus, my preoccupations shifted and, abandoning my hypothesis and its presuppositions, I simply asked myself: what are they writing about? What fields are covered and how?

Defining the sociology of work

It was Friedmann who had the privilege of providing a definition at the beginning. A difficult task — thirty-five large format pages are not enough: he continually skirts around the question and never comes up with a definition — or, to be precise, the one he finally gives is not one: 'The sociology of work must be considered at its broadest as the study, in their various guises, of all the human collectivities which are constituted when work is done' (FN: 26). Everything revolves around that word 'study': it was necessary to be precise about what that meant, yet each time Friedmann returns to the definition saying 'we must be precise here', he slides towards the subject matter, listing the fields of study. That much is clear: 'The plan of this *Traité* indicates well enough what questions seem to us to come under the sociology of work'. And again: 'We will see the main orientations . . .'.

In fact, what follows is a list of research programmes. There is never any conceptual development of the definition. Actually, that is not a total surprise: pushing the definition further implied, in a way, giving an idea of what *sociology*, the whole discipline, is, and you won't find that anywhere, except as a residual definition: sociology deals with subjects not specifically taken up by other established disciplines.

So the sociology of work, in the *Traités*, is a series of themes, of subjects. To limit ourselves for the moment to the most explicit, coherent and focused text, that is, the four chapters of G, the sociology of work has four subject areas, or themes, organized like a spiral: the machine; the worker and the work post; the collective workforce; out-of-work life (or what is left after work).

(1) *The machine, or 'the sociology of the techniques of production and labour'*. This concerns the evolution of technology, the description of the development of machines and the organization of production (Taylor and Ford), all linked around Touraine's three phases — from the craft to the work post, the evolution of skills and occupational structures. In there, too, but never explicit, is a discussion, never properly followed through, on technological determinism where a permanent denial is mixed up with ambiguous formulations.

(2) *The worker or 'the psycho-sociology of the workplace'*. Here, the Hawthorne experiments were to the sociology of work what the apple was, so it seems, to Newton's physics. The lighting is turned down and output continues to rise! There is something funny there, some link between the two — and *voilà*! the whole field of industrial sociology opens up. It is the elementary discovery that makes the first line of Gurvitch's *Traité*: 'The empirical[3] phase of industrial sociology was born . . .'

I agree that establishing that 'the workers think' is a telling criticism of Taylor's intentions and that, furthermore, the Hawthorne research is a remarkable teaching aid; all the same, from a distance, one is loath to accept that all previous knowledge is thus reduced to nothing simply because it did not have the seal of academic 'experimentation'. All those people working in the field who sometimes get the impression they are only 'discovering' what the workers have known all along will know what I mean.

So the workers *think*, despite all Taylor's efforts. What do they think? Now all of American psycho-sociology flies past: the Michigan school, Kahn, Bavelas, Roy, morale, satisfaction expectations.

(3) *The worker does not think in isolation, he or she joins the group*. The third chapter, the third subject of industrial sociology — unionism and working-class 'auto-gestion' (the meaning of this term has since altered: what is meant here is not what today we refer to as 'autogestion', or 'worker self-management', but rather what observers like André Philip were studying at the time under the heading of 'industrial democracy'). In the main, the chapter is descriptive. The corresponding sections of FN are more of a problem, the reader being invited to find his or her own way between Crozier's 'sociology of trade unionism' and the 'working class action' of Touraine and Mottez.

(4) *Finally, 'life at work and outside, industry and society'*. Under

this heading, one finds quite a ragbag (which was to be amply developed in FN): a word or two about a whole lot of things they feel they ought to discuss but which they do not have much to say about. These topics are listed, one after another: the problems of occupational choice, careers, retirement, leisure and so on. And, to conclude, there is a suggested programme of studies, because all these topics needed to be gone into more thoroughly.

Finally, we have a conclusion which serves as a foretaste of what is to run right through Friedmann's contribution to the FN *Traité*. Under the title 'Industry and Society' comes the question: 'What will happen to the relationship between work values and values of consumption?'

Thus, all this forges an extremely descriptive definition of the sociology of work according to its subject areas. There is little in the way of core issues ('problématique') but rather one great axis that the previous title from Friedmann sums up well: 'human problems of the use of machines in industry'.

Beyond the 'human problems' of industrial change, there is the clash of different rationalities in the workplace. It is necessary to study them and qualify them as partial rationalities, thus disclosing the ambitions of each one of them, attempting to present themselves as *the* Rationality with a capital R; and to show that they are conflictual and that ways must be found to handle these conflicts. All the same, there must be — and this is perhaps the project of the sociology of work — a metarationality which would form the basis of its contribution, 'because it is scientific, going as far as that reification of social relationships which is a feature of the modern world' (Friedmann in G: 442).

The first edition of G was dated the fourth quarter 1958. Since the manuscripts were probably solicited and drafted one or two years before that, they are now more than a quarter of a century old. The gap is long enough for criticism today to be easy: it might, for the same reason, even appear a little vain, if not presumptuous. Thus, one should take the following reactions not as a facile academic exercise but rather as an attempt to evaluate a heritage. So, rereading G and FN today, what did we find?

(1) Fascination with Hawthorne — or an entomologist's perspective of the world of the working class.

(2) The incursion of psychology and psycho-sociology into sociology, and their domination of it.

(3) A universe full of American (that is to say, US) references, and very undiscriminating ones at that; thus, Chester Barnard is cited more often than Alvin Gouldner, or even that Max Weber in the field of organizations.

(4) A scientific ambition in ways which today appear very naively positivistic, but which lent support to attempts at making sociology distinctive, which were aimed at all sorts of charlatans working in the same area.

(5) The temptation to try to be encyclopaedic. We encounter the idea, stated with more or less force depending on the author, that industrial sociology is in fact the sociology of industrial societies — sociology, tout court.

(6) An impressive lack of theoretical references judging by the list of authors cited in FN, though we appreciate that this sort of comment might result in similar criticisms of most books. But let us list them in order: Friedmann, 44 references; Naville 39; Marx 35; Touraine 23; Taylor 17; Crozier 16; Fourastié 16; Lewin 14; Colin Clark 13; Halbwachs 13; Durkheim 13; Chombard de Lauwe 12. Then come (still in order) Kerr, Maier, Morse, Sauvy, Aristotle, Balandier, Berle (and Means), Durand, Ombredane (and Faverge), Reynaud and Adam Smith, to limit ourselves to those quoted ten or more times. It is immediately obvious that the authors of the *Traité* get the lion's share. On the other hand, with none for Parsons, 1 for Sorokin, 2 for Sombart, 3 for Veblen and Simiand, 4 for Gurvitch, Merton, Proudhon and Ricardo and 6 for Weber, the sociology of work developed in something of a vacuum.

All this was intended to support two themes. The first refers to the idea that industrial sociology is in some way the sociology of industrial societies. Friedmann implies this but does not insist on it in G. It is left to Touraine to spell it out clearly in his 1965 article in the *Revue de l'Enseignement Supérieur* devoted to 'Industrial Sociology'. Touraine begins, like the *Traités*, by defining industrial sociology by reference to its subjects and fields of study. But these three fields are not added together. On the contrary, they bear witness to the dispersal of the discipline. The sociology of the firm is only a part of the sociology of organizations; the sociologies of working-class personality, and of social movements in industry, have no reason to focus on a particular social category or a particular social field: 'No form of work is more important than all others amongst all the social problems of industrial societies, any more than one social category, the manual worker, ought to be allotted a privileged role in the dynamics of society.' Hence the question: 'Is not the notion of industrial sociology a hindrance today to the development of analyses?' To which the founder of the Laboratoire de Sociologie Industrielle — Alain Touraine, no less — replies with a very nimble pirouette: 'Industrial sociology must not disappear for all that, since it is in reality the sociology of industrial societies.' QED!

Can we consider this text, coming a little after the *Traités*, as the raw expression of their hidden aim? A second factor points in this direction. The two *Traités* (G and FN) came out at roughly the same time. They sum up the state of the discipline at the turn of the 1950s and there was not to be another such attempt: much more selective collective works were to follow — see the following chapters of this book on *Tendances et Volontés*, Darras, etc.

Now, there is a marked difference between the contributors to the respective *Traités*. Of the 33 authors in G, 23 were university professors. Of the 25 in FN, only two came from universities and they are not professors; all the others belong to the CNRS, specialized research centres, some of them attached to government departments such as EPHE, INSEE, INED, CNAM, etc. We are looking at different, unconnected populations except, and this underlines the point, for the intrusion (punctuated by rather acid commentaries by Gurvitch himself) of Friedmann, Reynaud and Treanton into G. These three people end up looking like rivals to Gurvitch. Hence the distinct impression that, over and above the varying subject matter, it is less a case of a *Traité* on a special topic area (FN) versus a *Traité* on general sociology (G) than of one kind of sociology versus another:

FN	G
An up-to-date sociology for researchers	A decrepit sociology for professors
— empirical	— theoretical
— concrete	— abstract
— fieldwork-based	— armchair-based
— applicable	— purely academic
— marketable	— outside any market

They are not differentiated by *substantive* theory because there was no substantive theory, and the main contributors to FN were to set out their theories later in their doctoral theses. But perhaps there did not need to be, as what differentiates them is their apparent intended readership. FN is aimed at a different intellectual and professional clientele. Briefly, this was not the 'scientific community', especially its most academic elements, but the more dynamic sectors, especially the great professional training organizations and the large government departments. In fact, contact was to be made with both through the Commissariat au Plan, which was then a powerful body.

One can now ask if questions about our heritage ought to be directed towards the content or the work produced, or whether such content is not in some way secondary beside what the authors were trying to do. Each, after the FN *Traité*, was to try to define for him or herself a discrete field of specialization which diverges more and

Founders of the sociology of work 119

more clearly from anything we could call *the* sociology of work, thus working not so much to establish a discipline as to found a *profession*. And, it must be added, if the discipline remains something of a problem, the profession, for its part, is in good health. From this point of view, their success was total.

Notes

1. The French *Traités* are unlike 'treatises' in that they not only aim to provide comprehensive information but also to offer a kind of normative scaffolding of knowledge which may on occasion give them the air of an intellectual manifesto.

2. In discussing my exposé, some people have expressed surprise that I pick a quarrel with Friedmann, Naville et al. on the basis of quotes which merely express accepted facts. It is precisely this nature — the 'accepted fact' — rather than the content that I oppose. Work is perhaps all this: but — to mix genres — with Lafarge's *Le droit à la paresse* or Baudrillard's *Miroir de la production*, one can at least question the *fact* (and that is without looking up the abundant ethnological literature).

3. Gurvitch's own word was 'expérimental'. He seems to wish it to be understood in its broad, Baconian sense of deliberately planned enquiry. Gurvitch can hardly have believed that the Hawthorne studies met the criteria of controlled experimentation.

II. THE SOCIOLOGY OF GROWTH

10
Darras on 'the distribution of the pay-off'[1]
Catherine Paradeise*

We will introduce our paper by recalling the context in which this work by 'Darras' was conceived.

The action begins in 1965, that is, at a time when the Fifth Plan was developing an increasingly sophisticated conception of economic policy. Keynes was universally accepted: the Plan could no longer be considered subordinate to the imperatives of reconstruction, as it might have been immediately after the war; purely quantitative objectives on production were no longer sufficient to grasp the meaning of state intervention in the economic order. While economic policy had supplanted political economy, the goals of this policy in a context of growth and general optimism remained to be defined, in order to fix objectives and legitimacy (see Paradeise, Ch.3.1 in Laufer and Paradeise, 1981).

So we had a growth economy, still able to consider itself nationally independent and inducing considerable upheaval in social structures, but engendering the dual problem of how to manage social flux and the flow of resources, both of which result from this growth. It is now that we see the emergence of the notion of 'distributing the fruits of expansion' as a product of a society whose leaders see themselves as 'managers' of a democratic society — there is of course an immediate problem with this implied association — that is, following the national maxim, sharing the aim of ensuring the liberty, equality and solidarity of the citizens, now not only in the political order, but also in the economic order.

The action brings together economists and sociologists, the former belonging to a strong discipline, albeit one with internal divisions between technocratic planners and university liberals,[2] the latter from a weak discipline though a rapidly expanding one.[3] Among the economists, only the first group is represented (all the economist participants came from INSEE); among the sociologists Pierre Bourdieu brought together researchers and academics. This group of sociologists is quite distinct from the one that organized, around the

* University of Nantes and LERSCO

same time, the seminar on the *Tendances et Volontés de la Société Française* since only one person participated in both. Furthermore, on the sociologists' side, particularly in comparison with the economists, the sociologists' participants seem not yet to have found their institutional niche.

The action unfolds on neutral ground, graciously offered by the president of a provincial cultural association in the northern French town of Arras. This double 'move into the sticks' — by comparison with both the customary venues for academic and administrative discussion, and the mania for holding all meetings in Paris — probably demonstrates the double desire for innovation in co-operation and the rejection of eminent intellectual 'stars'.

So the exercise was highly original. It raises two questions:

(1) Is this the expression of the pre-existing unity of a 'socio-economic' school of thought, for which the context seems favourable, or is it rather a strategic exercise which everyone hopes to profit from? The answer requires an analysis of the principles of the homogeneity, as well as of the divergences, running through the text itself, in the paradigms of each of the groups present and the basis of the possible compromises that these paradigms make both feasible and necessary.

(2) What science of the economic sphere, and what science of the social sphere, can be discerned in the product of this encounter? Is the social science of the economists compatible with that of the sociologists? If so, at what price, and with what objective in mind?

Darras: the unity of a school of thought — or a strategic compromise?
The Darras volume is presented resolutely as a collective exercise from an undifferentiated group of authors. While each contributor signs his or her text, the work as a whole carries a *collective* signature. Similarly, the introductions, links and conclusions are not signed, even if their author is easily identifiable as Pierre Bourdieu. These rhetorical procedures clearly demonstrate the collective appropriation of the exercise by all the participants. This being the case, a first reading leads you to take the texts at face value, to treat each essay as a brick in a collective, homogeneous edifice in which the introduction, links and conclusions fulfil their normal role of neutrally holding together the substantive articles.

Nevertheless, if subsequently you relate back the stated propositions to their authors, you cannot fail to be struck by the implicit structuring of the text by discipline and institution. The discourse then sounds like a duet, the melody developing with the counter-melody. It loses its linearity. So how do the two voices come together? There is no doubt that they do, objectively, if only because a discourse is produced which claims to link two heterogeneous disciplines scientifically. Is this link-up based on inclusion or interdependence? If inclusion can be excluded due to the very form of cooperation, what is the nature of the interdependence? Is it to be located in the two disciplines, in the particular representatives of those disciplines at this seminar, or in both these at the same time? This takes us into the realm of the sociology of science: what implicit strategies organize the relationship between the actors? What sort of science do these make possible?

The science of the economists

The presuppositions
(1) Growth is an incontestable fact, identifiable by a single indicator (a rate) and related to an entity, 'French society'. So from the start the necessity of the measurement and the object to be measured are stated. Implicitly, then, French society is a totality, a system of interdependence limited to the nation, that is, a zone of sovereignty.

Growth is a boon because it allows change. That sums up the ideal of a mobile society, one which nonetheless requires purposeful action[4] to check the 'forces of inertia'. The system of interdependence is not therefore devoid of conflictual relations but these tend to be identified as 'friction', imperfections in the interdependence.

Growth cannot be considered a good in itself but only in relation to the opportunities it creates: more equality and more freedom (or fewer constraints), change being both what permits and results from growth.

(2) Growth can only bring benefits with the purposefully willed action of society operating on itself, because:

(i) by themselves, market forces tend neither towards more freedom nor more equality, and

(ii) the double aim of freedom and equality will only come about through more solidarity which society will construct, if need be against the friction engendered in some of its segments, in thè name of maximum benefits for all.

So the ideal is a managed society on the basis of a consensus organized around the double aim of growth and balanced distribution. This consensus defines the general interest and thus the legitimacy of the action undertaken in its name.

(3) The realization of this consensual objective (which crops up often in the various statements of the planners) requires the action of specialists of the general interest, that is, experts capable of identifying the ends in all ethical and social neutrality and developing the means to achieve them. The exercise of this expertise presumes a

science of the laws of growth and distribution, assisted by information on the real state of the system, to help fix the desired operational objectives and then organize them. This information must include data on objective social and economic needs, without which there would be no question of optimizing either growth or the distribution of resources.

Taken together, these presuppositions open up the field to two ranks of experts and fix their position relative to each other: on the one hand, the macroeconomists with their expertise on models of growth and distribution; and on the other, experts on needs who work out the morphology of society, which helps supply data for the models and even lets the latter incorporate certain variables initially held to be exogenous by the economists.

It is on this basis that a transaction between economic planners and sociologists becomes possible and desirable.

The blind spots in the economists' science
These are twofold:

(1) The objective conditions which make it possible to consider the management of the social sphere.

Internal interdependence and external independence are implicitly given as facts. French society is portrayed by the revealing metaphor of a 'machine' (p.36) with 'works': the speck of dirt is not forgotten either — this makes the machine 'seize up' and it then has to be 'oiled'. These mechanical images are typical of the period (see Marchal and Lecaillon, *Les Rouages de L'Économie Nationale*, among others). It is the vision of national accountancy. Society can be described as an economic table, the table of its interdependent units. It will gain in precision if one manages to divide it up according to the variability in needs. That is the very condition of any interventionist policy of managing the internal movements of the nation, in other words, of any Keynesian policy. But for this policy to be possible, it is also necessary for the internal interdependencies to win out over the external interdependencies. In other words, there has to be an ordering of positions between society and the *nation* — as the site of sovereign decision making, the only place where an organic will can apply or where the general interest can be defined.

If this is lacking, the will to action will be feeble. In fact, discussion of external interdependence, to become so crucial just a few years later, is almost totally absent from this text. This is why the economists can allow themselves their Faustian optimism.

Societal consensus on the objectives of growth is not questioned any more than is external interdependence. It is given a priori (p.34) either as blindingly obvious or as the product of objective knowledge.

Any divergence from this consensus, otherwise known as the general interest, is deemed a divergence from reason and identified with the seeking of personal gain, that speck of dirt in the cogs of general interest. The dissidents will be brought back into the fold of objective, optimizing reason by the correction of discrepancies and the fight against inflexibility — the objective of the planners.

(2) The status of the specialists of general interest.

The national economy, like all machines, needs its mechanics with their oil-cans to lubricate the works. Economic policy decided by experts can only be seen as legitimate if based on the objective knowledge of those experts, a knowledge of inter-relations informed by the study of needs. As experts, the economists situate themselves 'above society', endowed with an unquestioned capacity for social objectivity, escaping, as a consequence, all determinism (p.55–6).

This being the case, with the aims clear and the means assured, the specialists function as scientists and technicians, not politicians. As a result, they do not encroach upon democratic legitimacy, by which powers of decision are entrusted to elected representatives. Holding economic insights, they are well placed to pursue their task of technical arbitration in the service of reducing inequalities, which comes down to a moral imperative for all: surrender yourselves to the logic of the science of the collectivity.

The science of the social sphere among the economists

How do the macroeconomists situate themselves in relation to classic political economy? How does this affect what they ask of sociologists?

We will not dwell on the fundamental subversion of classic or neoclassic economic models by the planners who do not identify the general interest with the sum of individual interests. Instead, let us look at another subversion, just as essential (and related, anyway), this one aimed at the homogeneity of the individual which was a cornerstone of classic economic calculation. The participants here oppose the variability of the human groups which make up French society to the uniform reason of homo economicus. These groups, located statistically, are characterized by the constraints which define their situation (income, extent of participation in the market economy, values).

With this passage from the concept of preference in economic man to that of need related to social membership group, social variables make an appearance in economic thought. This science of the social sphere asserts: the objective variability of needs, and the need to measure differences by reference to a norm of needs (linked to the notion of the equalization of conditions).

It thus needs — and this is what is asked of the sociologist — the measurement of: the morphological differences between the groups, and the effects of the morphological changes in groups on their resources, needs and values, as a means of intervening against the pockets of resistance to modernity, defined as the optimization (as regards freedom and equality) of the distribution of growth. This vision will lead perfectly naturally to the definition of 'target groups' for state intervention beginning with the Sixth Plan.

In giving this role to the sociologist, the economist becomes exposed to many a complication when the former points out that not only does need vary from one group to another, but there is no objective reference to this need because:

(1) The relationship to goods and services is not uniform from one social group to another even when objective freedom of access increases with resources.

(2) Social preference or need only takes form within socially systemic relationships with goods. In other words, need is linked to the meaning given by groups to the various practices of consumption or investment. From this point onwards, the symbolic meaning of consumption is revealed.[5] Need has to be conceived of as subjective — which poses the problem of how to measure it (see Laufer and Paradeise, 1981).

The counterpoint to the economists' discourse

For the economists, the categorical imperative of balanced resource distribution is referred back to an ethical status, that of the researcher as person of knowledge, which blots out the problem of politics. For the sociologists, on the other hand, normative discourse is almost totally absent from the body of the text (just one example, p. 328). It is wholly to be found *between* the articles, in the linking sections written by Bourdieu, and can be attributed solely to the one man who edited them, even if it seems to be collectively appropriated by the groups of economists and sociologists, as suggested by the absence of any signature.

In this way, the editor, far from defining himself as above science, or in one specialist discipline, presents himself as the expert of experts, he who includes in his field of observation science itself and its conditions of production. He thus converts an objective weakness, as regards his discipline, into a position of strength since he proclaims his capacity for making objects of those who consider themselves the subjects of science par excellence, sociologists and economists alike; and also because he makes this very condition the absolute precept of all knowledge. This is a position of strength conquered by the strategic effort of capturing the high profile and credibility of economic discourse — via the collaboration and the preface of Pierre Gruson — in the cause of winning recognition for his discipline.

This discourse, in the form of a counterpoint, quite naturally assumes the task of questioning, point by point, the presuppositions enshrined in the body of the text, particularly those of the economists, but of the sociologists, too, as accessories. One might call it a double-edged strategy, first for the discipline as a 'name in common', second for a specific disciplinary tradition. Thus the principal 'accepted facts' of the text are questioned.

Growth is an incontestable fact characterizing French society, maybe. But what is French society? Growth may be a blessing because it allows change. But is change a universal value in French society?

Resistance to change, say the economists, is due to the forces of inertia. They may be analysed as frictions but if change is not a universal value, this analysis is erroneous; the behaviour, judged regrettable, unhealthy, inopportune and irrational, of some social groups in the face of the transformation of their world can only be analysed concretely by abandoning the assumption of a universal reason of the individual, a reason informed, moreover, by the nature and general interest of the search for an optimum defined by the economists as a collective one. At once the problem arises of the status of the societal consensus posited by the economists and the legitimacy of their position as experts. It is vital to analyse the social position of the experts to deduce the nature of their discourse as both a legitimizing and a scientific discourse.

Growth supposes solidarity: but what is solidarity?

Growth allows and supposes the reduction of inequalities. Can an inequality be defined by reference to an objective norm or does it not have to include the phenomenon of perception as a process and therefore the social conditions of perception such as scales of value?

What sociology is made possible by the compromise?

Agreement on the objects, agreement on the problems
As Bourdieu says in the introduction, you are struck on your first reading[6] by the existence of an agreement as to 'objects' and not on 'problems'. Perhaps we could go a step further in this direction and ask whether agreement on objects is not *already* in some ways agreement on problems, that is, on the framework accepted by the representatives of the two disciplines.

The agreement on objects can be seen in the way the sociologists agree, from the outset, to tackle the problem of the content of this general receptacle, French society, through a social morphology in liaison with the 'economic subsystem'. This accord has two distinct criteria:

(1) For the economists, a criterion of action: the need to segmentalize the macroeconomic models — an exercise that all the economists present were to lend themselves to, in particular by working out the FIFI models[7] for INSEE — which requires a refinement of knowledge about social structure, or as they put it, 'morphology'.

(2) For the sociologists (the editor, in any case), the criterion is a 'principle of method'. It is a question of fixing a research agenda: penetrating the reality of the social sphere through the economic subsystem is not to draw any conclusions about the autonomy of that subsystem (p. 425) nor even its supremacy.

The relative disagreement on the problems is shown in the desire of the economists to relate the joint elaborations of the two groups to a process of modelling and quantification (part II, Gruson) which the extreme complexity of the sociologists' theoretical models are ill-suited for, whether presented as descriptive or as models (for example, in the Darbel/Bourdieu text).

The objects as problems

The agreement on problems has to be located upstream, however, in the implicit sociological observation which accepts certain 'constructs' as objects and pushes aside others. What is accepted jointly as a problem?

First, it is a way of approaching social reality through statistical groups 'which owe their unity to their situation in global society' (p. 422), this situation defining by itself the nature of the interests and perceptions of the group (and more generally the ethos). This is a reading relying on statistics, which therefore excludes, provisionally at least, a construction of the object of sociological study relying on history or institutions (p. 15).

Second, it is a reading of the social sphere which bears on some groups deeply marked by change — the middle classes, peasants and farmers — practically excluding other numerically important groups like manual workers.

Third, it is a reading of the social sphere which, through its first two characteristics, practically excludes any look at the processes of collective action either within or outside institutional groupings (there is no mention of companies, onions, mobilization or negotiation). The primary statistic is the person, distinguished from economic man in that he or she shares specific attributes with other members of his or her social group, and that these attributes cannot be read just as products of rationality alone, even when behaviour is constrained. The social segments thus defined are, so to speak, treated as so many 'communities' in the ethnological sense, that is, as sufficiently distinct to be isolable, even if their particular position can only be understood by reference to those of all the others.

From all this emerges the picture of a determinist approach whose key concepts are identity, acculturation, diffusion and reproduction — all concepts appropriate to the 'common sense' of the time. It is also a taxonomic approach (p. 14), quite well adapted for linking up with the economists' concern for measuring differences (pp. 25, 77, 109, 136).

Finally, it is an approach which looks first and foremost at the problems of consumption and therefore of distribution which, as we have amply demonstrated earlier, were at the heart of the planners' problem.

Thus, themes which in the context of an interventionist economy might have caused conflict between the economists and sociologists were sidestepped: the potential contradictions between market society and state regulation were presented as secondary (p. 18) or put off for the time being (p. 227). Whether this is strategic or methodological, it is a clear example of the participants' de facto respect for neutrality in the handling of data. The phenomenon is all the more striking in that the term 'state' is absent from the lexicon of the sociologists while the economists use it incessantly. The state is absent; but nonetheless there is manifest agreement that goals recognized by both the sociologists and economists — more equality through growth — will not come about spontaneously (p. 14). Like the economists, the sociologists, by refraining from any reflection on the state, expel politics from their field of investigation.

Conclusion

It follows from our analysis that this work, monolithic at first sight, plays on a de facto ambiguity which is the basis of the possible compromise between sociologists and economists.

On the economists' side it is a matter of internalizing new variables to enrich models whose outlines are already traced. From this point of view, the sociologists are subordinate to the economists: they have to feed their models. They lose, on this ground, the specificity of their discipline (preface, III, IV). 'The risk presented by this union between sociologists and economists is that it comes about for the examination of global phenomena, an examination which may therefore remain sterile because it allows part of the essential to escape.'

On the sociologists' side, the strategy may be twofold.

(1) First, an attempt to gain legitimacy: the method consists of

following close in the footsteps of a strong discipline in the hope that some of its legitimacy will rub off.

(2) Second, as regards knowledge: the collaboration between the disciplines rests on the methodological act of fixing a research agenda, starting from a social morphology. From here, any amount of slippage is possible, including what happens if it leads to the displacement of macroeconomic models as algorithms of the thinking in social matters. This morphology is then conceived of only as a starting-point, not as a framework: it alone can permit a later return to the analysis of processes and institutions (pp. 12, 222).

The 'editor' replies in advance to the double risk that the sociologists are exposed, in the shape of two maxims:

(i) against the risk of subordination, the 'mutual respect of the specificity of each discipline and rigorous distinction of orders';

(ii) against the risk of ideological contagion, 'bracket off normative orientations'.

Notes

1. The title of the 1966 book, *Le Partage des bénéfices*, Paris: Editions de Minuit, a collective work attributed to 'Darras'.

2. We beg the reader to excuse the rather summary portrait — it is meant only to sketch the context of our remarks. On this particular point, see, for example, Fourquet, 1980.

3. The sociology degree had not long been in existence.

4. Volonté in the original. For a comment on this crucial and often misunderstood term, see the Note on Translation.

5. Books on the semiology of consumption flourished in the 1960s.

6. One exception is the piece by Darbel.

7. At the time, these econometric models of growth inspired great confidence.

ANNEX

ECONOMISTS

A. *Growth is a goal recognized as a value by all*

The personality of the new Planning Commissioner, the progress made in the technical quality of its work, the espousal of the themes of flexible planning by intermediary bodies and public opinion, international interest — all this gave a particular prestige to the planning exercise, and the high growth objective was adopted (34).

B. *Growth is a good which demands that resistance be crushed*

The reform of distribution circuits, the suppression of many obstacles to competition, the modernization of declining activities and the concentration of companies, the lack of housing and its consequences, the development of occupational training, the transformation of the education system... the reform of the administration and mode of public management... incomes policy, all these were the inexhaustible themes of administrative meetings, study groups, seminars, Sunday sermons and electoral meetings. The enduring nature of the talking was echoed by the permanence and discontinuity of the actions taken in this field as well as the enduring resistance of certain social groups to transformations

SOCIOLOGISTS

A. While it is true that the practice of economic forecasting has helped spread a philosophy of progress dominated by the eschatological vision of the society of abundance, is it certain that all social groups subscribe equally to this representation of society and its future? Just as it is important to examine the share of the benefits of development taken by different social groups, should we not also analyse the different ways of participating in the mystique of development, and more precisely in the ideology which confers on economic development the power, by itself, to reduce economic differences and social disparities?

B. Are transformations that French society is undergoing endured helplessly or accepted willingly, unconsciously lived through or consciously organized? Are the French resistant to change? Will they adapt only with regret or as if in spite of themselves, or are they in the process of accepting economic growth as *the* value around which to construct a project of civilization? The description of global transformations in production and distribution and the analysis of changes in the population and in work, raise the question of knowing what roles are effectively played by the various groups of agents (221).

which, though important, had only been reforms. One can see here the symptoms of the forces of inertia which inhabit French society, or at least the conservatism of the responsible elements of this society (36–7).

C. There is a great risk that the various economic actors do not have all the innovative willpower and imagination necessary to face up to the new situation, and that the structural reforms indispensable to reconcile behaviour patterns engendered by growth and stability will be embarked upon with neither more speed nor determination than in the past (38).

D. *This objective of growth calls for a managed economy*
One may well entertain doubts about the possibility of any spontaneous reduction in inequalities in a period of growth ... The experience of past years shows that the reduction of inequalities supposes the setting-up of appropriate instruments of action by the politicians (86).

In fact it is not enough simply to give everyone the same theoretical possibilities of consumption in order to reduce real differences automatically. For that, you need a much more radical remodelling of social structures and a modification of the mechanisms governing training and the transmission of cultural and material heritages (116).

But take note of the fact that at the lowest levels the chances of a successful school career are not the same for all social groups. This shows clearly that even if qualitative changes in education are necessary to ensure real democracy, real obstacles exist and have to be surmounted first (335).

C. Isn't there a grave danger of being lulled into the belief that increases in production and national income will by themselves bring all the benefits, particularly a reduction in economic and social inequalities? (17).

D. No-one today doubts that the state apparatus has become much more concerned with economic development and regulation, as well as much more interventionist, but the question is to know through whom, why and how. Is it enough to invoke the creation of ENA and the vocation for democracy which inspired it? Can change be accounted for by the existence of the Plan, defined as a clear creative synthesis of the doctrinaire/authoritarian and aesthetic/cultural tendencies of French culture?

Have top civil servants fundamentally altered their conception of the state? Through what channels does the Plan gain its effectiveness? Summoning up colourful abstractions such as the bourgeois family, Napoleonic authority or even the working class, or universal cultural facts such as the appearance of television or institutional innovations cannot account for the behaviour of social groups. What are the real attitudes of these groups as regards the phenomena of change? (223).

E. *... which requires information ...*

Since the interplay of qualitative growth factors can only be grasped, given the present state of our understanding, in a very imprecise way, the analysis of the past role of each of these can help throw only a little light on the future ... (48–9).

F. *... on a still autonomous, organic French society*

So with this evolution [in the external economic environment] comes the risk of increased economic dependence for [the weakest] and the allied risk that the unique character of their social organization and culture will be called into question (57).

G. *This management function is the work of experts, impartial, efficient technicians*

The reasons why western economies did not experience crises after the war are not yet fully clear ... But cannot the absence of crises be explained essentially by the fact that governments operated effective policies of economic fine tuning? If these policies worked, should not that be put down to the relative value of the economic analyses they were based on? ... Cannot the fact that these policies were put into effect be explained essentially by governments' role in economic regulation in market economies since the end of the war and by the increased competence of the leading groups in the economic administration? Certainly the extent of government

E. Uncovering sociological questions in the practice of the economist means first of all getting him or her not to treat certain variables as exogenous, provoking him or her into squeezing economic facts so that they reveal their relationship with the other social facts. In effect, any attempt at all at an answer presupposes, from mediation to mediation, that the relationship of the part to the whole of the system becomes clear (423).

G. Have greater economic knowledge and improved techniques of intervention conferred on those responsible for economic policy a position of judgment which, through decisions tailored to a perceived economic reality, could guide all of society in a direction which, unquestionably, would be in its interest? Will trials of strength give way to the equitable weighing-up of reasons and the rationalization of choices? In other words, are political battles between pressure groups just deceptive or a historic stage now transcended and must they give way to the harmonious fusion of constraints by the technocrat? Or again, does economic knowledge — and those who act by it — still, objectively, serve a social order and those who value it or are content to see it continue?

intervention, the correct dose of measures and when to take them, remain subject to varying appraisals and policy arguments, but certain basic principles of economic regulation are surely well-known and established . . . (56).

Faster technological progress, explained by an acceleration in scientific progress or faster diffusion of technical progress or both. A more rapid improvement than in the past of micro-and macroeconomic management and of social organization for productive ends would thus appear to make up the economic factors explaining, in part at least, the rapidity of French growth. The progress of economic and technical knowledge and information might thus have been a fundamental factor in the acceleration of growth after the Second World War (56–7, cf. also 60).

. . . Don't strategic decisions, however well-informed, still remain risky courses of action taken by people defined by a certain position in the social structure (and by reference to others in a different position) with a view to achieving ends which are necessarily defined by reference to socially distinct values? (16–17).

If you take into account the fact that the system of values is dependent on the economic order and that it has the strength and the right to determine conduct, even the most symbolic, then economic forecasting can claim to set itself up as a moral imperative and elevate itself to the level of prophecy. Anticipations of the future become imperatives of the present; the ethical and political orders are no longer distinct; the collective projects of organized groups confronting each other on the ground becomes incomprehensible and seem to be excluded from social reality just as much as from analysis . . . Hasn't the image of economic disorder which made such an impression on Durkheim been replaced today in the consciousness of observers by the all too reassuring image of order and by an exaggerated confidence in the idea that growth is not only a fact but also an end recognized as a value by all groups which then actually adapt their behaviour in line with the norms its strength and law impose on them?

H. *. . . whose task is to take decisions informed by the understanding of inequalities*

Do the structures of consumption reflect models of consumption differentiated according to social categories or are they simply a function of the average level of total consumption attained by each category? (109).

I. No doubt one must beware of believing that objective disparities as measured by statistics correspond exactly to perceived and experienced inequalities... We can in no way take for granted that the same revenue differential will have the same meaning after a general evaluation of levels of revenue capable of allowing access to hitherto impossible levels of consumption and therefore determining a redefinition of differences in the economic and symbolic use of revenues (98).

J. ... *and organized according to the norms of the econometric model*
For the moment [this joint description of sociologists and economists] does not go as far as quantitative explication. There is still a long way to go before that necessary objective is reached. Progress thus far is no less decisive: new explicative factors, better defined as to their real nature, are appearing ... (Up till now) the economists have done little more than trace the outline of what it was necessary to explain (II–III).

I. The economist who, at the end of a comparison of the economic methods and results of various countries, conclude that systems of regulation are equivalent, are acting as scientists or experts; since from the outset they brush aside politics and its conflicts, they cannot find it again at the end except in the form of moral concern. There is a great temptation for them to confuse objectivism or a philosophy of value neutrality with objectivity and to make them the principle of an exhortation to social and political consensus which thinks it is impartial and would like to think of itself as benevolent (425).

J. Economists' explanations always include a residual element which quantitative concepts and methods cannot handle... Can one, then, transfer a number of questions from an economic problematic to a sociological problematic, and what is the meaning of such an exercise? Any attempt to do this entails a reformulation of the question (442).

11
Trends and interventions in French society[1]
Pierre Tripier*

If it was necessary to prove that sociology moves forward (taking account of the place where it is developed) in a cultural language (*discours*) outside time and place, inspired by its great ancestors, featuring concepts which aspire to immortality or in words in the spirit of the times, preoccupied with the current convulsions of society, in statements akin to those of futurologists or experts, half-descriptive, half-prophetic, then one would merely have to jump back twenty years in time to have it confirmed.

In 1963, or four years after the publication of Gurvitch's *Traité* (see the foreword by Durand and Monjardet's chapter), the first conference of the French Sociological Society was held in Paris, and in 1965 a selection of the papers was to appear under the title *Tendances et Volontés de la Société Française*. We present here one interpretation of this collection to illustrate sociologists' sensitivity to the prevailing socioeconomic climate — other papers included could be used in a different way to show them ensnared in their presuppositions.

The grid we have used for our analysis is very simple — we sought to discover to what extent work and its technical evolution were significant variables in the interpretation of society or whether these factors were part of a larger interpretation, an underlying structure which served to embrace it.

The characteristics of the underlying sociology of the collection
Our diagnosis quickly led us to abandon any hypothesis about the leading position of work in the explanatory system represented in the majority of the papers, perhaps because more than half of the authors in the Friedmann–Naville *Traité* were not present here, be it as authors or as chairpeople or as rapporteurs of sessions. However, technological change has its place since the characteristic features of the underlying sociology are those of *a sociology devoid of memory, fascinated by change, both cultural and technological, which sees in America its own future, founded upon an interventionist economic policy.*

* Université Paris X and Groupe de Sociologie du Travail

Let us look at this appraisal in more detail. The sociology deployed in that work is devoid of memory, which may be explained by the age of the contributors but also, probably, by the spirit of the times. Apart from Raymond Aron, who wrote the preface, none of the authors was an adult before the war. That fact makes itself felt in all the papers — every development is said to date from 1945. The Third Republic in general, and the interwar years in particular, get the same treatment as the period running from the Middle Ages to the nineteenth century: depressing, empty years, periods of economic and political obscurantism (see the papers by Tavernier, Dumazedier, Adam and Maurice). As for Vichy, it is quite simply forgotten, there is not a single reference to it. So history begins in 1945 and everything that came before serves as a mythical foil to set off the new changes.

This way of reconstructing a misleading history makes for facile argumentation and renders possible some effects which seem exaggerated today, since we cannot forget the progress made by contemporary history over the last twenty years. One example is particularly striking to me, namely the notion of working-class unity. Gerard Adam and Marc Maurice present nineteenth-century society as (in their words) 'split neatly between the middle class and workers' — and working-class unity was based on this. Now in 1963 it was sensed that this unity was false, surveys showing a great diversity of situations. But what astonishes us today is that people could think — after the work of Rude, Duveau or Coornaert — that the working class was *ever* unified. There probably never was any historiographical material demonstrating such unity — it was perhaps more a case of this stereotypical reconstruction of the past which allows one to think of the present as different and throws research results into relief.

That is how we would interpret this piece of rhetorical bravura from Tavernier:

> Hesiod and Xenophon, Virgil and Columella described a way of life, a rural economy and type of man much like those of Olivier de Serres, Le Play and Jean Giono . . . Peasant society is dead and the young tenant farmer of today has less in common with his father than the latter had with his distant ancestors of the eighteenth century, the Renaissance or even antiquity (pp. 52–3).

Another form taken by amnesia is to reduce everything to the contemporary. All the same, it is remarkable that someone (Morin) should make that into a theory in this collection. We quote a passage from his article which helps to illustrate the views shared at the time:

> The disintegration of the past, the security of the future for individuals . . . therefore entail, in the context of a bourgeois (that is individualistic)

civilisation, a consumer society . . . the promotion and convergence of psychological and affective investment by individuals in the present. This focalisation may be termed 'contemporaneanism' (p. 404).

More generally, to synthesize many of the papers, the reasoning is as follows: the transformation of the church, its 'aggiornamento' as it was called at the time, is leading to dissipation of the 'apocalyptic vision of the Right' while the grand ideas of the Liberation are fading away in face of rising consumption, and revolutionary hopes are in decline: 'On the Left, the future isn't working.'

To sum up, becoming modern, thanks to the 'disintegration of its old demons', French society is becoming pragmatic and reasonable. Sociologists can study it without giving way to passion and since the past has disappeared, what better tool than systems analysis which presupposes, by definition, that all its elements are contemporaneous?

Thus there is a total fit between the observation the sociologist makes on society and the tool he or she uses to investigate it, functionalism, considered by many at the time to constitute the only possible scientific method.[2]

Moreover, to be without memory does not mean to be without future: a good many of the sociologists' papers try to throw light on the work of economists, notably those for the Plan. Each specialist seeks to highlight his or her particular area and analyses the present in order to draw out forecasts about the future.

These exercises in rational prophecy are common enough to allow one the thought that futurology is as prominent as history is absent, as if the former was in this period indissolubly linked to the sociologists' craft.

Two causal chains

What appearance did this modern and contemporary world take on for itself? And what lessons did sociological forecasting draw from what it saw? In answer to these twin questions the authors offer two lines of causality.

(1) The great upheavals in France over the previous twenty years have their origins in civil society. Largely rural at the beginning of the period, the nation has been urbanized. This France without peasants (there are a few farmers, all the same) is a transformed society: in becoming city dwellers, the peasants' sons strain the ties which held them in solidaristic primary groups and a hitherto dependable social equilibrium. These ties are loosening, the ideological apparatus which maintained or expressed the cohesion of the world is changing. In an effort to adapt to a situation that seems to be escaping it, the

Catholic church is transforming itself and beginning to produce activists. These, in turn, flood into the lay world and are highly influential in working-class and agricultural circles. Even if a majority of the authors do not go very deeply into the multiple consequences of this transformation, they are nonetheless struck by the metamorphosis of the CFTC into the CFDT which they interpret as yet another sign of the secularization of society.

Thus, the causal chain which corresponds to the 'tendencies' of civil society is quite naturally driving the peasants into the town, making them desert the church, transforming the more pious souls into activists and the apathetic ones into hedonists; these two modes of modernism work in the direction of increasing household consumption which, in turn (in a very Keynesian manner) encourages industrial restructuring and economies of scale, giving rise to an indefinite spiral of growth. This is circular reasoning, which makes benefits seem natural, the fruit of a general tendency to expand.

(2) Other non-sociologist authors — but some of the sociologists, too — formulate another view of development, parallel to this spontaneous one, which introduces that privileged actor of French history, the state. Here it is no longer a matter of a transformation whose origins might be found in the sum of individual actions (women's refusal to stay in the country, the structuring effects of publicity on consumption patterns, etc.) but of a transformation 'from above' due to planning à la française and starring the administrative elites of the nation as the heroes of growth and social transformation (it is about this time that Alain Touraine begins to talk of the *'historical subject'*[3] and the rationalizing model, precisely to describe this type of phenomenon).

Here, on this subject, is a state adviser (un Conseiller d'Etat, M. Grĕgoire):

> The old boys of ENA,[4] accepting implicitly the existing socioeconomic system, without doctrinal prejudices, totally allergic to liberalism, fundamentally hostile to the zero-growth mentality ('malthusianisme'), concerned exclusively with economic rationality, think that a good economic policy is likely to ensure permanent economic expansion and that the state is capable, by constant economic fine-tuning and the unfailing fight against whatever holds back the economy (bottle-necks, abuses, privileges), of ensuring growth in stable financial and social conditions.
>
> Created by men obsessed by expansion and productivity, ENA participated in the diffusion of these views amongst top civil servants. Born of the refusal to accept the continuation of the 1930s depression, it supplied allies for the artisans of victory in the 1950s.

To sum up, in a wholly national vision, the reasoning begins with what is now considered one of the resources of the French: the strength of their state (see Birnbaum, 1983). The opportunities for change are due to the state and the sociologists who comment on the transformations quite eagerly accept a combination of this interventionist and Promethean vision of history with the first schema. The only false note is sounded by Crozier, who argued against the possibility of a transformation of this type and demonstrated instead the risks, inherent in the form of action preferred by the authorities, of the system seizing up.

The place of work in the explication
Do these two great causal chains, which give rise to both the 'natural' trends of, and state interventionism in, French society, introduce work in any way in their explanatory schemes?

The answer is complex. While explanations of the trends refer freely to a certain type of evolutionism, that of the archaeologists and prehistorians of the first half of the century,[5] the articles about interventionism, on the other hand, consider the nature of the state as relatively ahistorical.

The argument which starts from the rural exodus pictures it as the result of technological transformations. The social sphere here is distinct from the technical. The latter develops under its own momentum, as if it were inscribed in the laws of nature. Society receives those impulses from without and adapts to them by transforming itself. The vehicle of this mutation is *change in the system of cultural meanings*.

Thus, the upheaval in peasant communities is analysed thanks to the revolution in agricultural techniques. The implications of this would seem to be the departure of idle hands, resulting in higher productivity, transformations in the temporal rhythm of country life; while these in turn are thought to have implications for family organization and the way rural enterprises are run.

The same sort of argument, involving (i) an independent technological variable, and (ii) a series of consequences, is used for other aspects of social life without the sociotechnical dimension of work and what that implies in terms of interactive analyses (society organizing and selecting technical solutions which lead to social upheaval) ever really being taken into consideration, except in one paper that we discuss later.

As in many evolutionist doctrines, society constitutes, at the given moment, the end result of history and the destiny of other nations is to follow it down the road it has opened up for them. What could be more natural than to consider the most opulent society, the United States, as the model and reference under present circumstances?

As for the papers dealing with interventionism, or 'volonté', even though they include the modernization of state activity in their commentary, they make no reference to work as a dynamic variable except in relation to indicative planning and what seemed then to be its success in France's effort to transform itself.

The only paper which explicitly puts work into its vision is that of Alain Touraine. He opposes those who see the tendencies of French society as a sort of Americanization, a view he denounces as 'the simplified, evolutionist vision which has always been the illusion of the rich, quick to identify their present with the future of others'. Then, more explicitly perhaps than in *Sociologie de l'Action* or *La Conscience Ouvrière* which he was at work on at the time, he puts forward a macroeconomic and social interpretation in which work, conceived as the creative activity par excellence, and the degree of control over it and what is produced by it, provides the key to understanding historical movement.

Strongly influenced by the Latin-American 'developmentalists' (Germani, 1955; and Furtado, 1961, for example), he explains the analysis of the volonté or state interventionist causal chain by reference to their brand of political economy:

> Over the last twenty years, the French have lived through a period of rapid, almost continuous growth. There are few people worse off today than they were before the war. Of course, the changes cause tensions and the abandonment of forms of social and cultural life that individuals were brought up in; more directly, it strikes a blow at ideologies apt to interpret their own shakiness as the decline of all society . . .
>
> Latin-American societies are undergoing extremely rapid social and cultural change, but they are not experiencing an economic expansion to compare with our own. And yet running through these societies is a national consciousness, an awareness that, even in the face of powerful obstacles, they are making their own history.

This vision confirms that, for the author, the ultimate analysis of a society consists of considering it as a superior type of individual,[6] whose manner of working has to be appreciated — that is, the way it creates material and symbolic wealth and then appropriates it.

Epilogue: fifteen years on
The texts we have presented all too briefly here are all the more interesting in that fifteen years later some of those who contributed to the collection came together again to weigh up what had happened in the meantime and to put the book into perspective.

The judgment (Mendras, 1980) aims at being both cutting and

discriminating. The main thesis seems to go like this. The year that *Tendances et Volontés* appeared, 1965, was the year that many of the trends which up till then were thought likely to persist actually began to take an unexpected course, or to diverge. A number of things continued, such as the trend towards secularization, in the church especially, but also in many other institutions (the army, justice, education). The authors draw a number of lessons from this which they use in conjunction with research findings — something quite alien to the method of *Tendances et Volontés*.

The first observation is perhaps the most cutting. In a chapter on 'The Watershed Year of 1965', Pavy shows that things which seemed amenable to control in the vision of planners of the day, quickly came up against the turbulence resulting from the increase in international trade following the 'Kennedy Round' and the drain on national savings due to the activities of multinational companies. The fall in gross fixed capital made France, from 1965, a nation in which the tertiary sector was bigger than the industrial sector. Thus, what might have looked at the start of the 1960s like national destiny, the fruit of actively imposed policies, turned out at the end of the 1970s to have been reversed by the very tendencies of that society.

The second observation is more ambiguous and the conclusions of the book are, in this respect, difficult to determine. At first, the diagnosis appears straightforward and we seem to see an illustration of a widely-spread doctrine in which the central place is taken by the market and all that bears upon the market, and possibly harms it in the way the state is organized.

> Institutions remain inflexible and anachronistic, stifling every initiative and reform (p. 43).

> French democracy has stabilized and modernized more outside Paris than in Paris, with its institutions, and the same goes for ways of behaving (p. 47).

> The company, as an institution . . . has been able to transform itself, mainly under American influence . . . Companies could work so well that they might attract to themselves much of their members' social life and play a more important role in the community. The company is exemplary and all-conquering (p. 49).

But elsewhere institutional crises do pose problems for the analysts. Witness this cry of alarm from Crozier, rehearsing his hypotheses on the ungovernable nature of western democracies:

> What is striking . . . is the fundamental questioning of the most respectable of society's institutions — the churches, the army, the educational institutions . . . The institutions that are disrupted are those which do not boast a function whose results are immediately comprehensible

and measurable. They survive and find a new equilibrium by withdrawing to a more precise and specialised function and by renouncing their role in social control over the whole society (p. 343).

Thus, we see that the arguments on non-economic institutions are two-edged: all society's rigidities are attributed to them, but at the same time there is concern that their regulatory powers are waning. In short, the reader is left to his or her own judgment as long as he or she chooses strictly between the conservative and the liberal interpretation.

Conclusions

The period of growth after the war saw the emergence of comprehensive explanatory systems, resulting from the fascination exerted by a modernity that could be measured every day in terms of the rural exodus, the consumption of household goods and cars, the transformation of production techniques and circuits of distribution, and the secularization of professions and institutions. In such a situation, highly general, universal pronouncements can have some meaning and the sociologist is not exempt from hazarding futurological projections or universal arguments. In a period when growth slows, sociologists rediscover the specific, the local, the individual trajectory, nuances, balance . . . No doubt that is because they now know much more about society as they have become 'professionalized' in the last fifteen years. But no doubt, too, this is proof that their arguments — that sometimes they like to think of as beyond time and space — are firmly rooted in the present actualities of their society.

Notes

1. Various authors (1965) *Tendances et Volontés de la Société Français*. Paris: SEDEIS.
2. For example, the first French edition of Michel Crozier's *The Bureaucratic Phenomenon* (London, Tavistock, 1964) is littered with phrases such as 'scientific, that is, functionalist'. These disappeared in subsequent editions.
3. In Touraine's scheme of analysis, there is always one social movement in any reasonably lengthy period of social history which sets the agenda for future social change: this movement forms its 'sujet historique'. The 'historic subject', in other words, is not what is sought collectively, but the vanguard social movement itself, which becomes more conscious of its own identity and destiny as a result. (This anthropomorphism explains why Touraine has sometimes been seen as a sociological existentialist.) Substantively, Touraine designated the labour movement as the sujet historique of capitalist industrialism until approximately 1950; at this point, he claimed, it began to cede its role as leading history-maker to the ecology movement or (as he seemed to be saying later, and more plausibly) the women's movement. See Rose (1985) for a fuller discussion of Touraine's social thought.
4. ENA — the *Ecole Nationale d'Administration* — is one of the supra-university

Grandes Ecoles, being founded at the end of the Second World War to train an elite of industrial and (especially) state experts and administrators. These 'enarques' were once regarded as a key factor in the rapid economic growth within the framework of state planning achieved between 1945 and 1970. More recently, their contribution, together with that of the Plan itself, have been questioned.

5. One thinks of Gordon Childe or W. G. Ogburn, for example.

6. This observation raises the difficulty in Touraine's approach of to what extent the sujet historique is to be viewed as a distinct 'counter individual' or merely a 'schizoid' aspect of society-as-individual.

12
Critics, outsiders and the dishonoured: from the seminar, 'Social Transformation in Contemporary France' to the book *Tendances et Volontés de la Société Française* (1965)

*Nicole Abboud**

A minor event begins to look less trifling if, restored to its appropriate context in a correctly reconstructed history of ideas, it manages both to confirm the general picture and make it more precise by throwing new light on it. It shows, on the one hand, the abstentions exercised and the opportunities grasped, and, on the other, the unmistakable acts of censorship which allowed a crystallization of specific ideologies to impose themselves more firmly as the truth.

It so happens that my own contribution to the seminar on 'Social Transformation in Contemporary France' fell under the knife of the editors of *Tendances et Volontés*. I had thought up till now that this was because it was too impressionistic, not academic enough (and so I never dared cite it in my list of publications!).

I had even forgotten the episode until, nearly twenty years later, I came upon Pierre Tripier's reading of *Tendances et Volontés de la Société Française*. Urged on by curiosity, I consulted the French Sociological Society's records of the seminar and compared them to the volume published by Futuribles. I was astonished to discover, by comparing the contents list of the two publications (see the Annex) that my little adventure was part of a bigger story, reconstructed well by Pierre Tripier and even more cleverly thought out than he might think.

The pruning process
Here is my first observation. The absence of sociologists of work at the seminar was even more complete than Tripier says — few of them (not even Touraine) presented a paper. One exception was Michelle Durand whose paper was published by Futuribles; we might add, in passing, that it dealt with the company and the behaviour of execu-

* Groupe de Sociologie du Travail

tives in the area of economic decisions (on production and marketing) and social decision (employment, training), which shows that one of the veins of the sociology of work of the time was already escaping from the 'Friedmannian paradigm'. The absence of sociologists of work was either due to critical abstention[1] or lack of motivation for a general theme which might have seemed too far removed from their interests.

Second observation: all — well, nearly all — the papers in the 'Education and Culture' section were excluded by the editors of *Tendances et Volontés*. Now, these were not just any old essays: among the papers given at the seminar was an analysis by Viviane Isambert-Jamati (see Annex for titles of seminar papers and book chapters) on the opposition, from teachers' unions, ministerial officials, education supervisors and various anti-democratic pressure groups, to the 1959 law which lengthened obligatory schooling and to the resulting distortions which soon showed up on the 'educational map': the under-funding of certain regions and zones, compounded by the inequality[2] of the teaching units set up.

Also figuring marginally in this section on 'Education and Culture' was a reflection by Bourdieu and Passeron going through a two-pronged critique of American 'culturalists' such as Margaret Mead and Jesse Pitts — though Lawrence Wylie was explicitly excluded — and the French theorists of the 'bureaucratic phenomenon' whose boss-man was Michel Crozier, with their pretentions of showing, through their respective grids, the conservatism of French higher education.[3]

The only paper in the 'Education and Culture' section to be retained in *Tendances et Volontés* was that of Dumazedier showing the decline of the traditional, ritual leisure pursuits of the French, and the parallel rise of 'cultural development' in such forms as 'tele-clubs', working-class tourism and popular culture, etc.

Final observation, perhaps of less interest: the elimination by the editors of those papers listed under 'Changes in Religious Life' which talked of something other than the crisis of the moral hold of traditional Catholicism and the 'aggiornamento' of the French clergy. Authors who adopted a critical approach which denied the sacred character of religious phenomena and presented themselves as 'heretics' talking about 'heretics' were ruled out.

One can detect the same ambiguity in the papers listed in the chapter on 'Political Problems'. Included in the book is the text of Leo Hamon, high priest and apostle of the collaboration between planners and sociologists. The content of the texts not included seems to me to indicate a clear and systematic bias on the part of the editors of *Tendances et Volontés* — they censored any analysis casting a critical eye over ideologies, treated as social facts, or over institutions, seen as 'non-natural', or over the phenomena of crisis and conflict, where cultural change and power struggles get mixed up in sociopolitical issues.

The status of work and the evolution of techniques among the critics and dishonoured

Outsiders
I will not repeat Pierre Tripier's accurate analysis of Touraine's conception of work, inseparable on the one hand from the pairing 'creation and control', but then broadened out, on the other, to the global action of the appropriation of material and symbolic wealth. I will merely recall, like Tripier, that this conception is totally alien and impervious to that which sees technological development as a natural process.

The authors in the seminar who speak of 'trends' or 'deliberate intervention' [volontés] in terms different from those of the dominant language[4] can certainly not be accused of regarding technical change in too 'naturalist' a way and to be open to criticism on that account; nor can their papers be defined as too far removed from those questions of work that it is right to introduce when one is dealing with technical and social change. Those are not the reasons for their disqualification.

Thus, the analyses of Isambert-Jamati and Bourdieu and Passeron of the phenomena of 'non-change' in the school and university system are clearly related to social relationships, to living institutions. The changes which feature in their theoretical framework are sociopolitical, and thrust at the social order, whether masked or not by the order of things. The techniques by which changes would be effected, if they were wanted, would essentially be techniques deployed in social relations: the exercise of power, the transmission of knowledge, communication by language.

For my part, I looked at the perceptions of 'change' of those adults holding power in the various institutions of social control aimed at the younger generation: government, political parties, the press, universities, churches, commercial groups, advertising, organizations of production. These visions of 'change' I tried to describe as reified representations — 'menace' or 'miracle'. The tidal wave, desired or dreaded, carried forward by the rising generation (cf. Sauvy's book, *La Montée des Jeunes*) was perceived as an external reality that had to be stemmed but by conceding as little as possible, through some freedom of choice as regards style of dress, forms of symbolic cultural expression, sung or otherwise. I also tried, though without really succeeding, it is fair to say, to distinguish clearly the myth of 'obsolescence' (imported from the United States) from what was really the structural inadequacy of the old Europe of the 1960s to certain social and technical changes useful for its development.

Looking at the content of the papers left out by the editors of *Tendances et Volontés* (especially those of Isambert-Jamati and Bourdieu and Passeron) it is possible to argue that there is indeed a relationship between the problematics of these authors and those of the sociology of work: if these papers had been included, Pierre Tripier's diatribe would have been less justified.[5] In fact, the themes of the division of labour, the relationship of knowledge to power in the firm and the evaluation of skill are not far away when you are analysing the processes of democratization or conservatism in the school and university system, or even the variations in visible symbols of authority relationships in the context of various socioeducational institutions, including the family and the school.

The critics, outsiders and the dishonoured are not acknowledged by the great ancestors[6]

Although more than one of those 'eliminated' referred to or explicitly utilized theoretical models and concepts constructed by academic sociologists recognized by French, German and American universities,[7] none figures among the contributors to Gurvitch's *Traité de Sociologie* mentioned by Monjardet and then by Tripier as an anti-model (academic, extra-temporal, etc.) of sociological production in the years from 1960 to 1965. It begins to look as if an unseen censor was operating against those who, anxious to remain sociologists and refusing the status of consultant, pursued the following objectives:

(1) An effort to adopt and retain a critical perspective — keeping at a distance, looking beyond surface 'realities' by analysing the processes of transformation and the social contradictions running through the areas of social facts explored;

(2) An endeavour to introduce a historical perspective and thereby some relativity, that is, an anti-historicist and anti-evolutionist perspective on the study of the transformations and elements of continuity observable in the French society of the time.

(3) An attempt to question the 'naturalness' of changes, contradictions and rigidities appearing in the fields of analysis, by situating them in systems of social relations constructed around ideological and political battles, which themselves were not interpreted in any volontariste way, that is as the product of political action supposedly expressing the general will, because it was also a

question of 'de-naturalizing' the legitimated institutions and ideologies of the period under study.

Conclusion: from an 'idea amongst friends' to an operation of self-legitimation

The few complementary pieces of information that I have added to the dossier opened by Tripier and others confirms very appropriately the feeling that the collection of articles, *Tendances et Volontés*, is the expression of an ideological current in the act of being born in a sociological milieu, many members of which opted from 1960 to 1965 to work as consultants, based on a more or less close collaboration with the Plan and financed by the contract system.

If that was all my paper contributed, it would hardly be worth publishing. Its main interest lies in the way it shows the work of pruning and censorship which an ideological pressure group in the process of formation can indulge in to establish its legitimacy more firmly in the eyes of the 'aware' public and to give the illusion that it presents a complete picture of the intellectual milieu that is made up of the young generation of a profession.[8]

Notes

1. As Tripier saw, the tone of Touraine's article is that of an external critic sought out after the event because of his intellectual authority in Parisian sociological circles. For him, as for many sociologists of 'work' or 'industrial society' at the time, the notion of growth had not only an interventionist connotation but an economic and political one, too, relating to social relationships, power relations at the national or world level (the notion of development).

2. Qualitative and quantitative.

3. The rigidities and fixed hierarchies, the distant internal relations in the system of social relations in the university are due, they say, to a tacit agreement between the professors (wishing to maintain the elitism of bourgeois France and transmit a 'class ethos' reproducing on a wider scale the caste of heirs — the book *Les Héritiers* appeared in 1964) and the students (wanting to be positively evaluated and selected even if the social role is hard for some of them originally from middle and lower classes).

4. That is, those whose papers were cut out of the book. I have called these the 'dishonoured outsiders'.

5. As Tripier notes, there is no treatment of work in this 'Keynesian' system of interpreting society.

6. cf. the 'cultural discourse' that Tripier alludes to, following Monjardet, when he contrasts *Tendances et Volontés* to the Gurvitch *Traité*.

7. e.g. Halbwachs, Durkheim, Weber, Marx, Erik K. Erikson, S. N. Eisenstadt, K. Keniston.

8. In this light, the presentation of the book as the concrete outcome of 'an idea which came to us one evening as we were chatting amongst friends' appears particularly specious.

Annex

Papers presented to the colloquium on 'Social Transformation in Contemporary France' organized by the French Sociological Society. (The papers marked with an asterisk also appeared in the book *Tendances et Volontés de la Société Française*.)

Session one (the French people and change)
Barbichon, G. and Moscovici, S. *Situations de changements et comportements collectifs.**
Crozier, M. *Le modèle d'action administrative à la française, est-il en voie de transformation?**
Girard, A. *Comportements et attitudes à l'égard du changement.**
Gregoire, R. *Note sur la haute administration: tradition et changements.**
Karpik, L. *Trois concepts sociologiques: le projet de référence, le statut social et le bilan individuel.**
Kesler, J.-F. *L'influence de l'Ecole Nationale d'Administration sur la rénovation de l'administration et ses limites.**
Morin, E. *L'avenir dans la société française.**

Session two (changes in religious life)
Adam, G. and Maurice, M. *L'église catholique et le monde ouvrier.**
Isambert, F. *'Nouveaux Prêtres' ou 'aggiornamento' du clergé français.**
Levitte, G. *Vers une étude des mutations de la population juive en France et du judaisme français.*
Maitre, J. *La consommation d'astrologie dans la France contemporaine.*
Mehl, R. *Modifications dans la structure et le comportement des églises protestantes en France à la suite du mouvement oecuménique.*
Seguy, J. *Les non-conformistes religieux et les transformations de la société française.*

Session three (education and culture)
Bourdieu, P. and Passeron, J.-C. *Les valeurs du système universitaire français. Quelques réflexions de méthode.*
Dumazedier, J. *Point de vue sociologique sur les nouvelles relations du loisir et du développement culturel en France depuis les années 1953–55.**
Isambert-Jamati, V. *La querelle du tronc commun.*
De Maupeou (Abboud), N. *Modèles de rapports inter-générations et attitudes a l'égard du changement social en France.*

Session four (political problems)
Brule, M. and Piret, J. *Réflexions sur vingt années de sondages politiques de l'IFOP, 1945–65.*
Burnier, M.-A. *Evolution idéologique et clivages des couches intellectuelles en France.*
Hamon, L. *Le plan et sa signification politique.**

Session five (economic actors)
Barbichon, G. *Note sur le passage de la population active de l'agriculture à l'industrie.**
Cuisenier, J. *Agents et systèmes d'action économique.**
Durand, M. *La rationalisation des politiques de formation, indice d'évolution des politiques de personnel.**

Gillon, J. *Médecine et santé.*

Kayser, B. and Ledrut, R. *La mobilité de croissance d'une population urbaine: le cas de Saint-Gaudens.**

Lautman, J. and Jacob, A. *Planification et changement dans l'Administration publique.**

Pitrou, A. *Présentation d'une recherche sur l'attitude des ménages français à l'égard des services de nature collective.**

Tavernier, Y. *L'évolution des structures agraires en France, 1945–1955. Attitudes des forces syndicales et politiques.**

Treanton, J.-R. and Kloekner, A. *Quelques problèmes psychologiques et sociaux des régions 'fermées'.**

III. THE SOCIOLOGY OF THE RECESSION

13
The division of labour — the Dourdan I colloquium[1]

*Michel Burnier**
Pierre Tripier†

The technical division of work into tasks, the division of the social world into roles, groups and classes — here is a theme which is never exhausted and which sums up the field of the sociology of work. In itself, it does not imply any explanatory grid but it does help to situate a set of problems, a problematic based on the analysis of social relations. At the very least it makes for a balanced view of the exercise of production and domination while always allowing the spotlight to be aimed at the most salient aspects of the organization of production at any given moment.

Proceedings at the first Dourdan seminar were based on the results of a series of studies into the organization of work in industry, the system of industrial training, trade unionism and management: fruitful studies, whose findings were enriched by international contributions and the observations of those present. But if you are trying to define the ground covered by current research and situate it in the history of sociology, or simply looking for gaps to see what remains to be done, it is useful to review the theoretical foundations of fieldwork.

The sociology of progress and the sociology of crisis:
from the Friedmann–Naville *Traité* to Dourdan I
In the 1950s and 1960s, French sociology of work focused less on the relations of production, preferring instead, as Friedmann says, 'the human collectivities which are constituted when work is done'. Naville notes, too, that 'it is less a matter of a sociology of work than work studied by sociology', a rather special conception which was always encumbered by two presuppositions:

* Maison des Sciences de l'Homme
† University of Paris X and Groupe de Sociologie du Travail

(1) A fascination with industrial growth which led to the organization of society being assimilated to that of the factory, as expressed in this sentence from the *Traité* (Friedmann and Naville, 1961–2: 37):

> Work, considered as the foundation on which rests the development of societies, is the most profound social mode in which human beings express desire for continuity. That is what makes the sociology of work one of the principal branches of sociology and . . . the one which weighs heavier than the others in the first instance, accepting what they have to contribute afterwards.

(2) An implicit belief in the liberation of workers by technology and in particular by the automation of work, with the industrial model being considered a progressive one in relation to 'archaic' models such as agriculture or craft work. There is no reason to believe that, twenty years on, these ideas have been wholly discarded. Certainly, at Dourdan, people refrained from reformulating or criticizing them.

On the division of labour, the *Traité* reflected an optimistic vision with the world of production being considered one of technical co-operation, to be contrasted with a social world split by antagonistic divisions. It is faithful to Durkheim's thesis (1886: 403):

> The division of labour produces solidarity [because] it creates between men a whole system of rights and duties which link them to each other in a lasting way . . . The division of labour gives rise to rules which ensure the peaceful and regular combination of divided functions.

Friedmann and Naville (1961–2) take up the idea:

> The division of labour is only the expression of a relationship made up of both antagonism and co-operation. In the workplace, the division of tasks is above all a form of technically efficient co-operation, while in society as a whole this co-operation is subject to opposition which is not easily subordinated to the practical objectives of the system

This conception has turned out to be useful for our understanding of the evolution of the work–worker relationship. From the end of the 1950s, with the study of the forms of task distribution, considered as a system with definable parameters, an evolving system, and not as a simple state of continually conflictual domination, people began to notice the growing autonomy of technical systems and of workers, and therefore their inevitable opposition.

Certain of the Dourdan papers go in the opposite direction to the *Traité*. It may be critical in appearance, but the idea according to which 'the division of labour is first of all, in its strongest form, the reduction of the individual to a productive body' (Le Tron) prevents any real understanding of the nature of the worker's integration and of his or her refusal of integration, which is based precisely on the separation of people from machines.

After Dourdan, this fear of the domestication of the workers by the productive system was to lead some analysts in a vain search for 'latent' (or 'tacit') skills or savoir-faire among workers who have actually been dispossessed of all real power in production. In this respect, the conclusions of the Groupe de Sociologie du Travail are radically opposed to those of a Linhart or a Bernoux. Thus, Durand (12 and 229): 'From craft work to industry one can confirm the gradual deskilling of the worker', and 'Automation and computerised programming have eliminated [for the worker] all forms of autonomy and initiative'.

However, Linhart (24) notes: 'Practical knowledge acquired on the job by production workers . . . widens out into a broader grasp of the process'. And we have Bernoux talking about (18): 'The worker's savoir-faire which is growing all the time . . .'.

Generally, it does look as if Dourdan, in abandoning the theses of Durkheim and Naville, fell prey to an a priori negation of the division of labour, probably brought on by the disputes involving semi-skilled mass production workers, drawing the battle lines almost exclusively at the level of the firm, where the forms of consensus had been erased.

On the other hand, the spirit of the *Traité* was kept alive in the form of the idea that work takes pride of place in human activity, and also in the empirical methods of studying present forms taken by the division of labour.

The dominance of a Proudhonian problematic

Naville, then Rolle, have accused Friedmann and his school of being Proudhonians. In a colloquium as varied as Dourdan I, can we find traces of the influence of the father of the *Political Capacity of the Working Class* on the sociology of work? And what should we understand by the term 'Proudhonism'?

In his introduction to the French text, Durand gives an excellent quotation which sums up well the viewpoint Proudhon shares with more than one worker of the nineteenth century: 'The division of labour, without which there is no progress, no wealth and no equality, turns the worker into somebody's subordinate, renders intelligence useless, wealth harmful and equality impossible.'

Elsewhere in this present volume Pierre Rolle gives us an overall view of the differences between Proudhon and Marx and there is no point in going over that ground again.

Here, we are interested in one aspect of Proudhon's work, that which deals with the metaphysic rooted in the work act as defined by someone who knows his writings well (Ansart, 1970: 218–19):

> He seeks to give the action of work a value in itself, to glorify productive activity, overlooking its outcome which might simply be physical comfort and well-being or the pleasures of consumption. No doubt he recognises that preoccupation with well-being has become general but he attributes precisely that interest to the bourgeoisie, not the class he wishes to defend . . .
>
> Work [for Proudhon] is not a necessity imposed on man by a transcendent law or by the biological laws of his needs. Work is in itself a free act, 'free by nature, a positive and internal freedom' (*De la justice*, Vol. 3, p. 81).
>
> . . . It constitutes, at the same time, the generative act par excellence: it engenders society itself which is only the organisation and the assembly of separate pieces of work. It transforms this society by the dynamism of its evolution . . . In other words, the act of production is the essentially 'real' act by contrast with the artificiality of politics or the emptiness of the arts of consumption; it is the 'total' act since, in working, the producer brings up to date both the social fact and justice.

In other words, and Ansart sees here the roots of his success as an ideologist, the philosophy of Proudhon is based on the metaphysical privilege granted to work in the explanation of the way the world turns.

Making the act of work the key to understanding society and human behaviour attributes to it the power to structure and make intelligible all other human manifestations — that is what we can call the Proudhonism of the sociology of work.

Several more or less direct consequences result from this central point. Thus, Ansart shows that Proudhon proposes two ways of establishing a society acceptable to all:

(1) On every occasion that it is possible, market or contractual relations must organize social relations. This is the necessary condition (already explored by liberal ideology) for an egalitarian, and therefore just, society.

(2) In all other circumstances justice is not equal. Based on competence, as in craft ideology, it governs the attributes and relations of masters and journeymen, journeymen and apprentices.

Thus, it seems that in this conception of the world, justice is established on the basis of market exchanges such as they would exist in a perfect market, between workshops; or, inside the workshops themselves, by respecting the hierarchy of competence. (Unlike Marx, Proudhon believes the relationship between simple and complex work is easy to establish.)

Thus, Proudhonism, with respect to the area we are interested in, seems to be a vision which gives a central place to the act of work in the interpretation of human behaviour in society, while denying any explanatory power to the sphere of consumption and bracketing off the political sphere. Finally, it combines a (liberal) belief in the virtues of the perfect market with an (anti-liberal) respect for the hierarchy of competence.

Proudhonism in Dourdan I: an effect of translation
If you want to find a Proudhonian problematic in the contemporary world, it could not have the same characteristics as in the nineteenth century. The leading role of large organizations, the extension of the wage-earning class and the multiple interventions of the state have, in the process of transposition, given the Proudhonian matrix a different shape. However, in their utterances, people at Dourdan I retained certain features of the first matrix, notably the centrality of the act of work and the assumption that a pay hierarchy based on craft lines is quite natural. In other words, what looks likely to appear 'Proudhonian' in Dourdan I is the belief in a working-class 'truth' pronounced by the workers themselves from within the frames of reference of their best organized and most vocal segment. In addition, there is the epistemological priority accorded to the work situation, since it is presented as the only conceivable starting point for anyone attempting a realistic examination of the division of labour.

Although this sort of exercise may be deceptive, we ought to note that only half of the subjects chosen for papers at the seminar lend themselves to a Proudhonian thesis. In other words, only half the papers had drawn on a systematic representation of the work situation and could on this occasion develop theses grounded in Proudhon's matrix.

Three papers were about job redesign, which at the time enjoyed the same sort of status as quality circles today. Two dealt with comparative structural analyses, two with the relationship between training and employment, and two others, finally, were methodological think-pieces. The other essays could be listed in three groups depending on how near they came to the following ideal model: there is a 'natural' state of the worker's condition defined by:

(1) intellectual control over the labour process;
(2) stability in the situation in which the labour process is located;
(3) respect for the hierarchy of workers according to a craft reference point (whose modern equivalent is to be found in the acceptance of an educational hierarchy and a relationship between qualifications and job position).

For all these authors, any situation close to this point of equilibrium is 'legitimate' and 'appropriate' in so far as it would give greater industrial clout to blue-collar workers in particular and wage-earners in general. Hypothetically, moving away from the ideal type would weaken their position.

The first group is made up of all those who subscribe to this equation and seek to illustrate it in their research material. These authors are ranked in a certain way: the more encompassing, phenomenological and illustrative the approach, and the more it tends towards a single diagnostic, the more this Utopian image influences the explanation.

Here are a few examples:

> The more the worker can deploy his intelligence in his work, the more he escapes the organisation and discipline of the employer (85).

> 'Polyvalency', or job enlargement via the ending of demarcation, has managed, inside the factory, to 'break' the near-monopoly of technical knowledge enjoyed by the specialist maintenance workers and as a result all means of resistance and restriction of output for each category of worker are under attack (119).

> To do their work they have to call on skills that experience or training has allowed them to acquire in another occupation. Thus, they are developing real skills in their work — but these are neither recognised nor rewarded (228).

All these quotations — and there are many more where they came from — are based on the same matrix which tends to denounce the social system by acting as if there had once been a period of justice when 'true' wage relationships existed, when genuine skills were recognized, and workers, thanks to their technical control, held a natural weapon which at least helped them get a just reward for their efforts.

This vision of a golden age must, in all logic, set the scene for a period of decadence, an iron age, when 'real skills' are not recognized, when the activities of workers, of all wage-earners, came under the control of management, when work is even more alienated than before, etc. In short, the typical craft argument against the rationalization of work (see, among others, Casella and Tripier, 1984).

The second group appears to adopt a more analytical approach, one less prone to jump to conclusions and making more use of the sophisticated methods of quantitative surveys. Although starting out from the same principles as the first group, it manages, through experiment, to 'deconstruct' the symbolic aspect by casting doubt on certain of the basic equations which go to make it up.

This is what happens in the research into worker autonomy which the authors detach from a perspective anchored in the work situation:

Workers' reactions in a factory cannot be explained by reference only to the work situation, by the characteristics of the work group alone. The analysis has to relate rather to a history of the group. The workers' reaction is inscribed in a cycle (66).

Hence this conclusion which relaunches the debate on working-class consciousness:

... the characteristics of the work situation, the composition of the group and the history of reactions in the sector do not determine the appearance of the most common reaction in any strictly mechanical way ... In this respect, the composition of the group and the history of the industrial action limit choices more than the work situation does (67).

If you are aware from their previous publications that these authors have shown, contrary to received opinion, that autonomy and responsibility are inconsistent, you see just how far their reasoning erodes the Proudhonian matrix since, contrary to what this infers, they say that power in negotiations cannot come from the conjunction of the two qualities.

In the same vein, the alleged invalidity of the Proudhonian equation is established by research into Taylorism. A more realistic approach (one more in line with what history teaches us) is substituted for the equation 'autonomy + responsibility = strong negotiating power': in this approach the dominated condition of the worker appears as a constant which, from one period to another, one sociotechnical system to the next, experiences some variation but nothing that might be considered upheaval: 'Companies tend to compensate for the autonomy totally lost by the worker in his occupational activity as a result of rationalization by changes on the level of relationships ... Thus, the authoritarian method of giving orders disappeared' (292).

Finally, a third group can be distinguished, which does not seem to follow the Proudhonian matrix at all — better, it actually opposes it.

Two tendencies are visible here:

(1) The first demonstrates its opposition to the mythical reconstruction of the past implied by the matrix by deploying methodological argument or through the presentation of results. For this group, reconstruction seems to involve the idealized image that the working-class aristocracy wants to give of its class. Here, there is no talk about deskilling, no reference to a golden age: the viewpoint is very specifically that of the subjugation of the working class in its different forms (more autonomy with increased control; more flexible methods of worker management). In one of the papers, the viewpoint defended is that of working-class unity seen through the eyes of its most vulnerable element, whose capacity for coalition is

weak and which cannot appeal to craft or community links, nor even to full membership of the national community — not even that other 'community', the great bureaucratic organization. This is an interesting paper (from Linhart) in that it leads into systematic consideration of labour market segmentation.

(2) The second tendency is that present in international comparisons. They contribute a weighty argument to the debate on the work situation and its central position in the analysis of the division of labour.

In effect, as soon as you show that the division and distribution of jobs is explained less by the technology used and its would-be imperatives than by societal variables such as the education system and the system of collective relations at work, you destroy the epistemological privilege which was attached to the empirical study of the company and workshop. The act of work loses its primary heuristic value. It remains an important factor to study, but it cannot contain wholly within itself all explanation as the Proudhonism of Friedmann sought to do.

As successive pieces of international research will confirm, the work situation[2] can teach us nothing if it is not examined in terms of a whole series of variables which explain and constrain it. In our societies, the act of work cannot be seen as the primary reality.

Here we see a radical break with the Proudhonian tradition — but will this fact be heeded by all those who, at one time or another, venture into the field of the sociology of work? To say the least, we cannot be sure because it is deeply rooted in our culture and French working-class tradition — so its persistence would seem to be guaranteed for a long time.

The lacunae of Dourdan I

In retrospect, the work of this seminar on the division of labour seems handicapped by divisions between disciplines (which have since become somewhat blurred). A whole series of consequences result from this.

Interest seems to centre on the subordination of jobs rather than the social relations of work in so far as these express the division of labour and the conditions of wage-work in its various manifestations and supra-industrial economic phenomena. Thus, issues such as competition between workers, incomes policies and 'free' time are only touched on incidentally, hence the absence of any work on age or sex discrimination. There is little on the expansion of bureaucracies, on methods of control, on organizations, on authority and resistance to power, on strikes, absenteeism, rotation, waste, and so on.

The debate on the crisis of Taylorism and Fordism, then at its height, finds few echoes at Dourdan, any more than some awareness of the impact of emerging information technology.

Are we entering a new phase in the history of work or are we simply seeing a simple, neo-Taylorist retouch? The researchers at Dourdan, perhaps scalded by the futurological prediction of the previous generation, did not hazard any opinion here.

One large gap is the division of labour outside the company (except as regards the links with the educational apparatus) and the spatial division (workplace/home, workplace/town, sites, local markets, international divisions, the world market) which follow on the whole set of relationships inherent in the hold of large organizations on the territory; nor is there anything on temporal divisions (work/out of work life, the distinction between immediate approaches and longitudinal data, differentiation in temporalities) which would entail the analysis of new types of social control and work policies with well-known effects on the labour market: differentiation of employment categories among non-workers (the unemployed, youth, women) as well as among workers ('precarious' workers or those in unstable jobs, illegal workers, immigrants and sub-contractors).

Conclusion

A year or two after the spectacular, inflationary rise in raw material prices, eight years after the 'cultural revolution' in the spring of 1968, the approach to the division of labour in Dourdan is at once negativist and timorous, marking both an increased professionalism by comparison with the preceding period but also some sensitivity to the spirit of the times (weren't people writing about the 'wreckage in the wake of progress' at the time?). This attitude is very well analysed by Durand: 'It is no longer the consequences of the division of labour or the bad way it is used that are questioned here but its very principle . . .'. What a contrast with Durkheim (1886: 385) who for his part, reckoned:

> People have been quite wrong to see in the division of labour the fundamental fact of all social life. Work is not divided out between independent, already differentiated individuals who get together and associate with each other to pool their different skills . . . Far from preceding collective life, [the forms taken by the division of labour] are derived from it.

Now, because it failed to raise the debate to a level as general as this, the Dourdan colloquium remained rather incoherent, leaving the whole exercise looking too disjointed and too empirical. We have asserted for a long time now that the focus on traditional industry (to the detriment of the tertiary sector in particular) and on crafts seems to justify the remark that a 'nostalgia for craft work' lives on in a large number of the contributions.

After the colloquium, we are still faced with the question of a properly sociological method separating the sociology of work from its technicist pole. Pierre Naville's appeal from 1961–2 (56) is still relevant today:

> A complete methodology in the sociology of work is far from having been elaborated today — not least because it is lacking in general sociology, too. That is why so many research studies contributing much detailed knowledge . . . sit uneasily together in bodies of work based on a specific method . . . The use of a clearly expressed methodology in the field of work requires as much intellectual courage as it did in other times to explain the mechanisms of the education system.

Notes

1. Various authors (1978) *La division du travail*, Colloque de Dourdan. Paris: Galilee.

2. 'Mechanised work, the level and method of payment plus the organisation and management methods of firms define a work situation and allow one to analyse the attitudes and action of workers' (Touraine and Mottez, 1962: 235).

14
Employment: the social and economic issues — the Dourdan II colloquium[1]

Sami Dassa*

The content

The second Dourdan seminar was held in December 1980 and all the papers were published by Maspero in 1982, carrying the title we have borrowed for our chapter.

The book comes in two parts and six main headings or chapters. The first part includes papers on employment and unemployment. In this context there are analyses of the development of company practices in employment matters, the meaning of new employment policies, how workers react to these and, finally, the development of the relationship between training and jobs. The main sociological themes appear to be as follows:

(1) The move, in the mid-1970s, from policies designed to tie the workforce to the company, the employer, and the locality, to policies aiming for flexibility, mobility and permanent adaptation to change.

(2) The disintegration of statuses and of the social relationships of work.

(3) The transformation of the real and legal content of the notions of employment and the enterprise.

(4) New industrial and legislative strategies aimed at removing the constraints and rigidity left over from the previous period.

(5) The relative break-up of social solidarities[2] among workers; the decomposition of the working class; new social divisions and the demobilization of collective strength.

(6) The transformation of training and education policies, the alternation of the times and places of study, of work and idleness; the growing intervention of employers in training.

The second part of the book consists, first, of a presentation of research methods illustrated by an analysis of career paths; and then a series of papers on the current problems bearing on skill and its effect on work and jobs. Longitudinal methods, and studies of work histories, are given as ways of elucidating the interactions and connections between the social sphere and the individual, as well as between the different levels and manifestations of the social sphere.

* Laboratoire de Sociologie du Travail et Relations Professionnelles, CNAM

The career paths that can thus be defined help in locating the mediating factors which lead to the elaboration of the rules and social structures which mark out, but also blur, the identity of individuals, at the same time that they construct the social field in which individuals are located.

The problems of skills and gradings are discussed to show a sort of correspondence between the jobs crisis and the crisis of work. The idea of a correlation between technical progress and development of skills is questioned, particularly as regards the effects of new technology on work. It is shown that action taken by workers for jobs and against unemployment is at the same time action for work and against deskilling. Flexibility in the workforce is sought not only through the setting up of new forms of employment but also through 'polyvalence' (workers doing jobs whose content crosses previous 'skill' or demarcation lines) and therefore the disintegration of traditional work groups (and the traditional units of organized worker action). The international comparisons and studies presented in the book demonstrate that identical technology and social and economic objectives do not have the same consequences for a labour force, for sociologically defined groupings, for conflicts or for real change; outcomes are different according to the specific national features of social structures, or union and employer strategies.

Methods

The seminar — and therefore the book — is rather lacking in cohesion. There is no real connection between the first part on 'Employment and Unemployment' and the second, on 'Career Paths and Skills'. As regards employment, there might have been scope for unity in the disassociations and combinations of the concepts of work (travail) and employment in the sense of regular jobs (emploi). Thus, one might distinguish the following sociological situations:

(1) Unemployment properly speaking, the absence of both work and jobs;

(2) Work without jobs, exemplified in 'precarious' or unstable work, activity in the underground economy, or mobile work;

(3) Jobs without work — a literary example is the hacks dear to the humorist Courteline,[3] but we have our counterpoints in those managers or journalists that continue to be paid even if there's no work for them to do, since redundancy money would work out dearer than the salary;

(4) Jobs with work — 'established posts' which are stable, productive and with real work to be done.

As for the methods which underlie the research presented here, it is noticeable that more often than not the projects are short, rapid and lightweight, as if proper, thorough fieldwork had been abandoned. There is an effort to construct typologies, a taste for qualitative studies concerned with analysing meanings, and less and less interest in quantitative, representative material.

In the same way, there are ideas and analyses but little in the way of demonstration. On occasions, social stereotypes are uncritically accepted as established fact when it ought to be a research principle to question this sort of conventional wisdom: this is the case, to take one example, with the idea that 'scientific production' determines in large part the future of our societies.

The analyses of personnel policy and the search for the social element in the technical, organizational and economic spheres
Numerous researchers have highlighted and analysed the move from a personnel policy designed to tie the worker to the firm (the famous paternalism of the employers) to a policy of mobility. But I wonder if that is really the right concept. When Raymond Barre explained unemployment at the end of the 1970s by the refusal of, or resistance to, mobility, one could be forgiven for thinking he was trying to be funny, such was the gap between jobs on offer and the numbers looking for work. But, after one has read this book, Barre's viewpoint is easier to understand since unemployment is not analysed as a form of social exclusion but, indeed, as the result of a policy of enforced mobility.

All the same, one has to say that what the employers are seeking is not to make the workforce more mobile but to control the wage bill and social security and related costs — and thus gain the possibility of getting rid of its social responsibilities. Mobility may result from that, but you have to go through redundancy and unemployment to get to that stage. Mobility per se does not explain this redundancy policy and neither is it the most immediate result. One could just as easily speak of a policy of destabilization, or social destructuring, or even a policy of regaining control of personnel matters including the numbers employed. We are witnessing a rather futile form of manoeuvring between unions with their demands and employers with their supply. Traditionally, the unions saw to the protection of workers' *employment* in the firm and now attempts are being made to take this role from them. On the other hand, the unions and workers in France played no part in the field of *work* and its organization. Now they are being drawn into this area, being made to participate and express themselves when they haven't asked for a thing. The employers are taking away what the workers have won in the field of employment as 'jobs' (emploi) and giving them what they've not asked for in the field of work (travail).

However, what is not said in the case of unemployment and mobility is expressed much more clearly as regards the policy of 'précarisation', or the destabilizing of job security. It is apparent that this policy does not have solely economic aims: it is stuffed full of social intentions and effects. We are dealing here with the social control of the workforce. By précarisation, just as with unemployment, you make people dependent on state benefits, you destroy collective resistance and the conditions of worker mobilization. Under the pretext of making management more fluid and attacking socioeconomic inflexibility, social organization is being dismantled and social gains attacked.

The analysis of collective action and identity
We are seeing a redefinition of social identity, of, in particular, the contours of communities of action. What counts most in collective action, just as in collective identification, is *being together* — rubbing shoulders — rather than the abstract membership of a class. In linguistic terms, one would say that the syntagma, metonymy and combination are paramount, over and above the paradigm, the metaphor and selection. The important thing in collective action and identity is contiguity — rubbing shoulders — including contiguity across and between classes, and not the similarity of the places and situations occupied in social structures which are identical but located in different places. One might put it another way: organization *in praesentia* takes precedence over structure *in absentia*.

This goes hand in hand with the idea of a contraction of the universe of reference — one is a former miner rather than a man, a woman or an immigrant.

The disappearance of company towns and employer paternalism which underpinned local units dominated by occupational interests brings in return a reawakening of local communities. The factory created the town and social life, but now the 'de-industrialized' area wants to live even without the factory. The industrial and occupational base may have gone but at least the culture that went with it and which gave life to the area can be saved. This is what has been happening in mining areas and steel towns. Thus, we are seeing identities rooted in work becoming regional or local identities.

The importance of cultural and social factors in collective identity is also showing through in the choice of jobs and retraining after redundancy. The main criteria in the search for new positions are social rather than occupational or economic. People look for the same type of company from the point of view of organization, management and personnel policies rather than the same type of production or occupation pursued in completely different social conditions.

Some sociological observations
It seems to me that in some of the papers there is a tendency to confuse the legal position with social reality or, at least, to attach too much importance to the legal in the definition of real social relations. It is perhaps a commonplace to recall the sociological distinction between the legal social relationship and the real social relationship — between property relations and the relations of real possession and utilization — but it still isn't accepted by everyone.

People have announced the death of the state as employer (*l'Etat-patron*) and the death of the working class; now they are announcing the death of the employer, or, at least, the death of the company. That's going a bit far. Lip[4] still exists despite its legal liquidation and there are strikes and other forms of action in firms which no longer have any legal existence.

As for the notion of the employer, one must distinguish between the legal relationship of the appropriation of labour power (the employer in the eyes of the law) and the real relationship of the possession and use of the labour force. We have here a distinction between the company that sells a labour force and the company that uses and consumes the labour power of those contracted workers. Employers and firms don't cease to exist simply because the employer's functions are split between several individuals and firms. Just as we talk about a collective worker, maybe we could also refer to a collective employer.[5]

Furthermore, the advantages to the employer of sub-contracting and non-secure jobs may have been demonstrated, as well as the disadvantages of these forms of work for those subjected to them — but it has been forgotten that there might be some *contented* temps, a few *happy* people in 'precarious' jobs. Even if you wouldn't go that far, you might agree that some workers, too, have found out how to exploit the situation. What about us researchers, for example? It is quite a different context, but we are well aware that the dissociation between our legal employer (the CNRS) and our real employer (the university, research centre or other organization) is often a very comfortable position to be in. In any case, there may be some benefit in being *in* a company without being *of* it.

Moreover, the dissociation between employer functions may be internal to the company rather than based on legally separate companies. This has been the case for years at Citroën, for example, where there is a careful distinction drawn between the person responsible for 'social' personnel matters and the supervisor who is concerned only with technical matters and gives the orders as regards work.

The dissociation, be it legal or organizational, is also aimed at regaining social control over the workforce. At this moment, we find the same intention behind the systematic establishment of parallel representative bodies or institutions originating with the employers or the management hierarchy. In a recent issue of *Syndicalisme CFDT* (17 February 1983) I saw that the Solmer group has appointed 'workshop assistants' ('assistants d'atelier') whose 'real raison d'être is to short-circuit the workers' representatives'. Similarly, at the Usinor steelworks in Dunkirk, 'a representative on the Health and Safety Committee is matched by a "safety foreman" and a staff representative (délégué du personnel) by a workshop assistant'.

Another idea is put over in certain of the papers in the second part, that of the dialectic of individual action and collective destiny, or alternatively of individual destiny and collective action. The debate is far from over but one might ask if sociologists are not abandoning the primacy and the very existence of the collective as such to turn towards an essentially nominalist approach to social reality.

Finally, a second, more general and critical observation, but a more fundamental one. It seems to me that in Dourdan II there is a lack of reflection at a further remove or 'second degree' on the ultimate goals or unconscious meanings implicit in social reality. Thus, unemployment is seen as an economic fact linked to economic policies. It is shown that its effect and its intention is the development of a social policy of worker mobility. Studies are done on how people adjust to, adapt to, get round or revolt against this fact. Moreover, in reality, as writers like Ganne and Motte show, it is the people most vulnerable to redundancy who have the most trouble finding a new job, even after retraining. So the problem is not to make these people more mobile but to eliminate them from production. The accumulation of handicaps is clear for the young, for women, for immigrants and for the unskilled. Unemployment, therefore, is a way for society to eliminate those surplus to requirements and in some sense to choose its dead. It is clear that research into unemployment and jobs will take quite a different direction depending on whether they are analysed in terms of mobility or the elimination of surplus labour capacity.

Notes
1. Various authors (1982) *L'emploi, enjeux économiques et sociaux*, colloque de Dourdan.
2. In the original, *désocialisation*. The writer wishes to characterize the growing individualism of the crisis period. The term coined, however, suggests a process that

would be the reverse of socialization; that is to say, it would be one in which shared meanings and values were abandoned altogether. Rather, what he is charting is a process of *re*-socialization, in which a solidaristic work culture is replaced by an individualistic work culture, i.e., this type of individualism is normative.

3. Pen-name of Georges Moinaux (1860–1917), a humorist and satirist who ridiculed *fin-de-siècle* officialdom, notably in his play 'Messieurs les Ronds-de-Cuir' of 1893, translated into English as 'The Bureaucrats'.

4. In one of the 'luttes exemplaires' of the 1970s self-management movement, the Lip watch company was occupied to prevent its closure. The watches made during the ensuing work-in were successfully offered for sale, to the scandal of the business world. The case attracted as much media coverage as the Upper Clyde Shipbuilders work-in in Britain a year or two earlier, and created more political steam. The solution of late 1975 was backed by the French government, but the firm disappeared finally a year or two later.

5. A complication here is that many temporary workers, or those who move between several sites as cleaners or maintenance staff, are in effect employed by labour brokers (such as Manpower, which in France has a very high profile indeed), whatever devices are resorted to in order to evade awarding (or to be sure, accepting) employee status in its strict legal sense.

15
The underlying sociology of the Dourdan II colloquium[1]

Danièle Linhart*

It is not easy to describe the sociology underlying the Dourdan II colloquium. The book is 450 pages long, with twenty-nine papers from sociologists, economists and jurists. Properly speaking, there is no theoretical school and no methodological school, but different survey practices, quite distinct research subjects and many diverse political and ideological orientations (even if they can all be grouped under the vocable 'Left').

Fortunately, Tripier and Paradeise tell us what the sociology of sociology is:

> The sociology of sociology's job is to uncover what is left unsaid by sociological discourse — the sub-sociology of that discourse, that is, all the implicit ontological presuppositions which make possible the explicit statement of assumptions and hypotheses. The sociology of sociology must account for the conditions of social organisation which ensure the hegemony of a given sociology in a given academic system at a given moment in time.

So first of all let us look at the assumptions and the hypotheses, then the ontological propositions, and finally the whys and wherefores of this hegemony.

The assumptions and hypotheses
The assumptions are clearly and 'honestly' announced in Claude Durand's introduction. The essays are linked by the themes of the recession and employment, defined as the priority of priorities.

The hypotheses: with the crisis and the jobs issue, we are experiencing a whole series of upheavals:

(1) at the level of company policies, with the definition of new social relations to do with work (precariousness, polyvalency, etc.); on the juridical level; at the level of the state — all of this defining a new employment relationship for wage-earners;

(2) at the level of the lived reality of those who 'live' the crisis through unemployment;

* Laboratoire de Sociologie du Travail et Relations Professionnelles, CNAM

(3) finally, at the level of the work situation, through skills and career paths.

In sum, the crisis leads us to analyse, through the prism of employment, the transformation of social actors, and to analyse how the employers, the state, the unions and the workers assume, live and act upon the situation.

It all seems perfectly clear. You define the subject, employment/crisis, then you study the dimensions and social strata this subject refers to.

And yet there is some shift of ground in the book which only really becomes clear in the second part: it is found in the way the notion of employment (emploi) evolves. At the start, it covers the classic definition of the way the work force is mobilized and used, looked at from the angle, first, of the law and the policies of companies and the state; then from the angle of workers confronted with the problem of employment. In the second part, employment, or *emploi*, becomes work post, skill, 'work situation'. This makes things problematic because the subject of analysis is no longer quite so clear: the workers only exist now through their individual histories, or those of the unions, but these are looked at from a highly global or almost theoretical angle, especially in the French/Italian/British comparisons.

The unsaid

What is left unsaid then emerges: it concerns the working class — or, at least, the curious way in which it is represented.

In the light of this statement, we can rapidly reinterpret the first and second parts of the book.

(1) There are two subsections in the first part.

(i) In the first subsection, indeed, we are given the destabilizing of jobs (précarisation), the regressive developments in personnel policies and the role of training for management, but we are told *nothing* about the way the unions confront this problem of the disintegration of the work collective and the crisis in employment; *nothing*, either, on the way the workers react or adapt.

Yet there was a great deal to say. Moreover, you cannot fully understand employer strategies if you do not put them alongside the reactions and attitudes of workers. Employer strategies are not conditioned solely by economic necessity and technological constraints but also by the form of social resistance. This is only mentioned by a few papers and even then only fleetingly. Unions and workers are absent in this first subsection — and this represents a break with the procedures adopted at Dourdan I.[2]

(ii) In the second subsection, on the other hand, we do find the workers. You can't say they're not there because it's all about them. And yet, not really. Because it is rather about the unemployed or the future unemployed — workers half-way to losing what defines them as workers, half-way to losing their work and leaving the collective of workers. But, paradoxically, it is not in this subsection that we find the papers on occupational biographies, individual histories and longitudinal data. The papers from Ganne and Motte, for example, are elsewhere. Is this mere chance? Is it by chance that one only shows interest in the workers when they lose what defines them, while continuing to analyse them from a collective point of view, in their impotence or violence; and is it chance, too, that the analysis of the individual, through biographies, is reserved until a second part more concerned with work situations? Here, there is a sort of methodological inversion: shouldn't the individual dimension be used rather to situate the unemployed who, precisely, have been expelled from the work collective?

So, in this first part, which seeks to define and analyse the social actors in the employment crisis, we find companies (and not any old companies — only the large groups are analysed here) and we find the state. We hardly see the workers, or only from the angle of their impotence when they are no longer working. In other words, they no longer constitute a positive collective social actor.

(2) So we come to the second part where there is discussion not so much about employment as work. Very good. But what is being analysed here? The industrial relations system at the highest level (international comparisons) and occupational careers. That's it. Nothing on the organization, content and conditions of work. Nothing on either side's strategies on this issue. Nothing, in short, on the workshop. That is, once more, the workers as a group are left out as a relevant body to analyse. Left out, to put it bluntly, is the working class.

Moreover, we find a remark in the last but one paper which supports this view. Azouvi comments:

> . . . underlying several of the papers presented here, but left unsaid, is the search for the system's degree of malleability: must economic laws be considered as a constraint applicable everywhere and always, without any nuance, and ultimately leaving the actors' strategies looking ridiculous; or on the other hand, does an unbiased examination of social reality reveal some diversity, a richness and a complexity which tend to rehabilitate the power and the games played by the social actors?

This diversity, this complexity that Azouvi pleads for does not appear in the Dourdan colloquium. Or rather, it only appears through a systematic search for specifics to the detriment of any analysis of the common lot of the workers.

When, in this seminar, this or that researcher has leaned towards the diversity, the richness and the complexity of the social actors, he or she has looked for it in the specificity dependent above all on the individual dimension. Can you really only come to grips with the complexity of the actors in what differentiates them (their individual history) rather than what makes them resemble each other (the common mould)? Is it not, on the contrary, the dialectical relationship between these two realities which is enlightening for the analysis?

In the observation that he makes, Azouvi brings to mind the third point we have to analyse for the sociology of sociology, relating to the notion of hegemony. Why was the conception that we have just described dominant at Dourdan at the end of 1980? Why didn't one of the papers really try to measure how malleable the system is?

Perhaps we should quite simply see in this the result of the researchers' interiorization of what might be called 'the constraints blackmail'. The crisis is now perceived only as a steamroller which transforms and flattens everything in its path. The researcher then finds him or herself up against the crisis, alone and defenceless, forced to turn back to his or her individuality and specificity like the worker excluded from the collectivity with whom he or she identifies — until eventually the isolated researcher no longer sees anything but the isolated worker.

Notes

1. Various authors (1982) *L'emploi, enjeux économiques et sociaux*. Colloque de Dourdan. Paris: Maspero.

2. Various authors (1978) *La division du travail*. Colloque de Dourdan. Paris: Galilée.

16
Conclusion: the sociological Utopia
*Dominique Monjardet**

Sociology is first and foremost about knowledge. It seeks out and establishes 'facts' that it treats like 'things'. Who marries whom? Are there social factors behind educational failure? Through what channels is technical innovation diffused in the agricultural sector? What links can be established between satisfaction and productivity at work? How are schemes drawn up in town planning? In firms, who makes what decisions? And so on. In this way, sociology is either answering questions which are put to it directly by such and such a 'sponsor' or questions which, thanks to academic freedom, the curiosity of researchers leads them to ask off their own bat. In this activity — which a section of the sociological community limits its horizons to, seeing it as the boundary of their discipline — sociology is increasingly facing competition from big institutions belonging more often than not to the government apparatus which have access to far greater research funds and are therefore sure of getting more credibility attached to the results they obtain. Sociology has therefore progressively abandoned the large-scale survey, restricting itself to more intensive, more carefully targeted research on questions which demand deeper observation in more limited areas. The end result of these studies most often takes the form of a monograph, sometimes embodies a historical dimension, and lends itself less systematically to quantification.

As a result, the old term 'social statistics' which used to sum up well this aspect of sociological activity and production has become quite anachronistic and it would be better to rehabilitate the notion of sociography, if we can all agree that it has no prejorative connotations. And it is just one aspect among others of sociological activity, neither the first nor the base which others, nobler or more scholarly, relate to in the hierarchy. On the contrary, one might even plead that it is still the touchstone — a necessary stage, an area for training and verification — of all more ambitious sociological work which would not be satisfied with 'incomplete' data.

All the same, it is difficult to escape the conclusion that it resembles an administrative science in the sense that its object is to

* Group de Sociologie du Travail

inform the Prince (or any group or institution concerned) of the social 'reality' that is likely to constrain, initiate or be affected by his actions. Proof of this comes precisely in the gradual and growing takeover of the activity of social statistics by institutions belonging directly to the administration. This slide can be observed in many fields: political sociology, which emerged in France from electoral sociology, finds itself in competition in this field with the large polling organizations and is gradually slipping towards narrowly defined issues. In the sociology of work, it is there, too: an essential part of its early activities — the study of skills, working conditions and technical change in the workplace — is today largely taken in hand by CEREQ, ANACT and other government bodies.

As I have said, one could well identify sociological activity with sociographic activity and fix one's attention exclusively on the administrative aspect of the discipline. As it develops, this 'administrative sociography' naturally ushers in a certain division of labour which it is difficult to argue against in principle and whose consequences, in terms of production and output, are, at least to begin with, positive. But the legitimacy of this position implies an equal legitimacy for the other aspect of sociological activity which we will call 'reflexive sociology'. This is reflexive in both senses of the term — it reflects upon, and then reflects back, the discourse of society about itself, as it appears in the meanings projected by a given group or institution, on the social relations which engender it and that it produces, on the nature of the social links which support it and that it weaves.[1] It is this aspect, more obscure, less sure of its instruments and its results, more inclined to internal polemics which are thus devoid of definite criteria, which interests us and whose aims or 'project' (or one possible project amongst others) it seems necessary to clarify.

The division of labour referred to above is not a simple, uncontentious and consensual delimitation of the various projects, tasks and ambitions; it also sketches the field of competition between distinct, even opposed, professional strategies bearing on the distribution within the labour market for sociology of the available means and rewards, whether one is talking of research contracts, staffing, posts, access to publishing or, more prosaically, careers. Consequently, the internal debates — methodological, theoretical, epistemological — are not only pious scholarly debates; they are also aimed, in some way or other, at the outside world, that is, at the real or potential sources of funds, posts and acclaim. 'Theoretical' quarrels they may be, but there is also a chair at the Collège de France at stake. It often happens that people affect a show of modesty in front of these 'sordid' realities underlying the debates about ideas, or rise up in righteous indignation when allusion is made to them. They pretend to believe that this unbecoming talk seeks improperly to reduce noble scientific questions to shabby commerce. Hardly a sociological attitude! It is not a matter of reducing the sociological field to mere economic transactions, but simply of recognizing the fact that the 'theoretical' field is similar in its construction to an inevitably competing professional field. And, it might be added, in passing, that it is more often than not the same people who, after achieving notoriety in the theoretical field, are often the first to praise any measure likely to strengthen selective and competitive devices in the professional field, or to denounce anything which might serve to uncouple scientific debate from the position in the labour market: 'Quality of French science', they say.

All this is meant to explain the nature of the plea which follows in the form of some propositions on reflexive, sociology. For many reasons, some of them quite clear (notably the role and the expectations of paying customers), the extension of the division of labour within sociology has, overall, been to the benefit of its 'governmental' or administrative wing and, within the reflexive wing, already in a minority, to the profit of those tendencies which, to my way of thinking, are the furthest from those we are trying to build up and practise.

While reflecting the discourse of society (of this group, that institution) about itself, scholarly discourse does not tell 'the truth' about it. Scholarly sociology does not state a truth which is the truth in the spontaneous sociology of the social actors. The two are not in any relationship of truth and error which presumes the existence of some yardstick by which either truth or error could be measured. This yardstick does not exist, whatever claims some might make, because there is no starting-point from which to define it.

The object of sociological discourse is to challenge, locate problems in, and thoroughly shake up the discourse of the actors — both the object of that discourse and its subject. But sociological discourse is itself just as soon the victim of a sociological discourse which challenges it, locates problems in it and unsettles it, and so on ad infinitum. This, one might add, accounts for the absence — so painful for positivists — of any cumulativeness of sociological wisdom.

This questioning of discourse, of all discourses, ad infinitum, which cuts across all social practices, constitutes in itself the work by which a society, or its different parts, thinks about itself or at least attempts to. Similarly there is a questioning, through the fault lines opened up in the discourse of each group, of their complicity or disjunction, and thus can occur a remodelling of the relationships between the speakers; at the very least they are thrown off balance. Moreover, that is what those institutions (naively) ask for when they sponsor or accept research because it will allow them access to an 'outside' opinion. It is not simply a matter here of questioning what socialization and routine have made unquestionable within the institution; it really is about knocking off balance the internal rationalization of the institution in such a way as to open up a gap through which an evolution, a change or an influence might be introduced into a field where social relations are blocked and therefore no longer aware of their own arbitrariness, or even, sometimes, of why they exist at all.

The criterion of the evaluation and pertinence of scholarly discourse is thus its capacity to question and knock off balance spontaneous discourse. This implies having recourse to certain techniques. The most widely used is the 'scientific' technique (generally summed up by the use of quantitative methods) in so far as sociologists are able to clothe themselves in dominant legitimacy by borrowing the form of discourse attributed with scientific status. In doing this, they are often caught in their own trap and lapse into a positivism which today is rejected by the 'true' sciences, by confusing the instrument through which its discourse claims a hearing with the object it is pursuing. The other instrument, at the other end of the spectrum, is consultancy, or *intervention*, which aims directly at its object but without making sure of the legitimacy of the treatment. There are endless variations between these two poles — the most unpardonable being without doubt the identification of sociologists with their subject, whose discourse they then only seek to fortify, refine, make more precise or complete, thereby denying their own valid social function.

This social function can be adopted deliberately for what it is, leading to a conscious effort to develop the relevant instruments. Often only a partial aspect of it is perceived which gives rise to two common forms of reflexive sociology.

First, there is a sociology of denunciation which certainly shakes the discourse of those denounced but from the point of view of Sirius, that is, of an a priori truth, external to the social relations which engender the discourse denounced and the discourse which denounces, itself safely outside the battle. The most common form, in its wildest versions, takes the shape of a summons to the denounced from the comfortable office of the denouncer to join the Revolution without a moment's delay, or else commit suicide — or, at least, show due guilt.

Second, we have a paradoxical sociology where the position stated is considered sociological simply because it runs counter to common sense. One could readily cite numerous examples of this — the success of some of Olsen's ideas, for instance, can surely be explained in part by this ambition, realized to some extent, to shock, not the bourgeoisie any more, but the intellectuals.

These two degraded forms express a portion of the sociological truth of reflexive sociology — that is, the fact that it can only be critical if it forgoes the production of any specific statement and thus must deny that it is just such a statement; in fact, the mistrust of anything specific, common among those who believed themselves endowed with both an exact social science and an infallible collective wisdom bore witness to the universality of this intention and this critical reach.

But at the same time this means that the inherent critical dimension disqualifies sociology and the sociologist from all claims to wisdom and any right to power. Sociologists have only an instrumental knowledge — their critical capacity which is variable, this variability reintroducing criteria and possibilities of evaluation — and they eliminate themselves in the figure of the Prince when they take a hand in advising him. Experience shows, moreover, that in this case they lose in knowledge what they think they are gaining in power.

Shaking up discourse, ad infinitum, that is, by repeating the exercise of challenging, showing there is no other sense to social action than interaction itself whose sense any partner can claim to speak for or corner — this is the permanent task of opening up the various levels of discourse, of relating them to each other, or at least allowing them to establish a connection. This is really pursuing a *Utopia*, based on an assumption that cannot be proved — that it is better to fight with words than fists.

The most determined opponents of reflexive sociology — who, if need be, take the most brutal measures against sociologists in flesh and blood — provide the proof themselves. A handful of professional sociologists, sometimes a few dozen, never more than a few hundred, ought not to constitute in themselves a serious threat to society (or to a government, a class, or a clan) whatever the evil intent — the omnipotence? — attributed to them. If each military coup d'etat, especially in Latin America, sees them hounded, imprisoned and exiled, there must be some other reason. When confronted by a group, class or clan determined to cross swords and impose its might through force, the sociological ambition — beyond its substantive statement — is a negation, a refutation, a de-legitimation. If I want to fight to halt all debate, I eliminate those whose social function, whose very raison d'etre, is just the opposite. I legitimize my fight by expelling from the social field ('cxiling') those whose function is to think and talk about this same social field as an area of debate, a system of interaction which persists and renews the social link to the infinity of its meanings, which constitutes the tissue from which social action, society, is possible. We are already charged with bleating pacifism or unprincipled liberalism: our message is neither, but rather the conviction that sociology is one of the instruments that society (groups and classes) gives itself to provide against mechanisms of exclusion, division and dissolution. The very history of sociology, coinciding with that of industrialization, and closely following its course, argues in the same direction. On the surface, but only there, it may seem paradoxical that this instrument consists precisely of dissolving certainties, breaking down the discourse of groups and classes which constitute the discourse of society about itself: it is in the gaps thereby opened up that the threads of the social bond reappear and that its permanent arbitrariness is remembered.

In this sense, reflexive sociology is indeed, as Durkheim would have had it, a form of morality, but a morality without principles, prescriptions or norms. It might be better to call it a form of hygiene. In this sense it is forever renewing its intellectual position, though that might not have been the intention of the original Sophists, for like them it runs the risk of being stoned to death from time to time when it exasperates the public too much. In ridiculing all thought, the Sophists bore witness to the very strength of thought; in unsettling the discourses which organize social life, sociology bears witness to the arbitrariness of the social and therefore its fragility.

Note

1. This characterization overlaps somewhat with the 'reflexive sociology' advocated by the late Alvin Gouldner in *The Coming Crisis of Western Sociology* (1971) London: Heinemann.

Bibliography

Ansart, P. (1970) *Naissance de l'Anarchisme*. Paris: PUF.
Aron, R. (1962) *Dix-Huit Leçons sur la Société Industrielle*. Paris: Gallimard.
Balle, C. (1980) 'Sociologie du travail et changement social', *Sociologie du Travail*, 1.
Barbichon, G. and Moscovici, S. (1962) *Modernisation des Mines, Conversion des Mineurs*. Paris: Ministère du Travail.
Birnbaum, P. (1983) *Logique de l'Etat*. Paris: Fayard.
Bloor, D. (1976) *Knowledge and Social Imagery*. London: Routledge and Kegan Paul.
Bourdieu, P. and Passeron, J.-C. (1979) *The Inheritors: French Students and their Relationship to Culture*. London: University of Chicago Press. First published in French in 1964 as *Les Héritiers*.
Braudel, F. (1981) *Civilisation and Capitalism*. London: Collins. First published in French in 1967 as *Civilisation Matérielle et Capitalisme*.
Caillé, A. (1981) *'La sociologie de l'intérêt, est-elle intéressante?'* in *Sociologie du Travail*, 3.
Camerlynck, G. H. and Lyon-Caen, G. (1972) *Précis de Droit de Travail*. Paris: Dalloz.
Casassus, C. and Erbès-Seguin, S. (1979) *L'Intervention Judiciaire et l'Emploi*. Paris: La Documentation Française.
Casella, P. and Tripier, P. (1984) 'La professionalisation des artisans du bâtiment'. Paper presented at Montreal conference on Neo-Corporatism.
Cohen, S. R. (1983) 'From Industrial Democracy to Professional Adjustment. The Development of Industrial Sociology in the United States, 1900–1955', *Theory and Society*, 12(1).
Commissariat Général du Plan (1980) *La Société Française et la Technologie*. Paris: La Documentation Française.
Crozier, M. (1964) *The Bureaucratic Phenomenon*. London: Tavistock.
'Darras': See Various authors (1966).
Desmarez, P. (1984) *Pareto et le Groupe de Harvard, à l'Origine de la Sociologie du Travail*. PhD thesis. Brussels: Université Libre de Bruxelles.
Dubois, P., Dulong, R., Durand, C., Erbès-Seguin, S. and Vidal, D. (1973) *Grèves Revendicatives ou Grèves Politiques?* Paris: Anthropos.
Dubois, P. (undated) *La Sociologie du Travail Ouvrier en France dans les Années 70*. Paris: GST.
Dull, K. (1975) *Industriesoziologie in Frankreich*. Frankfurt.
Durand, C. and Dubois, P. (1975) *La Grève*. Paris: Armand Colin.
Durkheim, E. (1886) *De la Division du Travail Social*. Paris: Alcan.
Durkheim, E. (1915) *The Elementary Forms of Religious Life*. London: Allen and Unwin. (2nd ed. 1976, with an introduction by R. Nisbet.)
Edelman, B. (1978) *La Légalisation de la Classe Ouvrière*. Paris: Bourgeois.
Erbès-Seguin, S. (1983) 'Le contrat de travail ou les avatars d'un concept', *Sociologie Du Travail*, 1.
Fourquet, F. (1980) *Les Comptes de la Puissance*. Paris: Encres.
Fraisse, R. (1981) 'Les sciences sociales: utilisation-dépendance-autonomie', *Sociologie du Travail*, 4.
Friedmann, G. and Naville, P. (1961) *Traité de Sociologie du Travail*. Paris: Armand Colin.

Bibliography 179

Furtado, C. (1961) *Desenvolvimiento e subdesenvolvimiento*. Mexico: Fondo de Cultura Economica.
Germani, G. (1955) *Integracion politica de las masas*. Buenos Aires: CLES.
Goetz-Girey, R. (1965) *Le Mouvement des Grèves en France, 1919–1962*. Paris: Sirey.
Goode, W. E. (1957) 'Community within a Community: the Professions', *American Sociological Review*, 22(2).
Gurvitch, G. (1960) *Traité de Sociologie*. Paris: PUF.
Hughes, E. C. (1952) 'Psychology: Science and/or Profession?', *The American Psychologist*, 7(2).
Hughes, E. C. (1954) 'Professional and Career Problems of Sociology', *Transactions of the Second World Congress of Sociology*. London.
Javillier, J.-C. (1976) *Les Conflits du Travail*. Paris: Que Sais-Je?
La Rosa, M. (1979) *La sociologia del lavoro in Italia e in Francia*. Milan: F. Angeli.
Laufer, R. and Paradeise, C. (1981) *Le Prince Bureaucrate*. Paris: Flammarion.
Legendre, P. (1977) 'Le droit et toute sa rigueur', *Communications*, No. 26.
Le Roy Ladurie, E. (1976) 'La crise et l'historien', *Communications*, No. 25.
Maisonneuve, J. (1950) *Psychologie Sociale*. Paris: Que Sais-Je?
Marx, K. (1848) *Wage-Labour and Capital*.
Marx, K. and Engels, F. (1848) *Communist Manifesto*.
Mendras, H. (ed.) (1980) *La Sagesse et le Désordre: France 1980*. Paris: Gallimard.
Ministère de la Recherche et de l'Industrie (1983) *Une Politique Industrielle pour la France*. Paris: La Documentation Française.
Olson, M. (1965) *The Logic of Collective Action*. Cambridge, Mass: Harvard University Press.
Palmade, G. (ed.) (1967) *L'Economique et les Sciences Humaines*. Paris: Dunod.
Parsons, T. (1952) 'A Sociologist Looks at the Legal Profession' in *Essays in Sociological Theory*. New York: Glencoe Free Press.
Parsons, T. (1959) 'Some Problems Confronting Sociology as a Profession', *American Sociological Review*, 24(4).
Perrot, M. (1974) *Les Ouvriers en Grève 1871–1890*. Paris: Mouton.
Polanyi, K., Arensberg, C. and Pearson, H. W. (eds) (1957) *Trade and Market in the Early Empires: Economics in History and Theory*. Glencoe, Illinois: Free Press.
Raguin, C. (1970) 'Le droit naissant et les luttes de pouvoir', *Sociologie du Travail*, 1.
Richet, D. (1968) 'Croissance et blocages en France du XV⁻ au XVIII⁻ siecle', *Annales ESC*, No. 23.
Rolle, P. (1971) *Introduction à la Sociologie du Travail*. Paris: Larousse.
Rose, M. (1985) *Industrial Behaviour*. Harmondsworth: Penguin.
Rose, M. (1979) *Servants of Post-industrial Power? Sociologie du Travail in Modern France*. London: Macmillan Press.
Starn, R. (1976) 'Metamorphoses de la notion de crise', *Communications*, No. 25.
Tilly, C. and Shorter, E. (1973) 'Les vagues de grèves en France, 1890–1968', *Les Annales*, July–August 1973. Published (1974) as *Strikes in France, 1830–1968*. Cambridge: Cambridge University Press.
Touraine, A. and Mottez, B. (1962) 'Classe Ouvrière et Société Globale' in G. Friedmann and P. Naville (eds) (1961) *Traité de Sociologie du Travail*. Paris: Armand Colin.
Touraine, A. (1963) *La Sociologie de l'Action*. Paris: Seuil.
Various authors (1965) *Tendances et Volontés de la Société Française*. Paris: SEDEIS.
Various authors (under collective name of 'Darras') (1966) *Le Partage des Bénéfices*. Paris: Minuit.
Various authors (1978) *La Division du Travail (Dourdan I)*. Paris: Galilée.

Various authors (1982) *L'Emploi: Enjeux Economiques et Sociaux (Dourdan II)*. Paris: Maspero.
Wieviorka, M. (1981) 'Les Effets Pervers de R. Boudon' in *Sociologie du Travail*, 3.

Index

Abboud, N., 8, 34
abstract work, 108, 109–10
Actions Thématiques Programmées, 64
actors, social, 170, 171
'administrative sociography', 173
'Agence Européenne de Productivité', 65
agreement, of sociologists, 126–8
Althusser, L., vii
ambiguities in labour legislation, 88–9
America/Americanization, 1, 17, 20, 35, 51, 77, 78, 81, 96, 116, 140, 141, 145
amnesia, sociological, 135–7
analysis, unity of, 32
Ansart, P., 154
Arensberg, C., 81
Aron, R., vii, 19, 136
'Assises de la recherche', 67
assumptions, economic, 78–83
Auroux Laws (1982), 17
authorities, and research, 71–2
autonomy, worker, 156–7
Azouvi, A., 170, 171

Barre, R., 163
behaviour at work, 41–2, 44, 45, 54–5
Bernoux, P., 153
Blauner, R., 2
blind spots, economists', 123–4
Bosquet, M., 15
Boudon, R., 82
Bourdieu, P., 120, 121, 126, 146
Braverman, H., 20–4
Britain, 1, 17, 18, 19, 20, 90, 167
Bulletin Signalétique, 58–64
Burnier, M.-A., 12–13

Cabet, E., 98
cadres, 62
Caillé, A., 82
'capitalism', 110
Castells, M., 18
Centre de Sociologie des Organisations, 65
change
social, 73, 84–5, 87, 126, 146–8

technological, 19–20, 67–8, 73
Chave, D., 14
Chevènement, J.-P., 68, 72, 76
church, Catholic, 137, 138, 145
Citroën, 165–6
class consciousness, 157
classes, socioeconomic, 86
classification by subject of research on work, 40–2, 43
Clausewitz, K. von, 109
collective action, 164
'comités d'entreprise', 89
communist party, French (PCF), 9
Comte, A., 85
conceptual issues in translation, viii–ix
concrete work, 108, 110
conditions, working, 61
Confédération Française Democratique du Travail (CFDT), 10
conflict, 86–7
concensus, social, 122, 123–4
'constituted value', 102, 105
Constitution, French (1946), 89
contracts, 103
  research under, 66–7, 72–3
control, social, 166
'corporatisme', x
coupons, work, 103
craft work, 21–2, 23–4, 104
credit, 100–1
crisis
  economic, 67
  of trade unionism, 50
  periods of, 83
Crozier, M., 8, 16, 33, 141–2, 145
Cuisenier, J., 80

'Darras', 6–7, 120–9
Dassa, S., 13, 14, 15
'dead labour', 107
demand, social, and research, 65–76
  dangers of, 69–75
  history of, 65–9
denunciation, sociology of, 175
Detraz enquiry, 69

'developmentalists', 140
discourse, sociological, 173–7
disputes *see* conflict; strikes
division of labour, 61, 104–5, 106, 151–60, 173
Dourdan colloquiums, 12–13, 14, 31–2, 34, 35
   I, 151–60
   II, 161–7, 168–71
Dubois, P., 14–15
Dumazedier, J., 145
Dupeux, G., 6
Durand, C., 24, 25–6, 168
Durand, M., 144–5, 153, 159
Durkheim, E., viii–ix, 27, 77, 78, 159

Ecole National d'Administration (ENA), 138, 142–3
economic policy, 124, 131–2
economic power, 1
economics, 18–20, 78–83
economists
   science of, 122–5
   v. sociologists, 42–3, 46, 79–83
Edelman, B., 89
EEC countries, 51
employers, 163, 165, 169
employment, 161–7, 169
energy, 107, 108–9
enterprises, research into, 40–1, 44, 45, 53–4
entropy, 109
environment of enterprises, 40, 44, 45, 53
Erbès-Seguin, S., 19
evolutionism, 139
exchange of goods, 102–3, 106
'experts', 124, 132–3
exploitation, 107

Fifth Plan, 120
firms, 165; *see also* enterprises, research into
'flexibilité', xii–xiii
flexibility, 15–18
Fordism, 13
Foucault, M., 32
Fourier, F., 98
Fraisse, R., 66
Friedmann, G., 2, 5, 13, 19, 21, 79, 86, 112, 113, 114, 116, 117, 151, 152
frontiers of sociology of work, 77–92

functionalist theory, 82
funding of research, 63, 74–5

Gaulle, C. de, 6, 12
Gaullism, 16
Gif conference, 2–4, 25
Giscard d'Estaing, V., 11, 25, 72
Giscardianism, sociological, 67
'global social phenomena', 81
Godelier, M., 3, 82
'golden age', 156
Gorz, A., 15, 110
Gouldner, A., 26
Grégoire, R., 138
Groupe de Sociologie du Travail (GST), 3, 11, 113
'groupes d'expression', xii
growth, economic, 33, 120, 122–3, 126, 131–2
Gurvitch, G., 5, 115

Hamon, L., 145
Hawthorne experiments, 115, 116
Henderson, L., 78
history/historians, 67, 86–7
   perspective of, 83
'homothemics', 77
Hopkins, T., 79, 81
Hughes, E.C., 95–6

identity, social, 164–5
independence of research, 72–5
individualism, 166–7
industrial relations, 71
injunctions, 90
Institut de Science Sociale du Travail (ISST), 65
integrity, scientific, 24–8, 69–70
intellectual power, 1–2
international research, 51
international trade *see* trade, international
interpretation, freedom of, 73
interventionism, 69–70, 71, 140
Isambert-Jamati, V., 145, 146
Italy, 17

Javillier, J.-C., 88–9
job security, 164

Kastoryano, R., 14–15

Laboratoire de Sociologie Industrielle, 65
Laboratoire d'Economie et de Sociologie du Travail (LEST), 18
labour legislation *see* law, civil
labour market, 41, 44, 45, 54, 61
labour process *see* process, labour
Lautman, J., 80
law, civil, 87–90
Le Roy Ladurie, E., 83
Legendre, P., 88
Linhart, D., 153
Lip watch company, 167

Maisonneuve, J., 77, 78
Mallet, S., 6
managed economy, 131–2
management, 62
manipulation, 25–6
Marx, K., 22, 23–4, 81–2, 86, 98–9, 107–11
Marxism, 21, 22, 23–4, 86
Maurice, M., 136
Mauss, M., 81
May 1968, events of, 9–10, 12, 33, 66, 159
mechanization, 105, 106–7, 115
methodological issues, 31–2, 35, 73–4
Ministry of Research and Industry, 68–9
Mitterrand, F., 24
mobility, 163–4, 166
monarchical prerogatives, ix
money, 103
Monjardet, D., 5, 26–7, 28
morality, 177

'naturalness', 147–8
Naville, P., 2, 3, 5, 68, 74–5, 86, 113, 151, 152, 160

occupational categories, 50
Olson, M., 78, 82
organization of work, scientific, 85
ownership, 99–100

Pagès, R., 77, 78
Palloix, C., 18
Paradeise, C., 6–7, 168
paradoxical sociology, 175–6
Parsons, T., 79, 80, 81, 82
Parti Socialiste Unifié (PSU), 10
Passeron, J.C., 146
Pavy, G., 141
pay, 61
Perrot, M., 83–4

persecution of sociology, 176–7
personnel policy, 163
Philip, A., 115
Pingaud, B., 6
Polanyi, K., 81–2
political commitment, 69–70
politicians, 96
'polyvalence', 162
population, working, 42, 44, 45, 55
power, 1–2
  balance of, 89, 90
'précarisation', xii, 164, 169
primacy of work, ontological, 2
process, labour, 41, 44, 45, 54, 104–5, 155–7
professions, 62
  v. sciences, 95–7
property, 99–100
Proudhon, P.-J., 22–3, 24, 98–111, 153–5
psychology, industrial, 77–8
public sector, 49
publication, types of, 62–3, 64

rationality, conceptions of, 79
references, theoretical, 117
reflexive sociology, 34–5, 173–7
research
  and authorities, 71–2
  and industrial relations, 71
  and social requirements, 65–76
  funding of, 63, 74–5
  future preferences for, 52–5
  in 1950s, 65–6
  in 1960s/1970s, 66–7
  in socialist era, 67–8
  independence of, 72–5
  institutions, 74
  international, 51
  interventionist, 69–70, 71
  inventory of, 39–57
  scientific rigour v. political commitment, 69–70
  subjects of, 39–57, 58–64
  under contract, 66–7, 72–3
  under Giscardianism, 67
resistance, social, 126, 130–1
'revolt against work', 13
Revolution, French, ix
Reynaud, J.-D., 16
Rolle, P., 22–3, 80, 86
rotas, 60

Saint-Simon, C., 98
'salariat', 110–11
Sartre, J.-P., vii, 11
Say, J.-B., 99, 100, 101–2, 103
sectors, economic, 49
series, notion of, 100–2, 106
sincerity, 26–7
size of companies, 49–50
skills, 21–2, 23–4, 61, 104, 156, 162
Smelser, N., 79
'social statistics', 172, 173
socialist era, research in, 67–8
society, change in *see* change, social
Sociologie du Travail, 31
soixante-huitards, 10–11
Solmer group, 166
Sophists, 27, 177
Starn, R., 83
state
   apparatus of, 131
   sponsorship of research, 24
status of researchers, 74
strikes, 61, 83–4, 88–9
stylistic issues in translation, vii–viii
sub-contracting, 165
subjects of research, 39–57, 58–64
supply and demand, 101–2

Tarde, G., 77
Tavernier, Y., 136
Taylorism, 85, 115, 157, 159
technology, effects of, 46–8; *see also* change, technological

theft, 99
Thierry, A., 98
Third Republic, French, 136
time, working, 60
Touraine, A., 12, 19, 80, 86–7, 117, 138, 140, 142, 148
trade, international, 141
Traités, 5, 112–19
Tripier, P., 7–8, 144, 146, 147, 148, 168
Trotskyites, 10–11

unemployment, 61, 163–4, 166, 170
union confederation, French (CGT), 9
unions, 50, 61, 84, 163
urbanization, 137–8
Usinor steelworks, 166
Utopia, sociological, 172–7

value of goods, 102–3, 105, 106
values, system of, 133
Vichy government, 136
vocational training, 61
'volontarisme', ix–x

war, 109
Weber, M., 81
women's work, 61
workers, 112, 115, 157, 169–70
working class, 9–12, 61
working population *see* population, working
Workplace Inspectors, 90